ABOUT THIS PUBLICATION

FOR SERVICE ASSISTANCE

Customer Service
1.704.898.0770

North Carolina General Statues is published by The Muliti-Media Group of Greater Charlotte in Charlotte, North Carolina. Copyright 2015 by the Multi-Media Group of Greater Charlotte. This book or parts thereof may not be reproduced in any form, stored in a retrieval system, or transmitted in any form by any means—electronic, mechanical, photocopy, recording or otherwise—without prior written permission of the publisher, except as provided by United States of America copyright law.

The records required by U.S. Code 2257(a) through (c) and the pertinent regulations 28 C.F.R. Cli. 1, Part 75 with respect to this publication and all materials associated with such records are maintained by The Multi-Media Group of Greater Charlotte, Publisher and available for review by Attorney General.

www.visionbooks.org

Copyright © 2015 by MMGGC
All rights reserved!

TID: 5064406
ISBN (10) digit: 1502934159
ISBN (13) digit: 978-1502934154

123-4-56789-01239-Paperback
123-4-56789-01239-Hardback

First Edition

090520140547

Printed in the United States of America

2015 EDITION

North Carolina Criminal Law And Procedure-Pamphlet # 57

Printed In conjunction with the Administration of the Courts

North Carolina Criminal Law and Procedure
Pamphlet Reference Guide

Chapters	Pamphlet
Chapter 1 Civil Procedure	1
Chapter 1 Civil Procedure (Continue)	2
Chapter 1A Rules of Civil Procedure	2
Chapter 1B Contribution.	2
Chapter 1C Enforcement of Judgments.	2
Chapter 1D Punitive Damages.	2
Chapter 1E Eastern Band of Cherokee Indians.	2
Chapter 1F North Carolina Uniform Interstate Depositions and Discovery Act.	2
Chapter 2 - Clerk of Superior Court [Repealed and Transferred.]	3
Chapter 3 - Commissioners of Affidavits and Deeds [Repealed.]	3
Chapter 4 - Common Law	3
Chapter 5 - Contempt [Repealed.]	3
Chapter 5A - Contempt	3
Chapter 6 - Liability for Court Costs	3
Chapter 7 - Courts [Repealed and Transferred.]	3
Chapter 7A – Judicial Department	3
Chapter 7A – Continuation (Judicial Department)	4
Chapter 7A – Continuation (Judicial Department)	5
Chapter 7B - Juvenile Code	5
Chapter 8 - Evidence	6
Chapter 8A - Interpreters for Deaf Persons [Recodified.]	6
Chapter 8B - Interpreters for Deaf Persons	6
Chapter 8C - Evidence Code	6
Chapter 9 - Jurors	6
Chapter 10 - Notaries [Repealed.]	6
Chapter 10A - Notaries [Recodified.]	6
Chapter 10B - Notaries	6
Chapter 11 - Oaths	6
Chapter 12 - Statutory Construction	6
Chapter 13 - Citizenship Restored	6
Chapter 14 - Criminal Law	7
Chapter 14 – Criminal Law (Continuation)	8
Chapter 15 - Criminal Procedure	9
Chapter 15A - Criminal Procedure Act (Continuation)	10
Chapter 15A - Criminal Procedure Act (Continuation)	11
Chapter 15B - Victims Compensation	11
Chapter 15C - Address Confidentiality Program	11
Chapter 16 - Gaming Contracts and Futures	11
Chapter 17 - Habeas Corpus	11

Chapter 17A - Law-Enforcement Officers [Recodified.]	11
Chapter 17B - North Carolina Criminal Justice Education and Training System [Recodified.] Chapter 17C - North Carolina Criminal Justice Education and Training Standards Commission	11 11
Chapter 17D - North Carolina Justice Academy	11
Chapter 17E - North Carolina Sheriffs' Education and Training Standards Commission	11
Chapter 18 - Regulation of Intoxicating Liquors [Repealed.]	12
Chapter 18A - Regulation of Intoxicating Liquors [Repealed.]	12
Chapter 18B - Regulation of Alcoholic Beverages	12
Chapter 18C - North Carolina State Lottery	12
Chapter 19 - Offenses against Public Morals	12
Chapter 19A - Protection of Animals	12
Chapter 20 - Motor Vehicles	13
Chapter 20 - Motor Vehicles (Continuation)	14
Chapter 20 - Motor Vehicles (Continuation)	15
Chapter 20 - Motor Vehicles (Continuation)	16
Chapter 21 - Bills of Lading	17
Chapter 22 - Contracts Requiring Writing	17
Chapter 22A - Signatures	17
Chapter 22B - Contracts Against Public Policy	17
Chapter 22C - Payments to Subcontractors	17
Chapter 23 - Debtor and Creditor	17
Chapter 24 – Interest	17
Chapter 25 – Uniform Commercial Code	18
Chapter 25 – Uniform Commercial Code (Continuation)	19
Chapter 25A – Retail Installment Sales Act	20
Chapter 25B - Credit	20
Chapter 25C - Sales of Artwork	20
Chapter 26 - Suretyship	20
Chapter 27 - Warehouse Receipts [Repealed.]	20
Chapter 28 - Administration [Repealed.]	20
Chapter 28A - Administration of Decedents' Estates	20
Chapter 28B - Estates of Absentees in Military Service	20
Chapter 28C - Estates of Missing Persons	20
Chapter 29 - Intestate Succession	21
Chapter 30 - Surviving Spouses	21
Chapter 31 - Wills	21
Chapter 31A - Acts Barring Property Rights	21
Chapter 31B - Renunciation of Property and Renunciation of Fiduciary Powers Act	21
Chapter 31C - Uniform Disposition of Community Property Rights at Death Act	21
Chapter 32 - Fiduciaries	21
Chapter 32A - Powers of Attorney	21
Chapter 33 - Guardian and Ward [Repealed and Recodified.]	21

Chapter 33A - North Carolina Uniform Transfers to Minors Act	21
Chapter 33B - North Carolina Uniform Custodial Trust Act	21
Chapter 34 - Veterans' Guardianship Act	22
Chapter 35 - Sterilization Procedures	22
Chapter 35A - Incompetency and Guardianship	22
Chapter 36 - Trusts and Trustees [Repealed.]	22
Chapter 36A - Trusts and Trustees	22
Chapter 36B - Uniform Management of Institutional Funds Act [Repealed.]	22
Chapter 36C - North Carolina Uniform Trust Code	22
Chapter 36D - North Carolina Community Third Party Trusts, Pooled Trusts	23
Chapter 36E - Uniform Prudent Management of Institutional Funds Act	23
Chapter 37 - Allocation of Principal and Income [Repealed.]	23
Chapter 37A - Uniform Principal and Income Act	23
Chapter 38 - Boundaries	23
Chapter 38A - Landowner Liability	23
Chapter 39 - Conveyances	23
Chapter 39A - Transfer Fee Covenants Prohibited	23
Chapter 40 - Eminent Domain [Repealed.]	23
Chapter 40A - Eminent Domain	23
Chapter 41 - Estates	23
Chapter 41A - State Fair Housing Act	23
Chapter 42 - Landlord and Tenant	23
Chapter 42A - Vacation Rental Act	23
Chapter 43 - Land Registration	23
Chapter 44 - Liens	24
Chapter 44A - Statutory Liens and Charges	24
Chapter 45 - Mortgages and Deeds of Trust	24
Chapter 45A - Good Funds Settlement Act	24
Chapter 46 - Partition	24
Chapter 47 - Probate and Registration	25
Chapter 47A - Unit Ownership	25
Chapter 47B - Real Property Marketable Title Act	25
Chapter 47C - North Carolina Condominium Act	25
Chapter 47D - Notice of Settlement Act [Expired.]	25
Chapter 47E - Residential Property Disclosure Act	25
Chapter 47F - North Carolina Planned Community Act	25
Chapter 47G - Option to Purchase Contracts	25
Chapter 47H - Contracts for Deed	25
Chapter 48 - Adoptions +	26
Chapter 48A - Minors	26
Chapter 49 - Bastardy	26
Chapter 49A - Rights of Children	26
Chapter 50 - Divorce and Alimony	26
Chapter 50A - Uniform Child-Custody Jurisdiction and	

Enforcement Act	26
Chapter 50B - Domestic Violence	26
Chapter 50C - Civil No-Contact Orders	26
Chapter 51 - Marriage	26
Chapter 52 - Powers and Liabilities of Married Persons	27
Chapter 52A - Uniform Reciprocal Enforcement of Support Act [Repealed.]	27
Chapter 52B - Uniform Premarital Agreement Act	27
Chapter 52C - Uniform Interstate Family Support Act	27
Chapter 53 - Banks	27
Chapter 53A - Business Development Corporations and North Carolina Capital Resource Corporations	28
Chapter 53B - Financial Privacy Act	28
Chapter 54 - Cooperative Organizations	28
Chapter 54A - Capital Stock Savings and Loan Associations [Repealed.]	28
Chapter 54B - Savings and Loan Associations	29
Chapter 54C - Savings Banks	29
Chapter 55 - North Carolina Business Corporation Act	30
Chapter 55A - North Carolina Nonprofit Corporation Act	31
Chapter 55B - Professional Corporation Act	31
Chapter 55C - Foreign Trade Zones	31
Chapter 55D - Filings, Names, and Registered Agents for Corporations, Nonprofit Corporations, and Partnerships	31
Chapter 56 - Electric, Telegraph and Power Companies [Repealed.]	31
Chapter 57 - Hospital, Medical and Dental Service Corporations [Recodified.]	31
Chapter 57A - Health Maintenance Organization Act [Recodified.]	31
Chapter 57B - Health Maintenance Organization Act [Recodified.]	31
Chapter 57C - North Carolina Limited Liability Company Act.	31
Chapter 58 - Insurance.	32
Chapter 58 - Insurance (Continuation)	33
Chapter 58 - Insurance (Continuation)	34
Chapter 58 - Insurance (Continuation)	35
Chapter 58 - Insurance (Continuation)	36
Chapter 58 - Insurance (Continuation)	37
Chapter 58 - Insurance (Continuation)	38
Chapter 58A - North Carolina Health Insurance Trust Commission [Recodified.]	38
Chapter 59 - Partnership.	39
Chapter 59B - Uniform Unincorporated Nonprofit Association Act.	39
Chapter 60 - Railroads and Other Carriers [Repealed and Transferred.]	39
Chapter 61 - Religious Societies	39
Chapter 62 - Public Utilities	39

Chapter 62 - Public Utilities (Continuation)	40
Chapter 62A - Public Safety Telephone Service And Wireless Telephone Service	40
Chapter 63 - Aeronautics	40
Chapter 63A - North Carolina Global TransPark Authority	40
Chapter 64 - Aliens	40
Chapter 65 – Cemeteries	40
Chapter 66 - Commerce and Business	41
Chapter 67 - Dogs	41
Chapter 68 - Fences and Stock Law	41
Chapter 69 - Fire Protection	41
Chapter 70 - Indian Antiquities, Archaeological Resources and Unmarked Human Skeletal Remains Protection	42
Chapter 71 - Indians [Repealed.]	42
Chapter 71A - Indians	42
Chapter 72 - Inns, Hotels and Restaurants	42
Chapter 73 - Mills	42
Chapter 74 - Mines and Quarries	42
Chapter 74A - Company Police [Repealed.]	42
Chapter 74B - Private Protective Services Act [Repealed.]	42
Chapter 74C - Private Protective Services	42
Chapter 74D - Alarm Systems	42
Chapter 74E - Company Police Act	42
Chapter 74F - Locksmith Licensing Act	42
Chapter 74G - Campus Police Act	42
Chapter 75 - Monopolies, Trusts and Consumer Protection	42
Chapter 75A - Boating and Water Safety	43
Chapter 75B - Discrimination in Business	43
Chapter 75C - Motion Picture Fair Competition Act	43
Chapter 75D - Racketeer Influenced and Corrupt Organizations	43
Chapter 75E - Unlawful Activities in Connection With Certain Corporate Transactions	43
Chapter 76 - Navigation	43
Chapter 76A - Navigation and Pilotage Commissions	43
Chapter 77 - Rivers, Creeks, and Coastal Waters	43
Chapter 78 - Securities Law [Repealed.]	43
Chapter 78A - North Carolina Securities Act	43
Chapter 78B - Tender Offer Disclosure Act [Repealed.]	43
Chapter 78C - Investment Advisers	43
Chapter 78D - Commodities Act	43
Chapter 79 - Strays [Repealed.]	43
Chapter 80 - Trademarks, Brands, etc.	44
Chapter 81 - Weights and Measures [Recodified.]	44
Chapter 81A - Weights and Measures Act of 1975.	44
Chapter 82 - Wrecks [Repealed.]	44
Chapter 83 - Architects [Recodified.]	44

Chapter 83A - Architects	44
Chapter 84 - Attorneys-at-Law	44
Chapter 84A - Foreign Legal Consultants	44
Chapter 85 - Auctions and Auctioneers [Repealed.]	44
Chapter 85A - Bail Bondsmen and Runners [Recodified.]	44
Chapter 85B - Auctions and Auctioneers	44
Chapter 85C - Bail Bondsmen and Runners [Recodified.]	44
Chapter 86 - Barbers [Recodified.]	44
Chapter 86A - Barbers	44
Chapter 87 - Contractors	44
Chapter 88 - Cosmetic Art [Repealed.]	44
Chapter 88A - Electrolysis Practice Act	44
Chapter 88B - Cosmetic Art	45
Chapter 89 - Engineering and Land Surveying [Recodified.]	45
Chapter 89A - Landscape Architects	45
Chapter 89B - Foresters	45
Chapter 89C - Engineering and Land Surveying	45
Chapter 89D - Landscape Contractors	45
Chapter 89E - Geologists Licensing Act	45
Chapter 89F - North Carolina Soil Scientist Licensing Act	45
Chapter 89G - Irrigation Contractors	45
Chapter 90 - Medicine and Allied Occupations	45
Chapter 90 - Medicine and Allied Occupations (Continuation)	46
Chapter 90 - Medicine and Allied Occupations (Continuation)	47
Chapter 90 - Medicine and Allied Occupations (Continuation)	48
Chapter 90A - Sanitarians and Water and Wastewater Treatment Facility Operators	48
Chapter 90B - Social Worker Certification and Licensure Act	48
Chapter 90C - North Carolina Recreational Therapy Licensure Act	48
Chapter 90D - Interpreters and Transliterators	48
Chapter 91 - Pawnbrokers [Repealed.]	48
Chapter 91A - Pawnbrokers Modernization Act of 1989	48
Chapter 92 - Photographers [Deleted.]	48
Chapter 93 - Certified Public Accountants	48
Chapter 93A - Real Estate License Law	49
Chapter 93B - Occupational Licensing Boards	49
Chapter 93C - Watchmakers [Repealed.]	49
Chapter 93D - North Carolina State Hearing Aid Dealers and Fitters Board.	49
Chapter 93E - North Carolina Appraisers Act	49
Chapter 94 - Apprenticeship	49
Chapter 95 - Department of Labor and Labor Regulations	49
Chapter 95 - Department of Labor and Labor Regulations (Continuation)	50
Chapter 96 - Employment Security	50
Chapter 97 - Workers' Compensation Act	50
Chapter 97 - Workers' Compensation Act (Continuation)	51

Chapter 98 - Burnt and Lost Records	51
Chapter 99 - Libel and Slander	51
Chapter 99A - Civil Remedies for Criminal Actions	51
Chapter 99B - Products Liability	51
Chapter 99C - Actions Relating to Winter Sports Safety and Accidents	51
Chapter 99D - Civil Rights	51
Chapter 99E - Special Liability Provisions	51
Chapter 100 - Monuments, Memorials and Parks	51
Chapter 101 - Names of Persons	51
Chapter 102 - Official Survey Base	51
Chapter 103 - Sundays, Holidays and Special Days	51
Chapter 104 - United States Lands	51
Chapter 104A - Degrees of Kinship	51
Chapter 104B - Hurricanes or Other Acts of Nature	51
Chapter 104C - Atomic Energy, Radioactivity and Ionizing Radiation [Repealed and Recodified.]	51
Chapter 104D - Southern States Energy Compact	51
Chapter 104E - North Carolina Radiation Protection Act	51
Chapter 104F - Southeast Interstate Low-Level Radioactive Waste Management Compact [Repealed]	51
Chapter 104G - North Carolina Low-Level Radioactive Waste Management Authority Act of 1987 [Repealed]	51
Chapter 105 - Taxation	51
Chapter 105 - Taxation (Continuation)	52
Chapter 105 - Taxation (Continuation)	53
Chapter 105 - Taxation (Continuation)	54
Chapter 105A - Setoff Debt Collection Act	55
Chapter 105B - Defaulted Student Loan Recovery Act	55
Chapter 106 - Agriculture	55
Chapter 106 - Agriculture (Continue)	56
Chapter 106 - Agriculture (Continue)	57
Chapter 107 - Agricultural Development Districts [Repealed.]	57
Chapter 108 - Social Services [Repealed and Recodified.]	57
Chapter 108A - Social Services	57
Chapter 108B - Community Action Programs	58
Chapter 108C Medicaid and Health Choice Provider Requirements.	58
Chapter 108D Medicaid Managed Care for Behavioral Health Services.	58
Chapter 109 - Bonds [Recodified.]	58
Chapter 110 - Child Welfare	58
Chapter 111 - Aid to the Blind	58
Chapter 112 - Confederate Homes and Pensions [Repealed.]	58
Chapter 113 - Conservation and Development	58
Chapter 113 - Conservation and Development (Continuation)	59

Chapter 113A - Pollution Control and Environment	59
Chapter 113A - Pollution Control and Environment (Continuation)	60
Chapter 113B - North Carolina Energy Policy Act of 1975	60
Chapter 114 - Department of Justice	60
Chapter 115 - Elementary and Secondary Education [Repealed.]	60
Chapter 115A - Community Colleges, Technical Institutes, and Industrial Education Centers [Repealed.]	60
Chapter 115B - Tuition and Fee Waivers	60
Chapter 115C - Elementary and Secondary Education	60
Chapter 115C - Elementary and Secondary Education (Continuation)	61
Chapter 115C - Elementary and Secondary Education (Continuation)	62
Chapter 115C - Elementary and Secondary Education (Continuation)	63
Chapter 115D - Community Colleges	63
Chapter 115E - Private Educational Facilities Finance Act [Recodified]	63
Chapter 116 - Higher Education	63
Chapter 116 - Higher Education (Continuation)	63
Chapter 116A - Escheats and Abandoned Property [Repealed.]	64
Chapter 116B - Escheats and Abandoned Property	64
Chapter 116C - Continuum of Education Programs	64
Chapter 116D - Higher Education Bonds	64
Chapter 117 - Electrification	64
Chapter 118 - Firemen's and Rescue Squad Workers' Relief and Pension Funds [Recodified.]	64
Chapter 118A - Firemen's Death Benefit Act [Repealed.]	64
Chapter 118B - Members of a Rescue Squad Death Benefit Act [Repealed.]	64
Chapter 119 - Gasoline and Oil Inspection and Regulation	64
Chapter 120 - General Assembly	65
Chapter 120 - General Assembly (Continuation)	66
Chapter 120 - General Assembly (Continuation)	67
Chapter 120C - Lobbying	67
Chapter 121 - Archives and History	67
Chapter 122 - Hospitals for the Mentally Disordered [Repealed.]	67
Chapter 122A - North Carolina Housing Finance Agency	67
Chapter 122B - North Carolina Agricultural Facilities Finance Act [Repealed.]	67
Chapter 122C - Mental Health, Developmental Disabilities, and Substance Abuse Act of 1985	67
Chapter 122C - Mental Health, Developmental Disabilities, and Substance Abuse Act of 1985 (Continuation)	68
Chapter 122D - North Carolina Agricultural Finance Act	68

Chapter 122E - North Carolina Housing Trust and Oil Overcharge Act	68
Chapter 123 - Impeachment	69
Chapter 123A - Industrial Development [Repealed.]	69
Chapter 124 - Internal Improvements	69
Chapter 125 - Libraries	69
Chapter 126 - State Personnel System	69
Chapter 127 - Militia [Repealed.]	69
Chapter 127A - Militia	69
Chapter 127B - Military Affairs	69
Chapter 127C - Advisory Commission on Military Affairs	69
Chapter 128 - Offices and Public Officers	69
Chapter 128 - Offices and Public Officers (Continuation)	70
Chapter 129 - Public Buildings and Grounds	70
Chapter 130 - Public Health [Repealed.]	70
Chapter 130A - Public Health	70
Chapter 130A - Public Health (Continuation)	71
Chapter 130A - Public Health (Continuation)	72
Chapter 130B - Hazardous Waste Management Commission [Repealed.]	72
Chapter 131 - Public Hospitals [Repealed.]	72
Chapter 131A - Health Care Facilities Finance Act	72
Chapter 131B - Licensing of Ambulatory Surgical Facilities [Repealed.]	72
Chapter 131C - Charitable Solicitation Licensure Act [Repealed.]	72
Chapter 131D - Inspection and Licensing of Facilities	72
Chapter 131E - Health Care Facilities and Services	72
Chapter 131E - Health Care Facilities and Services (Continuation)	73
Chapter 131F - Solicitation of Contributions	73
Chapter 132 - Public Records	73
Chapter 133 - Public Works	74
Chapter 134 - Youth Development [Recodified.]	74
Chapter 134A - Youth Services [Repealed.]	74
Chapter 135 - Retirement System for Teachers and State Employees; Social Security; Health Insurance Program for Children	74
Chapter 135 - Retirement System for Teachers and State Employees; Social Security; Health Insurance Program for Children	75
Chapter 136 - Transportation	75
Chapter 136 - Transportation (Continuation)	76
Chapter 137 - Rural Rehabilitation [Repealed.]	76
Chapter 138 - Salaries, Fees and Allowances	76
Chapter 138A - State Government Ethics Act	76
Chapter 139 - Soil and Water Conservation Districts	76

Chapter 140 - State Art Museum; Symphony and Art Societies	76
Chapter 140A - State Awards System	76
Chapter 141 - State Boundaries	76
Chapter 142 - State Debt	76
Chapter 143 - State Departments, Institutions, and Commissions	77
Chapter 143 - State Departments, Institutions, and Commissions (Continuation)	78
Chapter 143 - State Departments, Institutions, and Commissions (Continuation)	79
Chapter 143 - State Departments, Institutions, and Commissions (Continuation)	80
Chapter 143A - State Government Reorganization	80
Chapter 143B - Executive Organization Act of 1973	80
Chapter 143B - Executive Organization Act of 1973 (Continuation)	81
Chapter 143B - Executive Organization Act of 1973 (Continuation)	82
Chapter 143C - State Budget Act	83
Chapter 143D - The State Governmental Accountability and Internal Control Act	83
Chapter 144 - State Flag, Official Governmental Flags, Motto, and Colors	83
Chapter 145 - State Symbols and Other Official Adoptions.	83
Chapter 146 - State Lands	83
Chapter 147 - State Officers	83
Chapter 148 - State Prison System	84
Chapter 149 - State Song and Toast	84
Chapter 150 - Uniform Revocation of Licenses [Repealed.]	84
Chapter 150A - Administrative Procedure Act [Recodified.]	84
Chapter 150B - Administrative Procedure Act	84
Chapter 151 - Constables [Repealed.]	84
Chapter 152 - Coroners	84
Chapter 152A - County Medical Examiner [Repealed.]	84
Chapter 152A - County Medical Examiner [Repealed.] (Continuation)	85
Chapter 153 - Counties and County Commissioners [Repealed.]	85
Chapter 153A - Counties	85
Chapter 153B - Mountain Resources Planning Act	85
Chapter 153C - Uwharrie Regional Resources Act	85
Chapter 154 - County Surveyor [Repealed.]	85
Chapter 155 - County Treasurer [Repealed.]	85
Chapter 156 - Drainage	85
Chapter 156 – Drainage (Continuation)	86

Chapter 157 - Housing Authorities and Projects	86
Chapter 157A - Historic Properties Commissions [Transferred.]	86
Chapter 158 - Local Development	86
Chapter 159 - Local Government Finance	86
Chapter 159 - Local Government Finance (Continuation)	87
Chapter 159A - Pollution Abatement and Industrial Facilities Financing Act [Unconstitutional.]	87
Chapter 159B - Joint Municipal Electric Power and Energy Act	87
Chapter 159C - Industrial and Pollution Control Facilities Financing Act	87
Chapter 159D - The North Carolina Capital Facilities Financing Act	87
Chapter 159E - Registered Public Obligations Act	87
Chapter 159F - North Carolina Energy Development Authority [Repealed.]	87
Chapter 159G - Water Infrastructure	87
Chapter 159H - [Reserved.]	87
Chapter 159I - Solid Waste Management Loan Program and Local Government Special Obligation Bonds	87
Chapter 160 - Municipal Corporations [Repealed And Transferred.]	87
Chapter 160A - Cities and Towns	88
Chapter 160A - Cities and Towns (Continuation)	89
Chapter 160B - Consolidated City-County Act	89
Chapter 160C - Baseball Park Districts [Repealed.]	90
Chapter 161 - Register of Deeds	90
Chapter 162 - Sheriff	90
Chapter 162A - Water and Sewer Systems	90
Chapter 162B Continuity of Local Government in Emergency.	90
Chapter 163 Elections and Election Laws.	90
Chapter 163 Elections and Election Laws. (Continuation)	91
Chapter 164 Concerning the General Statutes of North Carolina.	92
Chapter 165 Veterans.	92
Chapter 166 Civil Preparedness Agencies [Repealed.]	92
Chapter 166A North Carolina Emergency Management Act.	92
Chapter 167 State Civil Air Patrol [Repealed.]	92
Chapter 168 Persons with Disabilities.	92
Chapter 168A Persons With Disabilities Protection Act.	92

Article 68A.

North Carolina Dairy Stabilization and Growth Program.

§ 106-812. Findings.
(a)   The General Assembly finds that North Carolina has suffered a significant loss of its traditional industrial and agricultural economic base. The State's dairy industry is at serious risk of total collapse unless milk prices reach levels sufficient to allow dairy farmers to meet production costs. At the same time, North Carolina is experiencing rapid population growth and urbanization. This growth and urbanization have fueled a rapid loss of prime agricultural land and green space, resulting in a decline in the quality of life for which the State is known.

(b)   The General Assembly finds that the dairy industry in North Carolina makes a substantial economic, environmental, and quality-of-life contribution to the well-being of the citizens of the State. The dairy industry, including both producers and processors, currently contributes over six hundred million dollars ($600,000,000) and 3,000 jobs to the State's economy. Properly managed dairy farms help maintain green space, keep prime agricultural land under production, maintain water quality, enhance food security, and provide a local supply of fresh milk at a reasonable cost to the consumer and to processors in the State. An adequate local milk supply has become increasingly important as transportation costs escalate, making the importation of milk from out-of-state increasingly expensive. The General Assembly finds, however, that despite its importance to the State's economic and environmental well-being, North Carolina's dairy industry is under severe economic pressure, and milk production is declining at an alarming rate. According to United States Department of Agriculture statistics, since 1985 the State has lost sixty-seven percent (67%) of its dairy farms and thirty-five percent (35%) of its processing facilities. North Carolina dairy farms no longer produce sufficient milk for North Carolina's processing facilities to operate. Milk must be imported 10 out of 12 months each year to keep these processing facilities functioning. Further, farm prices for milk exhibit great volatility, creating financial risk and discouraging investment. The General Assembly finds that it is essential to a viable North Carolina dairy industry to have locally produced milk available to processors in the State. The General Assembly further finds that it is essential to the well-being of the citizens of the State to have a local supply of fresh milk available at reasonable cost and not subject to the vagaries of transportation costs and production conditions in other regions of the country.

(c) The General Assembly finds that one of the primary reasons for the decline in milk production in the State is the gap between the price paid to farmers for milk under the federal milk programs and the actual cost of production. Inability to meet production costs combined with increasing land prices have led many milk producers to sell their farms for development and retire or turn to other employment. The General Assembly finds that the most effective means to ensure the continuation of a viable dairy industry in this State is to establish a price floor for milk to enable dairy farmers to meet their production costs. It is the intent of the General Assembly to establish a price support program that will stabilize and reverse the decline in the local milk supply and in the dairy industry in the State and encourage new producers to enter the dairy industry. Sustaining and growing North Carolina's dairy industry will advance the State's goals of preserving and enhancing its economic base and improving the quality of life in the State through maintaining green space and water quality and assuring an adequate local supply of fresh milk. (2006-139, s. 1.)

§ 106-813. North Carolina Dairy Stabilization and Growth Fund.

(a) The North Carolina Dairy Stabilization and Growth Fund is created as a nonreverting account in the Department of Agriculture and Consumer Services. The Fund shall consist of any money appropriated to the Fund by the General Assembly and money made available to it from grants, donations, and other sources. The Board of Agriculture shall actively seek donations, grants, and other sources of money for the Fund.

(b) The Board shall use the monies in the Fund as follows:

(1) Up to two percent (2%) of the money appropriated annually by the General Assembly may be used by the Department for the costs of administering the Dairy Stabilization and Growth Program. In the event that the General Assembly does not make an appropriation to the Fund in a given year, up to two percent (2%) of the balance remaining in the Fund may be used by the Department for the costs of administering the Program.

(2) The monies remaining after administrative expenses are deducted shall be used to provide assistance to North Carolina dairy farmers in accordance with the provisions of G.S. 106-814.

(3) At the end of any fiscal year in which the total payments to North Carolina dairy farmers under G.S. 106-814 are less than fifty percent (50%) of the amount appropriated by the General Assembly for the year, five percent (5%) of the unspent appropriation for the year may be set aside for use in that year and subsequent years for programs to support the development of the dairy industry. (2006-139, s. 1.)

§ 106-814. Dairy Stabilization and Growth Program.

(a) On July 1 of each year the Board of Agriculture shall set a milk support baseline price. The baseline price per hundredweight of milk shall be the average United States Department of Agriculture Federal Milk Market Order Class I price mover for the previous 10 years less fifty cents (50¢).

(b) The Board shall adopt rules implementing the provisions of this Article. The rules shall include criteria for eligibility for distributions from the Fund, procedures for applications for distributions from the Fund, the method by which the amount of a payment to a producer shall be calculated, and the manner of payment to producers.

(c) Each month the Board shall determine whether the monthly announced United States Department of Agriculture Federal Milk Market Order Class I price mover has dropped below the baseline price set for the year. If the monthly announced Class I price mover is lower than the baseline price, then each producer who meets the requirements of subsection (f) of this section shall become eligible for a distribution from the Fund in an amount equal to the difference between the baseline price and the monthly announced Class I price mover multiplied by the hundredweight of milk sold by the producer for the month.

(d) Under exceptional circumstances, and in the discretion of the Board, the amount of any monthly distribution as calculated by the formula set forth in subsection (c) of this section may be increased by an amount not to exceed one dollar ($1.00) per hundredweight of milk sold in that month.

(e) Distributions shall be made to eligible producers at least quarterly, unless in the judgment of the Board the payment amounts are trivial. All payments under the Program are subject to the availability of funds.

(f) To be eligible to receive assistance from the Dairy Stabilization and Growth Fund, a dairy farmer shall demonstrate to the satisfaction of the Board that they are in compliance with the following rules and regulations:

(1) For Grade A milk producers, the federal Grade A milk regulations.

(2) For non-Grade A producers, Article 26 of Chapter 106 of the General Statutes and the rules implementing that Article.

(g) Farmers who fail to demonstrate compliance with applicable rules and regulations shall become ineligible for assistance from the Fund until compliance is attained. (2006-139, s. 1.)

§ 106-815. Report.

The Commissioner of Agriculture shall file a report no later than 31 March of each year with the Chairs of the House of Representatives Appropriations Subcommittee on Natural and Economic Resources and Senate Appropriations Committee on Natural and Economic Resources, the Chair of the House of Representatives Agriculture Committee, and the Chair of the Senate Committee on Agriculture, Environment, and Natural Resources which shall include the following:

(1) The short- and long-term problems associated with maintaining a viable dairy industry in the State.

(2) Ways to sustain the existing dairy industry in the State.

(3) Opportunities to expand the dairy industry, including attracting both new dairy producers and new processors to the State.

(4) The contribution of dairy farms to the maintenance of prime agricultural land and the quality of life in the State.

(5) An analysis of the effectiveness of the Dairy Stabilization and Growth Program in achieving the goals of maintaining a local supply of fresh milk for processing and consumption, facilitating the entry of young farmers into the dairy industry, and preserving green space along the urban fringe.

(6) Other factors that impact the dairy industry in the State. (2006-139, s. 2; 2007-495, s. 21.)

§ 106-816. Reserved for future codification purposes.

§ 106-817. Reserved for future codification purposes.

§ 106-818: Reserved for future codification purposes.

§ 106-819: Reserved for future codification purposes.

Article 69.

Horse Industry Promotion Act.

§ 106-820. Title.

This Article may be cited as the Horse Industry Promotion Act. (1998-154, s. 1.)

§ 106-821. Findings.

The General Assembly finds that the horse industry makes an important contribution to the State's economy, and that it is appropriate for the State to provide a means for horse owners to voluntarily assess themselves in order to provide funds to promote the interests of the horse industry. (1998-154, s. 1.)

§ 106-822. Definitions.

As used in this Article:

(1) "Commercial horse feed" means any commercial feed, as defined in G.S. 106-284.33, labeled for equine use.

(2) "Council" means the North Carolina Horse Council.

(3)   "Department" means the Department of Agriculture and Consumer Services.

(4)   "Equine" means a horse, pony, mule, donkey, or hinny.

(5)   "Horse owner" means a person who (i) is a North Carolina resident and (ii) owns or leases an equine. (1998-154, s. 1.)

§ 106-823. Referendum.

(a)   The Council may conduct a referendum among horse owners upon the question of whether an assessment shall be levied consistent with this Article.

(b)   The Council shall determine all of the following:

(1)   The amount of the proposed assessment, not to exceed two dollars ($2.00) per ton of commercial horse feed.

(2)   The period for which the assessment shall be levied, not to exceed three years.

(3)   The time and place of the referendum.

(4)   Procedures for conducting the referendum and counting votes.

(5)   Any other matters pertaining to the referendum.

(c)   The amount of the proposed assessment and the method of collection shall be set forth on the ballot.

(d)   All horse owners are eligible to vote in the referendum. The Council shall send press releases about the referendum to at least 10 daily and 10 weekly or biweekly newspapers having general circulation in a county in the State, and to any trade journals deemed appropriate by the Council. Notice of the referendum also shall be posted in every place the Council identifies as selling commercial horse feed. Any questions concerning eligibility to vote shall be resolved by the board of directors of the Council. (1998-154, s. 1.)

§ 106-824. Majority vote required; collection of assessment.

(a) The assessment shall not be collected unless a majority of the votes cast in the referendum are in favor of the assessment. If a majority of the votes cast in the referendum are in favor of the assessment, the Department shall notify all commercial horse feed manufacturers and distributors of the assessment. The assessment shall apply to all commercial horse feed subject to the provisions of G.S. 106-284.40(b), and the assessment shall be remitted to the Department with the inspection fee imposed by G.S. 106-284.40. The Department shall provide forms for reporting the assessment. Persons who purchase commercial horse feed on which the assessment has not been paid shall report these purchases and pay the assessment to the Department.

(b) The Council may bring an action to collect unpaid assessments against any feed manufacturer or distributor who fails to pay the assessment. (1998-154, s. 1.)

§ 106-825. Use of funds; refunds.

(a) The Department shall remit all funds collected under this Article to the Council at least quarterly. The Council shall use these funds to promote the interests of the horse industry and may use these funds for those administrative expenses that are reasonably necessary to carry out this function.

(b) Any person who purchases commercial horse feed upon which the assessment has been paid shall have the right to receive a refund of the assessment by making demand in writing to the Council within one year of purchase of the feed. This demand shall be accompanied by proof of purchase satisfactory to the Council. (1998-154, s. 1.)

§ 106-826: Reserved for future codification purposes.

§ 106-827: Reserved for future codification purposes.

§ 106-828: Reserved for future codification purposes.

§ 106-829: Reserved for future codification purposes.

Article 70.

North Carolina Sustainable Local Food Advisory Council.

§§ 106-830 through 106-833: Expired. See note.

§ 106-834: Reserved for future codification purposes.

§ 106-835: Reserved for future codification purposes.

§ 106-836: Reserved for future codification purposes.

§ 106-837: Reserved for future codification purposes.

§ 106-838: Reserved for future codification purposes.

§ 106-839: Reserved for future codification purposes.

Article 71.

Soil and Water Conservation Commission.

§ 106-840. Soil and Water Conservation Commission - creation; powers and duties; compliance inspections.

(a) There is hereby created the Soil and Water Conservation Commission of the Department of Agriculture and Consumer Services with the power and duty to adopt rules to be followed in the development and implementation of a soil and water conservation program.

(1) The Soil and Water Conservation Commission has all of the following powers and duties:

a. To approve petitions for soil conservation districts.

b. To approve application for watershed plans.

c. Such other duties as specified in Chapter 139.

d. To conduct any inspections in accordance with subsection (b) of this section.

(2) The Commission shall adopt rules consistent with the provisions of this Chapter. All rules not inconsistent with the provisions of this Chapter heretofore adopted by the Soil and Water Conservation Committee shall remain in full force and effect unless and until repealed or superseded by action of the Soil and Water Conservation Commission. All rules adopted by the Commission shall be enforced by the Department of Agriculture and Consumer Services.

(b) An employee or agent of the Soil and Water Conservation Commission or the Department of Agriculture and Consumer Services may enter property, with the consent of the owner or person having control over property, at reasonable times for the purposes of investigating compliance with Commission or Department programs when the investigation is reasonably necessary to carry out the duties of the Commission. If the Commission or Department is unable to obtain the consent of the owner of the property, the Commission or Department may obtain an administrative search warrant pursuant to G.S. 15-27.2.

(c) Any person who refuses entry or access to property by an employee or agent of the Commission or the Department or who willfully resists, delays, or obstructs an employee or agent of the Commission or the Department while the employee or agent is in the process of carrying out official duties after the employee or agent has obtained the consent of the owner or person having control of the property or, if consent is not obtained, after the employee or agent has obtained an administrative search warrant, shall be guilty of a Class 1 misdemeanor. (1973, c. 1262, s. 34; 1977, c. 771, s. 4; 1989, c. 727, s. 194; 1997-173, s. 1; 1997-443, s. 11A.119(a); 2011-145, s. 13.22A(e), (f).)

§ 106-841. Soil and Water Conservation Commission - members; selection; removal; compensation; quorum; services.

(a) The Soil and Water Conservation Commission of the Department of Agriculture and Consumer Services shall be composed of seven members appointed by the Governor. The Commission shall be composed of the following members:

(1) The president, first vice-president, and immediate past president of the North Carolina Association of Soil and Water Conservation Districts. Vacancies arising in any of these positions shall be filled through appointment by the Governor upon the nomination by the executive committee of the North Carolina Association of Soil and Water Conservation Districts;

(2) Three supervisor members nominated by the North Carolina Association of Soil and Water Conservation Districts from its own membership representing the three major geographical regions of the State and appointed by the Governor;

(3) One member appointed at large by the Governor.

(b) The members of the Commission, except those members serving in an ex officio capacity, shall be appointed for terms of three years and shall serve until their successors are appointed and qualified. Any appointment to fill a vacancy on the Commission created by the resignation, dismissal, death or disability of a member shall be for the balance of the unexpired term.

(c) The office of member of the Soil and Water Conservation Commission may be held concurrently with any other elective or appointive office, in addition to the maximum number of offices permitted to be held by one person under G.S. 128-1.1.

(d) The Governor shall have the power to remove any member of the Commission from office for misfeasance, malfeasance, and nonfeasance according to the provisions of G.S. 143B-13.

(e) The members of the Commission shall receive per diem and necessary travel and subsistence expenses in accordance with the provisions of G.S. 138-5.

(f) A majority of the Commission shall constitute a quorum for the transaction of business.

(g) All clerical and other services required by the Commission shall be supplied by the Department of Agriculture and Consumer Services. (1973, c. 1262, s. 35; 1977, c. 771, s. 4; 1989, c. 727, s. 218(136); 1997-443, s. 11A.119(a); 2002-176, s. 2; 2003-198, s. 1; 2011-145, s. 13.22A(e), (g).)

§ 106-842. Soil and Water Conservation Commission - officers.

The Soil and Water Conservation Commission shall have a chair and a vice-chair. The chair shall be designated by the Governor from among the members of the Commission to serve as chair at the pleasure of the Governor. The vice-chair shall be elected by and from the members of the Commission and shall serve for a term of two years or until the expiration of the vice-chair's regularly appointed term. (1973, c. 1262, s. 36; 2006-79, s. 7; 2011-145, s. 13.22A(e).)

§ 106-843. Soil and Water Conservation Commission - meetings.

The Soil and Water Conservation Commission shall meet at least quarterly and may hold special meetings at any time and place within the State at the call of the chair or upon the written request of at least four members. (1973, c. 1262, s. 37; 2006-79, s. 8; 2011-145, s. 13.22A(e).)

§ 106-844. Soil and Water Conservation Account.

The Soil and Water Conservation Account is established as a nonreverting account within the Department of Agriculture and Consumer Services. The Account consists of revenue credited to the Account from the sale of soil and water conservation special license plates. The Commission shall use the revenue from the account to fund environmental education and water quality education in North Carolina. (1997-477, s. 5; 1997-443, s. 11A.123; 2011-145, s. 13.22A(e), (dd).)

§ 106-845: Reserved for future codification purposes.

§ 106-846: Reserved for future codification purposes.

§ 106-847: Reserved for future codification purposes.

§ 106-848: Reserved for future codification purposes.

§ 106-849: Reserved for future codification purposes.

Article 72.

Nonpoint Source Pollution Control Program.

§ 106-850. Agriculture cost share program.

(a) There is created the Agriculture Cost Share Program for Nonpoint Source Pollution Control. The program shall be created, implemented, and supervised by the Soil and Water Conservation Commission.

(b) The program shall be subject to the following requirements and limitations:

(1) The purpose of the program shall be to reduce the input of agricultural nonpoint source pollution into the watercourses of the State.

(2) The program shall initially include the present 16 nutrient sensitive watershed counties and 17 additional counties.

(3) Subject to subdivision (7) of this subsection, priority designations for inclusions in the program shall be under the authority of the Soil and Water Conservation Commission. The Soil and Water Conservation Commission shall retain the authority to allocate the cost share funds.

(4) Areas shall be included in the program as the funds are appropriated and the technical assistance becomes available from the local Soil and Water Conservation District.

(5) Funding may be provided to assist practices including conservation tillage, diversions, filter strips, field borders, critical area plantings, sedimentation control structures, sod-based rotations, grassed waterways, strip-cropping, terraces, cropland conversion to permanent vegetation, grade control structures, water control structures, closure of lagoons, emergency spillways, riparian buffers or equivalent controls, odor control best management practices, insect control best management practices, and animal waste management systems and application. Funding for animal waste management shall be allocated for practices in river basins such that the funds will have the greatest impact in improving water quality.

(6) Except as provided in subdivision (8) of this subsection, State funding shall be limited to seventy-five percent (75%) of the average cost for each

practice with the assisted farmer providing twenty-five percent (25%) of the cost, which may include in-kind support of the practice, with a maximum of seventy-five thousand dollars ($75,000) per year to each applicant.

(7) Priority designation for inclusion in the program for State funding shall be given to projects that improve water quality. To be eligible for cost share funds under this subdivision, a project shall be evaluated before funding is awarded and after the project is completed to determine the impact on water quality.

(8) For practices that are eligible for funding from the federal Conservation Reserve Enhancement Program, State funding from the program shall be limited to seventy-five percent (75%) of the average cost of each practice, with the remainder paid from funding from the Conservation Reserve Enhancement Program, other available federal funds, other State funds, or the assisted farmer, whose contribution may include in-kind support of the practice. This subdivision is subject to subdivision (9) of this subsection.

(9) When the applicant is either (i) a limited-resource farmer, (ii) a beginning farmer, or (iii) a person farming land that is located in an enhanced voluntary agricultural district and is subject to a conservation agreement under G.S. 106-743.2 that remains in effect, State funding shall be limited to ninety percent (90%) of the average cost for each practice with the assisted farmer providing ten percent (10%) of the cost, which may include in-kind support of the practice, with a maximum of one hundred thousand dollars ($100,000) per year to each applicant. The following definitions apply in this subdivision:

a. Beginning farmer. - A farmer who has not operated a farm or who has operated a farm for not more than 10 years and who will materially and substantially participate in the operation of the farm.

b. Enhanced voluntary agricultural district. - A district established by a county or a city by ordinance under Part 3 of Article 61 of this Chapter.

c. Limited-resource farmer. - A farmer with direct and indirect annual gross farm sales that do not exceed one hundred thousand dollars ($100,000) and with an adjusted household income in each of the previous two years that is at or below the greater of the county median household income, as determined by the United States Department of Housing and Urban Development, or two times the national poverty level based on the federal poverty guidelines established by the United States Department of Health and Human Services and revised each April 1.

d. Materially and substantially participate.

1. In the case of an individual, for the individual, including members of the immediate family of the individual, to provide substantial day-to-day labor and management of the farm, consistent with the practices in the county in which the farm is located.

2. In the case of an entity, for all members of the entity, to participate in the operation of the farm, with some members providing management and some members providing labor and management necessary for day-to-day activities such that if the members did not provide the management and labor, the operation of the farm would be seriously impaired.

(10) To be eligible for cost share funds under this program, each applicant must establish that he or she is engaged in farming by providing any of the following to the Soil and Water Conservation Commission with his or her application:

a. A copy of the farm owner's or operator's federal tax Schedule F (Form 1040) or an equivalent form for the most recent tax year showing the owner's or operator's profit or loss from farming.

b. A copy of the farm's agricultural exemption certificate issued to the farm owner or operator by the Department of Revenue.

c. For forestland actively engaged in the commercial growing of trees under a sound management program as defined in G.S. 105-277.2(6), a copy of the sound forest management plan described in G.S. 105-277.3(g).

(11) In extraordinary circumstances, the Commission may permit an applicant to establish that he or she is engaged in farming with an alternate form of documentation if the farm has a conservation plan that meets the statutory purposes of the program.

(c) The program shall be reviewed, prior to implementation, by the Committee created by G.S. 106-852. The Technical Review Committee shall meet quarterly to review the progress of this program.

(d)   State funds for the program shall remain available until expended for the program.

(e)   The Soil and Water Conservation Commission shall report on or before 31 January of each year to the Environmental Review Commission, the Department of Agriculture and Consumer Services, and the Fiscal Research Division. This report shall include a list of projects that received State funding pursuant to the program, the results of the evaluations conducted pursuant to subdivision (7) of subsection (b) of this section, findings regarding the effectiveness of each of these projects to accomplish its primary purpose, and any recommendations to assure that State funding is used in the most cost-effective manner and accomplishes the greatest improvement in water quality. (1985 (Reg. Sess., 1986), c. 1014, s. 149(a); 1987, c. 827, s. 154; c. 830, s. 102; 1995 (Reg. Sess., 1996), c. 626, ss. 9, 10; 1996, 2nd Ex. Sess., c. 18, s. 27.22(a), (b); 1997-496, s. 15; 1998-221, s. 3.1; 2002-165, s. 2.18; 2003-284, s. 11.6; 2004-124, s. 12.6; 2005-390, s. 8; 2007-495, s. 18; 2011-145, ss. 13.22A(a), (t)-(w), 13.23A(a); 2011-391, s. 32; 2012-142, s. 11.2A(a).)

§ 106-851. Program participation.

Participation in the program shall be voluntary.

All participants in the program shall be required to match State funds at the same rate, and assistance from the Agriculture Extension Service at North Carolina State University shall also be used. (1985 (Reg. Sess., 1986), c. 1014, s. 149(a); 2011-145, s. 13.22A(t).)

§ 106-852. Committee established.

Detailed plans for implementing the program shall be reviewed and suggested changes and reasons therefor shall be given by a committee consisting of the Master of the North Carolina State Grange, President of the North Carolina Farm Bureau Federation, the North Carolina Commissioner of Agriculture, the Dean of the School of Agriculture and Life Sciences at North Carolina State University, the Dean of the School of Agriculture at North Carolina Agricultural and Technical State University, the Chairman of the State Soil and Water Conservation Commission, the President of the North Carolina Association of

Soil and Water Conservation Districts, the Executive Director of the Wildlife Resources Commission or a designee, and the Director of the Division of Marine Fisheries or a designee. The committee shall review the program prior to expenditure of any funds for the program. Certification documenting the committee's review of the program shall be made in writing to the Speaker of the House of Representatives, the President of the Senate, the Chairmen of the Appropriations Committees of the Senate and the House of Representatives, the Director of the Fiscal Research Division of the Legislative Services Office, and the Legislative Library. (1985 (Reg. Sess., 1986), c. 1014, s. 149(a); 1989, c. 500, s. 117; 1993, c. 321, s. 261; 2011-145, s. 13.22A(t).)

§ 106-853: Reserved for future codification purposes.

§ 106-854: Reserved for future codification purposes.

§ 106-855: Reserved for future codification purposes.

§ 106-856: Reserved for future codification purposes.

§ 106-857: Reserved for future codification purposes.

§ 106-858: Reserved for future codification purposes.

§ 106-859: Reserved for future codification purposes.

Article 73.

Community Conservation Assistance Program.

§ 106-860. Community Conservation Assistance Program.

(a) Program Established. - There is established the Community Conservation Assistance Program. The Program shall be implemented and supervised by the Soil and Water Conservation Commission of the Department of Agriculture and Consumer Services.

(b) Purposes. - The purpose of the Program shall be to reduce the input of nonpoint source pollution into the waters of the State. The Program shall be subject to the following requirements and limitations:

(1) Subject to subdivision (5) of this subsection, priority designations for inclusion in the Program for State funding shall be established by the Soil and Water Conservation Commission. The Soil and Water Conservation Commission shall allocate the cost share and technical assistance funds under the Program.

(2) Areas shall be included in the Program as the funds are appropriated and technical assistance becomes available from the local Soil and Water Conservation District.

(3) Funding may be provided to assist community conservation practices approved by the Soil and Water Conservation Commission.

(4) State funding shall be limited to seventy-five percent (75%) of the average cost for each practice with the assisted applicant providing twenty-five percent (25%) of the cost, which may include in-kind support of the practice, with a maximum of seventy-five thousand dollars ($75,000) per year to each applicant.

(5) Priority designation for inclusion in the Program for State funding shall be given to projects that improve water quality. To be eligible for cost-share funds under this subdivision, a project shall be evaluated before funding is awarded and after the project is completed to determine the impact on water quality.

(6) Participation in the Program shall be voluntary.

(c) Availability of Funds. - State funds for the Program shall remain available until expended.

(d) Advisory Committee. - The Program shall be reviewed, prior to implementation, by the Community Conservation Assistance Program Advisory Committee. The Advisory Committee shall meet quarterly to review the progress of the Program. The Advisory Committee shall consist of the following members:

(1) The Director of the Division of Soil and Water Conservation of the Department of Agriculture and Consumer Services or the Director's designee, who shall serve as the Chair of the Advisory Committee.

(2) The President of the North Carolina Association of Soil and Water Conservation Districts or the President's designee.

(3) The Director of the Cooperative Extension Service at North Carolina State University or the Director's designee.

(4) The Executive Director of the North Carolina Association of County Commissioners or the Executive Director's designee.

(5) The Executive Director of the North Carolina League of Municipalities or the Executive Director's designee.

(6) The State Conservationist of the Natural Resources Conservation Service of the United States Department of Agriculture or the State Conservationist's designee.

(7) The Executive Director of the Wildlife Resources Commission or the Executive Director's designee.

(8) The President of the North Carolina Conservation District Employees Association or the President's designee.

(9) The President of the North Carolina Association of Resource Conservation and Development Councils or the President's designee.

(10) Repealed by Session Laws 2013-413, s. 57(e). For effective date, see note.

(11) The Assistant Commissioner of the North Carolina Forest Service of the Department of Agriculture and Consumer Services or the Assistant Commissioner's designee.

(12) The Director of the Division of Energy, Mineral, and Land Resources of the Department of Environment and Natural Resources or the Director's designee.

(13) The Director of the Division of Coastal Management of the Department of Environment and Natural Resources or the Director's designee.

(14) The Director of the Division of Water Resources of the Department of Environment and Natural Resources or the Director's designee.

(15) The President of the Carolinas Land Improvement Contractors Association or the President's designee.

(e) Report. - The Soil and Water Conservation Commission shall report no later than 31 January of each year to the Environmental Review Commission, the Department of Agriculture and Consumer Services, and the Fiscal Research Division. The report shall include a summary of projects that received State funding pursuant to the Program, the results of the evaluation conducted pursuant to subdivision (5) of subsection (b) of this section, findings regarding the effectiveness of each project to accomplish its primary purpose, and any recommendations to assure that State funding is used in the most cost-effective manner and accomplishes the greatest improvement in water quality. (2006-78, s. 1; 2011-145, ss. 13.22A(x)-(z), (aa), 13.25(vv), (xx); 2012-143, s. 1(f); 2013-155, s. 10; 2013-413, s. 57(e).)

§ 106-861: Reserved for future codification purposes.

§ 106-862: Reserved for future codification purposes.

§ 106-863: Reserved for future codification purposes.

§ 106-864: Reserved for future codification purposes.

§ 106-865: Reserved for future codification purposes.

§ 106-866: Reserved for future codification purposes.

§ 106-867: Reserved for future codification purposes.

§ 106-868: Reserved for future codification purposes.

§ 106-869: Reserved for future codification purposes.

Article 74.

Acquisition and Control of State Forests and State Recreational Forests.

§ 106-870. Policy and plan to be inaugurated by Department of Agriculture and Consumer Services.

(a) In this Article, unless the context requires otherwise, "Department" means the Department of Agriculture and Consumer Services and "Commissioner" means Commissioner of Agriculture.

(b) For purposes of this Chapter, "State recreational forest" means a forest managed primarily for natural resource preservation, scenic enjoyment, and recreational purposes.

(c) The Department shall inaugurate the following policy and plan looking to the cooperation with private and public forest owners in this State insofar as funds may be available through legislative appropriation, gifts of money or land, or such cooperation with landowners and public agencies as may be available:

(1) The extension of the forest fire prevention organization to all counties in the State needing such protection.

(2) To cooperate with federal and other public agencies in the restoration of forest growth on land unwisely cleared and subsequently neglected.

(3) To furnish trained and experienced experts in forest management, to inspect private forestlands and to advise with forest landowners with a view to the general observance of recognized and practical rules of growing, cutting, and marketing timber. The services of such trained experts of the Department must naturally be restricted to those landowners who agree to carry out so far as possible the recommendations of said Department.

(4) To prepare and distribute printed and other material for the use of teachers and club leaders and to provide instruction to schools and clubs and other groups of citizens in order to train the younger generation in the principles of wise use of our forest resources.

(5) To acquire small areas of suitable land in the different regions of the State on which to establish small, model forests which shall be developed and used by the said Department as State demonstration forests for experiment and demonstration in forest management. (2011-145, s. 13.25(o).)

§ 106-871. Growing of timber on unused State lands authorized.

The Department of Administration may allocate to the Department, for management as a State forest, any vacant and unappropriated lands, any marshlands or swamplands, and any other lands title to which is vested in the State or in any State agency or institution, where such lands are not being otherwise used and are not suitable for cultivation. Lands under the supervision of the Wildlife Resources Commission and designated and in use as wildlife management areas, refuges, or fishing access areas and lands used as research stations shall not be subject to the provisions of this section. The Department shall plant timber-producing trees on all lands allocated to it for that purpose by the Department of Administration. The Commissioner may contract with the appropriate prison authorities for the furnishing, upon such conditions as may be agreed upon from time to time between such prison authorities and the Commissioner, of prison labor for use in the planting, cutting, and removal of timber from State forests which are under the management of the Department. (2011-145, s. 13.25(o).)

§ 106-872. Use of lands acquired by counties through tax foreclosures as demonstration forests.

The boards of county commissioners of the various counties of North Carolina are herewith authorized to turn over to the said Department title to such tax-delinquent lands as may have been acquired by said counties under tax sale and as in the judgment of the Commissioner may be suitable for the purposes named in subdivision (5) of subsection (c) of G.S. 106-870. (2011-145, s. 13.25(o).)

§ 106-873. Procedure for acquisition of delinquent tax lands from counties.

In the carrying out of the provisions of G.S. 106-872, the several boards of county commissioners shall furnish forthwith on written request of the Department a complete list of all properties acquired by the county under tax sale and which have remained unredeemed for a period of two years or more. On receipt of this list, the Commissioner shall have the lands examined and, if any one or more of these properties is in the Commissioner's judgment suitable for the purposes set forth in G.S. 106-872, request shall be made to the county commissioners for the acquisition of such land by the Department at a price not to exceed the actual amount of taxes due without penalties. On receipt of this request, the county commissioners shall make permanent transfer of such tract or tracts of land to the Department through fee-simple deed or other legal transfer, said deed to be approved by the Attorney General of North Carolina, and shall then receive payment from the Department as above outlined. (2011-145, s. 13.25(o).)

§ 106-874. Purchase of lands for use as demonstration forests.

Where no suitable tax-delinquent lands are available and, in the judgment of the Department, the establishment of a demonstration forest is advisable, the Department may purchase sufficient land for the establishment of such a demonstration forest at a fair and agreed-upon price, the deed for such land to be subject to approval of the Attorney General, but nothing in G.S. 106-870 to G.S. 106-875 shall allow the Department to acquire land under the right of eminent domain. (2011-145, s. 13.25(o).)

§ 106-875. Forest management appropriation.

Necessary funds for carrying out the provisions of G.S. 106-870 and G.S. 106-872 to G.S. 106-875 shall be set up in the regular budget as an item entitled "forest management." (2011-145, s. 13.25(o).)

§ 106-876. Power to acquire lands as State forests; donations or leases by United States; leases for recreational purposes.

(a) The Governor may, upon recommendation of the Department, accept gifts of land to the State to be held, protected, and administered by the Department as State forests, and to be used so as to demonstrate the practical utility of timber culture and water conservation, and as refuges for game. The gifts of land must be absolute except in cases where the mineral interest on the land has previously been sold. The Department may purchase lands in the name of the State, suitable chiefly for the production of timber, as State forests, for experimental, demonstration, educational, and protection purposes, using for these purposes any special appropriations or funds available. The Department may acquire by condemnation under the provisions of Chapter 40A of the General Statutes areas of land in different sections of the State that may in the opinion of the Department be necessary for the purpose of establishing or developing State forests and other areas and developments essential to the effective operation of the State forestry activities under its charge. Condemnation proceedings shall be instituted and prosecuted in the name of the State, and any property so acquired shall be administered, developed, and used for experiment and demonstration in forest management, for public recreation, and for other purposes authorized or required by law. Before any action or proceeding under this section can be exercised, the approval of the Governor and Council of State shall be obtained and filed with the clerk of the superior court in the county or counties where the property is located. The Attorney General shall ensure that all deeds to the State for land acquired under this section are properly executed before the gift is accepted or payment of the purchase money is made.

(b)   The Department may accept as gifts to the State any forest and submarginal farmland acquired by the federal government that is suitable for the purpose of creating and maintaining State forests or enter into longtime leases with the federal government for the areas and administer them with funds secured from their administration in the best interest of longtime public use, supplemented by any appropriations made by the General Assembly. The Department may segregate revenue derived from State hunting and fishing licenses, use permits, and concessions, and other proper revenue secured through the administration of State forests, to be deposited in the State treasury to the credit of the Department to be used for the administration of these areas.

(c)   The authority granted to the Department under this section is in addition to any authority granted to the Department under any other provision of law. (2011-145, s. 13.25(o).)

§ 106-877. State timber may be sold by Department; forest nurseries; operation of public service facilities; concessions to private concerns; authority to charge fees and adopt rules.

(a)   Timber and other products of State forests may be sold, cut, and removed under rules of the Department. The Department may establish and operate forest tree nurseries and forest tree seed orchards. Forest tree seedlings and seed from these nurseries and seed orchards may be sold to landowners of the State for purposes of forestation under rules adopted by the Department. When the Commissioner determines that a surplus of seedlings or seed exists, this surplus may be sold, and the sale shall be in conformity with the following priority of sale: first, to agencies of the federal government for planting in the State of North Carolina; second, to commercial nurseries and nurserymen within this State; and third, without distinction, to federal agencies, to other states, and to recognized research organizations for planting either within or outside of this State. The Department shall make reasonable rules governing the use by the public of State forests under its charge. These rules shall be posted in conspicuous places on and adjacent to the properties of the State and at the courthouse of the county or counties in which the properties are located. A violation of these rules is punishable as a Class 3 misdemeanor.

(b) The Department may construct, operate, and maintain within the State forests and other areas under its charge suitable public service facilities and conveniences, and may charge and collect reasonable fees for the use of these facilities and conveniences. The Department may also charge and collect reasonable fees for hunting privileges on State forests and fishing privileges in State forests, provided that these privileges shall be extended only to holders of State hunting and fishing licenses who comply with all State game and fish laws.

(c) The Department may grant to private individuals or companies concessions for operation of public service facilities for such periods and upon such conditions as the Department deems to be in the public interest. The Department may adopt reasonable rules for the regulation of the use by the public of the lands and waters under its charge and of the public service facilities and conveniences authorized under this section. A violation of these rules is punishable as a Class 3 misdemeanor.

(d) The authority granted to the Department under this section is in addition to any authority granted to the Department under any other provision of law. (2011-145, s. 13.25(o).)

§ 106-878. Applications of proceeds from sale of products.

(a) Application of Proceeds Generally. - Except as provided in this section, all money received from the sale of wood, timber, minerals, or other products from the State forests shall be paid into the State treasury and to the credit of the Department; and such money shall be expended in carrying out the purposes of this Article and of forestry in general, under the direction of the Commissioner.

(b) Tree Cone and Seed Purchase Fund. - A percentage of the money obtained from the sale of seedlings and remaining unobligated at the end of a fiscal year shall be placed in a special, continuing, and nonreverting Tree Cone and Seed Purchase Fund under the control and direction of the Commissioner. The percentage of the sales placed in the Fund shall not exceed ten percent (10%). At the beginning of each fiscal year, the Commissioner shall select the percentage for the upcoming fiscal year depending upon the anticipated costs of tree cones and seeds which the Department must purchase. Money in this Fund shall not be allowed to accumulate in excess of the amount needed to purchase a four-year supply of tree cones and seed and shall be used for no purpose other than the purchase of tree cones and seeds.

(c) Forest Seedling Nursery Program Fund. - The Forest Seedling Nursery Program Fund is created within the Department of Agriculture and Consumer Services, North Carolina Forest Service, as a special revenue fund. Except as provided in subsection (b) of this section, this Fund shall consist of receipts from the sale of seed and seedlings as authorized in G.S. 106-877 and any gifts, bequests, or grants for the benefit of this Fund. No General Fund appropriations shall be credited to this Fund. Any balance remaining in this Fund at the end of any fiscal year shall not revert. The Department may use this Fund only to develop, improve, repair, maintain, operate, or otherwise invest in the Forest Seedling Nursery Program.

(d) Bladen Lakes State Forest Fund. - The Bladen Lakes State Forest Fund is created within the Department of Agriculture and Consumer Services, North Carolina Forest Service, as a special revenue fund. This Fund shall consist of receipts from the sale of forest products from Bladen Lakes State Forest as authorized in G.S. 106-877 and any gifts, bequests, or grants for the benefit of this Fund. No General Fund appropriations shall be credited to this Fund. Any balance remaining in this Fund at the end of any fiscal year shall not revert. The Department may use this Fund only to develop, improve, repair, maintain, operate, or otherwise invest in the Bladen Lakes State Forest. (2011-145, s. 13.25(o); 2011-391, s. 33(b); 2013-155, s. 11.)

§ 106-879. Legislative authority necessary for payment.

Nothing in this Article shall operate or be construed as authority for the payment of any money out of the State treasury for the purchase of lands or for other purposes unless by appropriation for said purpose by the General Assembly. (2011-145, s. 13.25(o).)

§ 106-880. Distribution of funds from sale of forestlands.

All funds paid by the National Forest Commission, by authority of an act of Congress, approved May 23, 1908, (35 Stat. 260), for the Counties of Avery, Buncombe, Burke, Craven, Haywood, Henderson, Hyde, Jackson, Macon, Montgomery, Swain, Transylvania, Watauga, and Yancey, shall be paid to the proper county officers, and said funds shall, when received, be placed in the account of the general county funds: Provided, however, that in Buncombe County said funds shall be entirely for the use and benefit of the school administrative unit in which said national forestlands shall be located.

All funds which may hereafter come into the hands of the State Treasurer from like sources shall be likewise distributed. (2011-145, s. 13.25(o).)

§ 106-881. License fees for hunting and fishing on government-owned property unaffected.

No wording in G.S. 113-307.1(a), or any other North Carolina public, local, or special act, shall be construed to abrogate the vested rights of the State of North Carolina to collect fees for license for hunting and fishing on any government-owned land or in any government-owned stream in North Carolina including the license for county, State, or nonresident hunters or fishermen; or upon any lands or in any streams hereafter acquired by the federal government within the boundaries of the State of North Carolina. The lands and streams within the boundaries of the Great Smoky Mountains National Park are exempt from this section. (2011-145, s. 13.25(o).)

§ 106-882. Donations of property for forestry purposes; agreements with federal government or agencies for acquisition.

The Department may accept gifts, donations, or contributions of land suitable for forestry purposes and to enter into agreements with the federal government or other agencies for acquiring by lease, purchase, or otherwise such lands as in the judgment of the Department are desirable for State forests and State recreational forests. (2011-145, s. 13.25(o).)

§ 106-883. Expenditure of funds for development, etc.; disposition of products from lands; rules.

When lands are acquired or leased under G.S. 106-882, the Department may make expenditures from any funds not otherwise obligated, for the management, development, and utilization of such areas; to sell or otherwise dispose of products from such lands, and to make such rules as may be necessary to carry out the purposes of G.S. 106-882 to G.S. 106-886. (2011-145, s. 13.25(o).)

§ 106-884. Disposition of revenues received from lands acquired.

All revenues derived from lands now owned or later acquired under the provisions of G.S. 106-882 to G.S. 106-886 shall be set aside for the use of the Department in acquisition, management, development, and use of such lands until all obligations incurred have been paid in full. Thereafter, fifty percent (50%) of all net profits accruing from the administration of such lands shall be applicable for such purposes as the General Assembly may prescribe and fifty percent (50%) shall be paid into the school fund to be used in the county or counties in which lands are located. (2011-145, s. 13.25(o).)

§ 106-885. State not obligated for debts created hereunder.

Obligations for the acquisition of land incurred by the Department under the authority of G.S. 106-882 to G.S. 106-886 shall be paid solely and exclusively from revenues derived from such lands and shall not impose any liability upon the general credit and taxing power of the State. (2011-145, s. 13.25(o).)

§ 106-886. Disposition of lands acquired.

The Department shall have full power and authority to sell, exchange, or lease lands under its jurisdiction when in its judgment it is advantageous to the State to do so in the highest orderly development and management of State forests: Provided, however, said sale, lease, or exchange shall not be contrary to the terms of any contract that it has entered into. (2011-145, s. 13.25(o).)

§ 106-887. Management of DuPont State Recreational Forest.

(a) DuPont State Forest is designated as a State Recreational Forest. The Department shall manage DuPont State Recreational Forest: (i) primarily for natural resource preservation, scenic enjoyment and recreational purposes, including horseback riding, hiking, bicycling, hunting, and fishing; (ii) so as to provide an exemplary model of scientifically sound, ecologically based natural resource management for the social and economic benefit of the forest's diverse community of users; and (iii) consistent with the grant agreement that designates a portion of the forest as a North Carolina Nature Preserve. In addition, the Department may use the forest for the demonstration of different forest management and resource protection techniques for local landowners, natural resource professionals, students, and other forest visitors.

(b) The Department shall adopt a land management plan for DuPont State Recreational Forest, which shall be periodically revised as needed, to (i) provide the ecological context within which management of the forest will be conducted; (ii) describe the desired future condition of natural resources throughout the forest toward which management will be directed; and (iii) outline appropriate management techniques to achieve those desired future conditions.

(c) Notwithstanding subsection (a) of G.S. 106-877, with respect to DuPont State Recreational Forest, the Department may cut and remove timber for forest management purposes only, including for the purposes of fire, pest, and disease prevention and control. The Department may cut, remove, and sell timber for the purpose of revenue generation only upon approval of the Governor and the Council of State.

(d) Notwithstanding G.S. 106-886, with respect to property comprising DuPont State Recreational Forest, the Department may sell, lease, or exchange such property only upon approval of the Governor and the Council of State.

(e) The Department may acquire inholdings or lands adjacent to DuPont State Recreational Forest for recreational purposes, natural resource protection or scenic enjoyment purposes, and other purposes described in G.S. 106-876 as appropriate for a recreational forest, and such acquisitions shall be made in accordance with the provisions of G.S. 106-876.

(f) In accordance with subsection (b) of G.S. 106-877, the Department may construct, operate, and maintain within DuPont State Recreational Forest suitable public service facilities and conveniences, and may charge and collect reasonable fees for the use of these facilities and conveniences. The Department may also charge and collect reasonable fees for hunting and fishing privileges in the forest, provided that these privileges shall be extended only to holders of State hunting and fishing licenses who comply with all State game and fish laws.

(g) In accordance with subsection (c) of G.S. 106-877, the Department may grant to private individuals or companies concessions for operation of public service facilities for such periods and upon such conditions as the Department deems to be in the public interest.

(h) The Department shall adopt rules for operation and management of DuPont State Recreational Forest in consultation with interested parties, including, but not limited to, local governments with jurisdiction over the area, the Friends of DuPont Forest, and other stakeholders with interests in the property for recreation and protection of its wildlife populations, water quality, biodiversity, or historical and cultural value.

(i) The Department shall report no later than October 1 of each year to the Joint Legislative Commission on Governmental Operations, the House and Senate Appropriations Subcommittees on Natural and Economic Resources, the Fiscal Research Division, and the Environmental Review Commission on the Department's management activities at DuPont State Recreational Forest during the preceding fiscal year and plans for management of DuPont State Recreational Forest for the upcoming fiscal year. (2011-145, s. 13.25(o); 2013-155, s. 12; 2013-360, s. 14.3(h).)

§ 106-888: Reserved for future codification purposes.

§ 106-889: Reserved for future codification purposes.

§ 106-890: Reserved for future codification purposes.

§ 106-891: Reserved for future codification purposes.

§ 106-892: Reserved for future codification purposes.

§ 106-893: Reserved for future codification purposes.

§ 106-894: Reserved for future codification purposes.

Article 75.

Protection and Development of Forests; Fire Control.

§ 106-895. Powers of Department of Agriculture and Consumer Services.

(a) The Department of Agriculture and Consumer Services may take such action as it may deem necessary to provide for the prevention and control of forest fires in any and all parts of this State, and it is hereby authorized to enter into an agreement with the Secretary of Agriculture of the United States for the protection of the forested watersheds of streams in this State.

(b) In this Article, unless the context requires otherwise:

(1) "Commissioner" means the Commissioner of Agriculture.

(2) "Department" means the Department of Agriculture and Consumer Services. (1915, c. 243, s. 1; C.S., s. 6133; 1925, c. 122, s. 22; 1973, c. 1262, s. 28; 1977, c. 771, s. 4; 1989, c. 727, s. 60; 1997-443, s. 11A.119(a); 2011-145, s. 13.25(p), (q).)

§ 106-896. Forest rangers.

The Commissioner may appoint one county forest ranger and one or more deputy forest rangers in each county of the State in which, after careful investigation, the amount of forestland and the risks from forest fires shall, in his judgment, warrant the establishment of a forest fire organization. (1915, c. 243, s. 2; C.S., s. 6134; 1925, c. 106, s. 1; c. 122, s. 22; 1927, c. 150, s. 1; 1935, c.

178, s. 1; 1951, c. 575; 1973, c. 1262, s. 28; 1977, c. 771, s. 4; 1989, c. 727, s. 61; 2011-145, s. 13.25(p), (q).)

§ 106-897. Forest laws defined.

The forest laws consist of:

(1) G.S. 14-136 to G.S. 14-140;

(2) Articles 74 through 84 of this Chapter;

(3) G.S. 77-13 and G.S. 77-14;

(4) Other statutes enacted for the protection of forests and woodlands from fire, insects, or disease and concerning obstruction of streams and ditches in forests and woodlands; and

(5) Regulations and ordinances adopted under the authority of the above statutes. (1983, c. 327, s. 1; 2011-145, s. 13.25(p), (q).)

§ 106-898. Duties of forest rangers; payment of expenses by State and counties.

Forest rangers shall have charge of measures for controlling forest fires, protection of forests from pests and diseases, and the development and improvement of the forests for maximum production of forest products; shall post along highways and in other conspicuous places copies of the forest fire laws and warnings against fires, which shall be supplied by the Commissioner; shall patrol and man lookout towers and other points during dry and dangerous seasons under the direction of the Commissioner; and shall perform such other acts and duties as shall be considered necessary by the Commissioner in the protection, development and improvement of the forested area of each of the counties within the State. No county may be held liable for any part of the expenses thus incurred unless specifically authorized by the board of county commissioners under prior written agreement with the Commissioner; appropriations for meeting the county's share of such expenses so authorized by the board of county commissioners shall be provided annually in the county budget. For each county in which financial participation by the county is authorized, the Commissioner shall keep or cause to be kept an itemized account of all expenses thus incurred and shall send such accounts periodically to the board of county commissioners of said county; upon approval by the board of the correctness of such accounts, the county commissioners shall issue or cause to be issued a warrant on the county treasury for the payment of the county's share of such expenditures, said payment to be made within one month after receipt of such statement from the Commissioner. Appropriations made by a county for the purposes set out in Articles 75, 76, 78, and 82 of this Chapter in the cooperative forest protection, development and improvement work are not to replace State and federal funds which may be available to the Commissioner for the work in said county, but are to serve as a supplement thereto. Funds appropriated to the Department for a fiscal year for the purposes set out in Articles 75, 76, 78, and 82 of this Chapter shall not be expended in a county unless that county shall contribute at least twenty-five percent (25%) of the total cost of the forestry program. (1915, c. 243, s. 4; C.S., s. 6136; 1925, c. 106, s. 1; 1927, c. 150, s. 3; 1935, c. 178, s. 2; 1943, c. 660; 1947, c. 56, s. 1; 1951, c. 575; 1961, c. 833, s. 17; 1963, c. 312, s. 1; 1973, c. 1262, s. 86; 1975, c. 620, s. 1; 1977, c. 771, s. 4; 1983, c. 327, s. 2; 1989, c. 727, s. 62; 1991 (Reg. Sess., 1992), c. 1039, s. 23; 2011-145, s. 13.25(p), (q).)

§ 106-899. Powers of forest rangers to prevent and extinguish fires; authority to issue citations and warning tickets.

(a) Forest rangers shall prevent and extinguish forest fires and shall have control and direction of all persons and equipment while engaged in the extinguishing of forest fires. During a season of drought, the Commissioner or his designate may establish a fire patrol in any district, and in case of fire in or threatening any forest or woodland, the forest ranger shall attend forthwith and use all necessary means to confine and extinguish such fire. The forest ranger or deputy forest ranger may summon any resident between the ages of 18 and 45 years, inclusive, to assist in extinguishing fires and may require the use of crawler tractors and other property needed for such purposes; any person so summoned and who is physically able who refuses or neglects to assist or to allow the use of equipment and such other property required shall be guilty of a Class 3 misdemeanor and upon conviction shall only be subject to a fine of not less than fifty dollars ($50.00) nor more than one hundred dollars ($100.00). No action for trespass shall lie against any forest ranger, deputy forest ranger, or person summoned by him for crossing lands, backfiring, burning out or performing his duties as a forest ranger or deputy forest ranger.

(b)   Forest rangers are authorized to issue and serve citations under the terms of G.S. 15A-302 and warning tickets under the terms of G.S. 106-901 for offenses under the forest laws. This subsection may not be interpreted to confer the power of arrest on forest rangers, and does not make them criminal justice officers within the meaning of G.S. 17C-2. (1915, c. 243, s. 6; C.S., s. 6137; 1925, c. 106, ss. 1, 2; c. 240; 1927, c. 150, s. 4; 1951, c. 575; 1963, c. 312, s. 2; 1973, c. 108, s. 65; c. 1262, s. 86; 1975, c. 620, s. 2; 1977, c. 771, s. 4; 1983, c. 327, s. 3; 1989, c. 727, s. 63; 1993, c. 539, s. 832; 1994, Ex. Sess., c. 24, s. 14(c); 2011-145, s. 13.25(p), (q).)

§ 106-900. Powers of forest law-enforcement officers.

The Commissioner is authorized to appoint as many forest law-enforcement officers as he deems necessary to carry out the forest law-enforcement responsibilities of the Department. Forest law-enforcement officers shall have all the powers and the duties of a forest ranger enumerated in G.S. 106-898 and G.S. 106-899. Forest law-enforcement officers shall, in addition to their other duties, have the powers of peace officers to enforce the forest laws. Any forest law-enforcement officer may arrest, without warrant, any person or persons committing any crime in his presence or whom such officer has probable cause for believing has committed a crime in his presence and bring such person or persons forthwith before a district court or other officer having jurisdiction. Forest law-enforcement officers shall also have authority to obtain and serve warrants including warrants for violation of any duly promulgated rule of the Department. (1975, c. 620, s. 3; 1977, c. 771, s. 4; 1983, c. 327, s. 5; 1989, c. 727, s. 64; 2011-145, s. 13.25(p), (q).)

§ 106-901. Warning tickets for violations of the forest laws.

(a)   To encourage the cooperation of the public in achieving the objectives of the forest laws, the Commissioner may provide for the issuance of warning tickets instead of the initiation of criminal prosecution by forest rangers and forest law-enforcement officers. Issuance of the warning tickets shall be in accordance with criteria administratively promulgated by the Commissioner within the requirements of this section. These criteria are exempt from Article 2A of Chapter 150B of the General Statutes.

(b)   No warning ticket may be issued unless all of the following conditions are met:

(1)   The forest ranger or the forest law-enforcement officer must be convinced that the offense was not committed intentionally.

(2)   The offense is not one, or a type of offense, for which the Commissioner has prohibited the issuance of warning tickets.

(3)   At the time of the violation it was not reasonably foreseeable that the conduct of the offender could result in any significant destruction of forests or woodlands or constitute a hazard to the public.

(c)   A warning ticket may not be issued if the offender has previously been charged with, or issued a warning ticket for, the same or a similar offense within the preceding three years. A list of persons who have been issued warning tickets under this section within the preceding three years shall be maintained and periodically updated by the Commissioner.

(d)   This section does not entitle any person who has committed an offense to the right to be issued a warning ticket, and the issuance of a warning ticket does not prohibit the later initiation of criminal prosecution for the same offense for which the warning ticket was issued. (1983, c. 327, s. 6; 1987, c. 827, s. 6; 2000-189, s. 8; 2011-145, s. 13.25(p), (q).)

§ 106-902. Compensation of forest rangers.

Forest rangers shall receive compensation from the Department at a reasonable rate to be fixed by said Department for the time actually engaged in the performance of their duties; and reasonable expenses for equipment, transportation, or food supplies incurred in the performance of their duties, according to an itemized statement to be rendered the Commissioner every month, and approved by him. Forest rangers shall render to the Commissioner a statement of the services rendered by the men employed by them or their deputy rangers, as provided in this Article, within one month of the date of service, which bill shall show in detail the amount and character of the service performed, the exact duration thereof, the name of each person employed, and any other information required by the Commissioner. If said bill be duly approved by the Commissioner, it shall be paid by direction of the Department out of any funds provided for that purpose. (1915, c. 243, s. 7; C.S., s. 6138; 1924, c. 60; 1925, c. 106, ss. 1, 3; c. 122, s. 22; 1947, c. 56, s. 2; 1951, c. 575; 1963, c. 312, s. 3; 1973, c. 1262, ss. 28, 86; 1977, c. 771, s. 4; 1989, c. 727, s. 65; 2011-145, s. 13.25(p), (q).)

§ 106-903. Overtime compensation for forest fire fighting.

The Department shall, within funds appropriated to the Department, provide overtime compensation to the professional employees of the North Carolina Forest Service involved in fighting forest fires. (1983, c. 761, s. 119; 1989, c. 727, s. 66; 2005-386, s. 1.5; 2011-145, s. 13.25(p); 2013-155, s. 13.)

§ 106-904. Woodland defined.

For the purposes of this Article, woodland is taken to include all forest areas, both timber and cutover land, and all second-growth stands on areas that have at one time been cultivated. (1915, c. 243, s. 11; C.S., s. 6139; 2011-145, s. 13.25(p).)

§ 106-905. Misdemeanor to destroy posted forestry notice.

Any person who shall maliciously or willfully destroy, deface, remove, or disfigure any sign, poster, or warning notice, posted by order of the Commissioner, under the provisions of this Article, or any other act which may be passed for the purpose of protecting and developing the forests in this State, shall be guilty of a Class 3 misdemeanor. (1915, c. 243, s. 5; C.S., s. 6140; 1963, c. 312, s. 4; 1973, c. 1262, s. 86; 1977, c. 771, s. 4; 1989, c. 727, s. 67; 1993, c. 539, s. 833; 1994, Ex. Sess., c. 24, s. 14(c); 2011-145, s. 13.25(p), (q).)

§ 106-906. Cooperation between counties and State in forest protection and development.

The board of county commissioners of any county is hereby authorized and empowered to cooperate with the Department in the protection, reforestation, and promotion of forest management of their own forests within their respective counties, and to appropriate and pay out of the funds under their control such amount as is provided in G.S. 106-898. (1921, c. 26; C.S., s. 6140(a); 1925, c. 122, s. 22; 1945, c. 635; 1963, c. 312, s. 5; 1973, c. 1262, s. 86; 1977, c. 771, s. 4; 1989, c. 727, s. 68; 2011-145, s. 13.25(p), (q).)

§ 106-907. Instructions on forest preservation and development.

(a) It shall be the duty of all district, county, township rangers, and all deputy rangers provided for in this Chapter to distribute in all of the public schools and high schools of the county in which they are serving as such fire rangers all such tracts, books, periodicals and other literature that may, from time to time, be sent out to such rangers by the State and federal forestry agencies touching or dealing with forest preservation, development, and forest management.

(b) It shall be the duty of the various rangers herein mentioned under the direction of the Commissioner, and the duty of the teachers of the various schools, both public and high schools, to keep posted at some conspicuous place in the various classrooms of the school buildings such appropriate bulletins and posters as may be sent out from the forestry agencies herein named for that purpose and keep the same constantly before their pupils; and said teachers and rangers shall prepare lectures or talks to be made to the pupils of the various schools on the subject of forest fires, their origin and their destructive effect on the plant life and tree life of the forests of the State, the development and scientific management of the forests of the State, and shall be prepared to give practical instruction to their pupils from time to time and as often as they shall find it possible so to do. (1925, c. 61, s. 3; 1951, c. 575; 1963, c. 312, s. 6; 1973, c. 1262, s. 86; 1977, c. 771, s. 4; 1989, c. 727, s. 69; 2011-145, s. 13.25(p), (q).)

§ 106-908. Authority of Governor to close forests and woodlands to hunting, fishing and trapping.

During periods of protracted drought or when other hazardous fire conditions threaten forest and water resources and appear to require extraordinary precautions, the Governor of the State, upon the joint recommendation of the Commissioner and the Executive Director of the North Carolina Wildlife Resources Commission, may by official proclamation:

(1)   Close any or all of the woodlands and inland waters of the State to hunting, fishing and trapping for the period of the emergency.

(2)   Forbid for the period of the emergency the building of campfires and the burning of brush, grass or other debris within 500 feet of any woodland in any county, counties, or parts thereof.

(3)   Close for the period of the emergency any or all of the woodlands of the State to such other persons and activities as he deems proper under the circumstances, except to the owners or tenants of such property and their agents and employees, or persons holding written permission from any owner or his recognized agent to enter thereon for any lawful purpose other than hunting, fishing or trapping. (1953, c. 305; 1973, c. 1262, s. 86; 1977, c. 771, s. 4; 1989, c. 727, s. 70; 2011-145, s. 13.25(p), (q).)

§ 106-909. Publication of proclamation; annulment thereof.

Such proclamation shall become effective 24 hours after certified time of issue, and shall be published in such newspapers and posted in such places and in such manner as the Governor may direct. It shall be annulled in the same manner by another proclamation by the Governor when he is satisfied, upon joint recommendation of the Commissioner and the Executive Director of the North Carolina Wildlife Resources Commission, that the period of the emergency has passed. (1953, c. 305; 1973, c. 1262, s. 86; 1977, c. 771, s. 4; 1989, c. 727, s. 71; 2011-145, s. 13.25(p), (q).)

§ 106-910. Violation of proclamation a misdemeanor.

Any person, firm or corporation who enters upon any woodlands or inland waters of the State for the purpose of hunting, fishing or trapping, or who builds a campfire or burns brush, grass or other debris within 500 feet of any woodland, after a proclamation has been issued by the Governor forbidding such activities, or who violates any other provisions of the Governor's proclamation with regard to permissible activities in closed woodlands shall be guilty of a Class 1 misdemeanor. (1953, c. 305; 1993, c. 539, s. 834; 1994, Ex. Sess., c. 24, s. 14(c); 2011-145, s. 13.25(p).)

§ 106-911. Annual report on wildfires.

No later than October 1 of each year, beginning October 1, 2012, the Commissioner shall submit a written report on wildfires in the State to the chairs of the House Appropriations Subcommittee on Natural and Economic Resources and the Senate Appropriations Committee on Natural and Economic Resources, the Joint Legislative Commission on Governmental Operations, and the Fiscal Research Division of the General Assembly. The report shall include the following information for all major or project wildfires during the prior fiscal year:

(1) The date, location, and impacts (property damage and any casualties) from the wildfire.

(2) The following data for firefighters and related support personnel involved in fighting the wildfire:

a. Total overtime hours worked.

b. Total compensation paid for overtime.

c. The portion of compensation paid that was reimbursed to the State.

(3) The fiscal impact of the wildfire, including total costs, reimbursable costs, and costs incurred by the State. (2012-142, s. 11.2.)

§ 106-912: Reserved for future codification purposes.

§ 106-913: Reserved for future codification purposes.

§ 106-914: Reserved for future codification purposes.

§ 106-915: Reserved for future codification purposes.

§ 106-916: Reserved for future codification purposes.

§ 106-917: Reserved for future codification purposes.

§ 106-918: Reserved for future codification purposes.

§ 106-919: Reserved for future codification purposes.

Article 76.

Protection of Forest Against Insect Infestation and Disease.

§ 106-920. Purpose and intent.

(a) The purpose of this Article is to place within the Department of Agriculture and Consumer Services the authority and responsibility for investigating insect infestations and disease infections which affect stands of forest trees, the devising of control measures for interested landowners and others, and taking measures to control, suppress, or eradicate outbreaks of forest insect pests and tree diseases.

(b) In this Article, unless the context requires otherwise, the expression "Department" means the Department of Agriculture and Consumer Services, and "Commissioner" means the Commissioner of Agriculture. (1953, c. 910; 1969, c. 342, s. 3; 1973, c. 1262, ss. 28, 86; 1977, c. 771, s. 4; 1989, c. 727, s. 72; 1997-443, s. 11A.119(a); 2011-145, s. 13.25(r), (s).)

§ 106-921. Authority of the Department.

The authority and responsibility for carrying out the purpose, intent and provisions of this Article are hereby delegated to the Department. The administration of the provisions of this Article shall be under the general supervision of the Commissioner. (1953, c. 910; 1969, c. 342, s. 3; 1973, c.

1262, ss. 28, 86; 1977, c. 771, s. 4; 1989, c. 727, s. 73; 1997-261, s. 109; 2011-145, s. 13.25(r), (s).)

§ 106-922. Definitions.

As used in this Article, unless the context clearly requires otherwise:

(1) "Control zone" means an area of potential or actual infestation or infection, boundaries of which are fixed and clearly described in a manner to definitely identify the zone.

(2) "Forestland" means land on which forest trees occur.

(3) "Forest trees" means only those trees which are a part and constitute a stand of potential immature or mature commercial timber trees, provided that the term "forest trees" shall be deemed to include shade trees of any species around houses, along highways, and within cities and towns, if the same constitute insect and disease menaces to nearby timber trees or timber stands.

(4) "Infection" means attack by any disease affecting forest trees which is declared by the Commissioner to be dangerously injurious thereto.

(5) "Infestation" means attack by means of any insect, which is by the Commissioner declared to be dangerously injurious to forest trees. (1953, c. 910; 1973, c. 1262, s. 86; 1977, c. 771, s. 4; 1989, c. 727, ss. 74, 75; 2011-145, s. 13.25(r), (s).)

§ 106-923. Action against insects and diseases.

Whenever the Commissioner, or his agent, determines that there exists an infestation of forest insect pests or an infection of forest tree diseases, injurious or potentially injurious to the timber or forest trees within the State of North Carolina, and that said infestation or infection is of such a character as to be a menace to the timber or forest growth of the State, the Commissioner shall declare the existence of a zone of infestation or infection and shall declare and fix boundaries so as to definitely describe and identify said zone of infestation or infection, and the Commissioner or his agent shall give notice in writing by mail or otherwise to each forest landowner within the designated control zone advising him of the nature of the infestation or infection, the recommended control measures, and offer him technical advice on methods of carrying out controls. (1953, c. 910; 1973, c. 1262, s. 86; 1977, c. 771, s. 4; 1989, c. 727, s. 76; 2011-145, s. 13.25(r), (s).)

§ 106-924. Authority of Commissioner and his agents to go upon private land within control zones.

The Commissioner or his agents shall have the power to go upon the land within any zone of infestation or infection and take measures to control, suppress or eradicate the insect, infestation or disease infection. If any person refuses to allow the Commissioner or his agents to go upon his land, or if any person refuses to adopt adequate means to control or eradicate the insect, infestation or disease infection, the Commissioner may apply to the superior court of the county in which the land is located for an injunction or other appropriate remedy to restrain the landowner from interfering with the Commissioner or his agents in entering the control zone and adopting measures to control, suppress or eradicate the insect infestation or disease infection, provided the cost of court or control thereof shall not be a liability against the forest landowner nor constitute a lien upon the real property of such infested area. (1953, c. 910; 1973, c. 1262, s. 86; 1977, c. 771, s. 4; 1989, c. 727, s. 77; 2011-145, s. 13.25(r), (s).)

§ 106-925. Cooperative agreements.

In order to more effectively carry out the purposes of this Article, the Department is authorized to enter into cooperative agreement with the federal government and other public and private agencies, and with the owners of forestland. (1953, c. 910; 1973, c. 1262, s. 86; 1977, c. 771, s. 4; 1989, c. 727, s. 78; 2011-145, s. 13.25(r), (s).)

§ 106-926. Annulment of control zone.

Whenever the Commissioner determines that the forest insect or disease control work within a designated control zone is no longer necessary or feasible, then the Commissioner shall declare the zone of infestation or infection no longer pertinent to the purposes of this Article and such zone will then no longer be recognized. (1953, c. 910; 1973, c. 1262, s. 86; 1977, c. 771, s. 4; 1989, c. 727, s. 79; 2011-145, s. 13.25(r), (s).)

§ 106-927: Reserved for future codification purposes.

§ 106-928: Reserved for future codification purposes.

§ 106-929: Reserved for future codification purposes.

Article 77.

Southeastern Interstate Forest Fire Protection Compact.

§ 106-930. Execution of Compact authorized; terms of Compact.

The legislature on behalf of this State is hereby authorized to execute a Compact, in substantially the following form, with any one or more of the states of Alabama, Florida, Georgia, Kentucky, Mississippi, South Carolina, Tennessee, Virginia, and West Virginia, and the legislature hereby signifies in advance its approval and ratification of such Compact:

SOUTHEASTERN INTERSTATE FOREST FIRE PROTECTION COMPACT

ARTICLE I.

The purpose of this Compact is to promote effective prevention and control of forest fires in the Southeastern region of the United States by the development of integrated forest fire plans, by the maintenance of adequate forest fire-fighting services by the member states, by providing for mutual aid in fighting forest fires among the compacting states of the region and with states which are party to other regional forest fire protection compacts or agreements, and for more adequate forest protection.

ARTICLE II.

This Compact shall become operative immediately as to those states ratifying it whenever any two or more of the states of Alabama, Florida, Georgia, Kentucky, Mississippi, North Carolina, South Carolina, Tennessee, Virginia, and West Virginia, which are contiguous have ratified it and Congress has given consent thereto. Any state not mentioned in this Article which is contiguous with any member state may become a party to this Compact, subject to approval by the legislature of each of the member states.

ARTICLE III.

In each state, the state forester or officer holding the equivalent position who is responsible for forest fire control shall act as compact administrator for that state and shall consult with like officials of the other member states and shall implement cooperation between such states in forest fire prevention and control.

The compact administrators of the member states shall coordinate the services of the member states and provide administrative integration in carrying out the purposes of this Compact.

There shall be established an advisory committee of legislators, forestry commission representatives, and forestry or forest products industries representatives which shall meet from time to time with the compact administrators. Each member state shall name one member of the Senate and one member of the House of Representatives who shall be designated by that state's commission on interstate cooperation, or if said commission cannot constitutionally designate the said members, they shall be designated in accordance with laws of that state; and the governor of each member state shall appoint two representatives, one of whom shall be associated with forestry or forest products industries to comprise the membership of the advisory committee. Action shall be taken by a majority of the compacting states, and each state shall be entitled to one vote.

The compact administrators shall formulate and, in accordance with need, from time to time, revise a regional forest fire plan for the member states.

It shall be the duty of each member state to formulate and put in effect a forest fire plan for that state and take such measures as may be necessary to integrate such forest fire plan with the regional forest fire plan formulated by the compact administrators.

ARTICLE IV.

Whenever the state forest fire control agency of a member state requests aid from the state forest fire control agency of any other member state in combating, controlling or preventing forest fires, it shall be the duty of the state forest fire control agency of that state to render all possible aid to the requesting agency which is consonant with the maintenance of protection at home.

ARTICLE V.

Whenever the forces of any member state are rendering outside aid pursuant to the request of another member state under this Compact, the employees of such state shall, under the direction of the officers of the state to which they are rendering aid, have the same powers (except the power of arrest), duties, rights, privileges and immunities as comparable employees of the state to which they are rendering aid.

No member state or its officers or employees rendering outside aid pursuant to this Compact shall be liable on account of any act or omission on the part of such forces while so engaged, on account of the maintenance, or use of any equipment or supplies in connection therewith: Provided, that nothing herein shall be construed as relieving any person from liability for his own negligent act or omission, or as imposing liability for such negligent act or omission upon any state.

All liability, except as otherwise provided hereinafter, that may arise either under the laws of the requesting state or under the laws of the aiding state or under the laws of a third state on account of or in connection with a request for aid, shall be assumed and borne by the requesting state.

Any member state rendering outside aid pursuant to this Compact shall be reimbursed by the member state receiving such aid for any loss or damage to, or expense incurred in the operation of any equipment answering a request for aid, and for the cost of all materials, transportation, wages, salaries, and subsistence of employees and maintenance of equipment incurred in connection with such request: Provided, that nothing herein contained shall prevent any assisting member state from assuming such loss, damage, expense or other cost or from loaning such equipment or from donating such service to the receiving member state without charge or cost.

Each member state shall provide for the payment of compensation and death benefits to injured employees and the representatives of deceased employees in case employees sustain injuries or are killed while rendering outside aid pursuant to this Compact, in the same manner and on the same terms as if the injury or death were sustained within such state.

For the purposes of this Compact the term employee shall include any volunteer or auxiliary legally included within the forest fire fighting forces of the aiding state under the laws thereof.

The compact administrators shall formulate procedures for claims and reimbursement under the provisions of this Article, in accordance with the laws of the member states.

ARTICLE VI.

Ratification of this Compact shall not be construed to affect any existing statute so as to authorize or permit curtailment or diminution of the forest fire fighting forces, equipment, services or facilities of any member state.

Nothing in this Compact shall be construed to limit or restrict the powers of any state ratifying the same to provide for the prevention, control and extinguishment of forest fires, or to prohibit the enactment or enforcement of state laws, rules or regulations intended to aid in such prevention, control and extinguishment in such state.

Nothing in this Compact shall be construed to affect any existing or future cooperative relationship or arrangement between any federal agency and a member state or states.

ARTICLE VII.

The compact administrators may request the United States Forest Service to act as a research and coordinating agency of the Southeastern Interstate Forest Fire Protection Compact in cooperation with the appropriate agencies in each state, and the United States Forest Service may accept responsibility for preparing and presenting to the compact administrators its recommendations with respect to the regional fire plan. Representatives of any federal agency engaged in forest fire prevention and control may attend meetings of the compact administrators.

ARTICLE VIII.

The provisions of Articles IV and V of this Compact which relate to mutual aid in combating, controlling or preventing forest fires shall be operative as between any state party to this Compact and any other state which is party to a regional forest fire protection compact in another region: Provided, that the legislature of such other state shall have given its assent to such mutual aid provisions of this Compact.

ARTICLE IX.

The Compact shall continue in force and remain binding on each state ratifying it until the legislature or the governor of such state, as the laws of such state shall provide, takes action to withdraw therefrom. Such action shall not be effective until six months after notice thereof has been sent by the chief executive of the state desiring to withdraw to the chief executives of all states then parties to the Compact. (1955, c. 803, s. 1; 2011-145, s. 13.25(t).)

§ 106-931. When Compact to become effective; authority of Governor.

When the legislature shall have executed said Compact on behalf of this State and shall have caused a verified copy thereof to be filed with the State Secretary, and when said Compact shall have been ratified by one or more of the states named in G.S. 106-930, then said Compact shall become operative and effective as between this State and such other state or states. The Governor is hereby authorized and directed to take such action as may be necessary to complete the exchange of official documents as between this State and any other state ratifying said Compact. (1955, c. 803, s. 2; 2011-145, s. 13.25(t), (xx).)

§ 106-932. Assent of legislature to mutual aid provisions of other compacts.

The legislature of this State hereby gives its assent to the mutual aid provisions of Articles IV and V of the South Central Interstate Forest Fire Protection Compact in accordance with Article VIII of that Compact relating to interregional mutual aid; and the legislature of this State also hereby gives its assent to the mutual aid provisions of Articles IV and V of the Middle Atlantic Interstate Forest Fire Protection Compact in accordance with Article VIII of that Compact relating to interregional mutual aid. (1955, c. 803, s. 3; 2011-145, s. 13.25(t).)

§ 106-933. Compact Administrator; North Carolina members of advisory committee.

The Commissioner of Agriculture is hereby designated as Compact Administrator for this State and shall consult with like officials of the other member states and shall implement cooperation between such states in forest fire prevention and control.

At some time before the adjournment of each regular session of the General Assembly, the Governor shall choose one person from the membership of the House of Representatives, and shall choose one person from the membership of the Senate, who shall serve on the advisory committee of the Southeastern Interstate Forest Fire Protection Compact as provided for in Article III of said Compact. At the time of the selection of the House and Senate members of such advisory committee, the Governor shall choose one alternate member from the House of Representatives and one from the Senate who shall serve on such advisory committee in case of the death, absence or disability of the regular members so chosen. (1955, c. 803, s. 4; 1973, c. 1262, s. 86; 1977, c. 771, s. 4; 1989, c. 727, s. 218(51); 1997-443, s. 11A.119(a); 2011-145, s. 13.25(t), (u).)

§ 106-934. Agreements with noncompact states.

The Department of Agriculture and Consumer Services is hereby authorized to enter into written agreements with the State forest fire control agency of any other state or any province of Canada which is party to a regional forest fire protection compact. The provisions of any written agreement entered into pursuant to this Article shall be substantially in the form of the authority heretofore granted under the provisions of this Article, Southeastern Interstate Forest Fire Protection Compact. (1971, c. 1171; 1973, c. 1262, s. 28; 1977, c. 771, s. 4; 1989, c. 727, s. 218(52); 1997-443, s. 11A.119(a); 2011-145, s. 13.25(t), (v).)

§ 106-935: Reserved for future codification purposes.

§ 106-936: Reserved for future codification purposes.

§ 106-937: Reserved for future codification purposes.

§ 106-938: Reserved for future codification purposes.

§ 106-939: Reserved for future codification purposes.

Article 78.

Regulation of Open Fires.

§ 106-940. Purpose and findings.

The purpose of this Article is to regulate certain open burning in order to protect the public from the hazards of forest fires and air pollution and to adapt such regulation to the needs and circumstances of the different areas of North Carolina. The General Assembly finds that open burning in proximity to woodlands must be regulated in all counties to protect against forest fires and air pollution. The General Assembly further finds that in certain counties a high percentage of the land area contains organic soils or forest types which may pose greater problems of forest fire and air pollution controls, and that in counties in which a great amount of land-clearing operations is taking place on these organic soils or these forest types, additional control of open burning is required. The counties subject to the need for additional control are classified as high hazard counties for purpose of this Article. (1981, c. 1100, s. 2; 1981 (Reg. Sess., 1982), c. 1385, s. 1; 2011-145, s. 13.25(w).)

§ 106-941. Definitions.

As used in this Article:

(1)   "Department" means the Department of Agriculture and Consumer Services.

(2)   "Forest ranger" means the county forest ranger or deputy forest ranger designated under G.S. 106-896.

(3)   "Person" means any individual, firm, partnership, corporation, association, public or private institution, political subdivision, or government agency.

(4)   "Woodland" means woodland as defined in G.S. 106-904. (1981, c. 1100, s. 2; 1989, c. 727, s. 218(53); 1991 (Reg. Sess., 1992), c. 890, s. 3; 1997-443, s. 11A.119(a); 2011-145, s. 13.25(w), (x).)

§ 106-942. High hazard counties; permits required; standards.

(a) The provisions of this section apply only to the counties of Beaufort, Bladen, Brunswick, Camden, Carteret, Chowan, Craven, Currituck, Dare, Duplin, Gates, Hyde, Jones, Onslow, Pamlico, Pasquotank, Perquimans, Tyrrell, and Washington which are classified as high hazard counties in accordance with G.S. 106-940.

(b) It is unlawful for any person to willfully start or cause to be started any fire in any woodland under the protection of the Department or within 500 feet of any such woodland without first having obtained a permit from the Department. Permits for starting fires may be obtained from forest rangers or other agents authorized by the county forest ranger to issue such permits in the county in which the fire is to be started. Such permits shall be issued by the ranger or other agent unless permits for the area in question have been prohibited or cancelled in accordance with G.S. 106-944 or G.S. 106-946.

(c) It is unlawful for any person to willfully burn any debris, stumps, brush or other flammable materials resulting from ground clearing activities and involving more than five contiguous acres, regardless of the proximity of the burning to woodland and on which such materials are placed in piles or windrows without first having obtained a special permit from the Department. Areas less than five acres in size will require a regular permit in accordance with G.S. 106-942(b).

(1) Prevailing winds at the time of ignition must be away from any city, town, development, major highway, or other populated area, the ambient air of which may be significantly affected by smoke, fly ash, or other air contaminates from the burning.

(2) The location of the burning must be at least 500 feet from any dwelling or structure located in a predominately residential area other than a dwelling or structure located on the property on which the burning is conducted unless permission is granted by the occupants.

(3) The amount of dirt or organic soil on or in the material to be burned must be minimized and the material arranged in a way suitable to facilitate rapid burning.

(4) Burning may not be initiated when it is determined by a forest ranger, based on information supplied by a competent authority that stagnant air

conditions or inversions exist or that such conditions may occur during the duration of the burn.

(5)   Heavy oils, asphaltic material, or items containing natural or synthetic rubber may not be used to ignite the material to be burned or to promote the burning of such material.

(6)   Initial burning may be commenced only between the hours of 8:00 A.M. and 4:00 P.M. and no combustible material may be added to the fire between 4:00 P.M. on one day and 8:00 A.M. on the following day, except that when favorable meteorological conditions exist, any forest ranger authorized to issue the permit may authorize in writing a deviation from the restrictions. (1981, c. 1100, s. 2; 1981 (Reg. Sess., 1982), c. 1165; c. 1385, s. 2; 2002-132, s. 1; 2011-145, s. 13.25(w), (x); 2013-265, s. 15.)

§ 106-943. Open burning in non-high hazard counties; permits required; standards.

(a)   The provisions of this section apply only to the counties not designated as high hazard counties in G.S. 106-942(a).

(b)   It shall be unlawful for any person to start or cause to be started any fire or ignite any material in any woodland under the protection of the Department or within 500 feet of any such woodland during the hours starting at midnight and ending at 4:00 P.M. without first obtaining a permit from the Department. Permits may be obtained from forest rangers or other agents authorized by the forest ranger to issue such permits in the county in which the fire is to be started. Such permits shall be issued by the ranger or other agent unless permits for the area in question have been prohibited or cancelled under G.S. 106-944 or G.S. 106-946. (1981, c. 1100, s. 2; 2011-145, s. 13.25(w), (x).)

§ 106-944. Open burning prohibited statewide.

During periods of hazardous forest fire conditions or during air pollution episodes declared pursuant to Article 21B of Chapter 143 of the General Statutes, the Commissioner is authorized to prohibit all open burning regardless of whether a permit is required under G.S. 106-942 or G.S. 106-943. The

Commissioner shall issue a press release containing relevant details of the prohibition to news media serving the area affected. (1981, c. 1100, s. 2; 2011-145, s. 13.25(w), (x).)

§ 106-945. Permit conditions.

Permits issued under this Article shall be issued in the name of the person undertaking the burning and shall specify the specific area in which the burning is to occur, the type and amount of material to be burned, the duration of the permit, and such other factors as are necessary to identify the burning which is allowed under the permit. (1981, c. 1100, s. 2; 2011-145, s. 13.25(w).)

§ 106-946. Permit suspension and cancellation.

Upon a determination that hazardous forest fire conditions exist the Commissioner is authorized to cancel any permit issued under this Article and suspend the issuance of any new permits. Upon a determination by the Environmental Management Commission or its agent that open burning permitted under this Article is causing significant contravention of ambient air quality standards or that an air pollution episode exists pursuant to Article 21B of Chapter 143 of the General Statutes, the Commissioner shall cancel any permits issued under authority of this Article and shall suspend the issuance of any new permits. (1981, c. 1100, s. 2; 2011-145, s. 13.25(w), (x).)

§ 106-947. Control of existing fires.

(a) If a fire is set without a permit required by G.S. 106-942, 106-943, or 106-944, and is set in an area in which permits are prohibited or cancelled at the time the fire is set, the person responsible for setting the fire or causing the fire to be set shall immediately extinguish the fire or take such other action as directed by any forest ranger authorized to issue permits under G.S. 106-942(c). In the event that the person responsible does not immediately undertake efforts to extinguish the fire or take such other action as directed by the forest ranger, the Department may enter the property and take reasonable steps to extinguish or control the fire and the person responsible for setting the fire shall reimburse the Department for the expenses incurred by the Department. A showing that a fire is associated with land-clearing activities is prima facie evidence that the person undertaking the land clearing is responsible for setting the fire or causing the fire to be set.

(b)   If a fire requiring a permit under G.S. 106-942(c) is set without a permit and a forest ranger authorized to issue such permits determines that a permit would not have been issued for the fire at the time it was set, the person responsible for setting the fire or causing the fire to be set shall immediately take such action as the forest ranger directs to extinguish or control the fire. In the event the person responsible does not immediately undertake efforts to extinguish the fire or take such other action as directed by the forest ranger, the Department may enter the property and take reasonable steps to extinguish or control the fire and the person responsible for setting the fire shall reimburse the Department for the expenses incurred by the Department. A showing that a fire is associated with land-clearing activities is prima facie evidence that the person undertaking the land clearing is responsible for setting the fire or causing the fire to be set.

(c)   If a fire is set in accordance with a permit but the burning is taking place contrary to the conditions of the permit, any forest ranger with authority to issue permits in the area in question may order the permittee in writing to undertake the steps necessary to comply with the conditions of his permit. If the permittee is not making a reasonable effort to comply with the order, the forest ranger may enter the property and take reasonable steps to extinguish or control the fire and the permittee shall reimburse the Department for the expenses incurred by the Department. (1981, c. 1100, s. 2; 2011-145, s. 13.25(w), (x).)

§ 106-948. Penalties.

Any person violating the provisions of this Article or of any permit issued under the authority of this Article shall be guilty of a Class 3 misdemeanor. It is not a violation of this Article or any permit issued under the authority of this Article if a person unintentionally fails to comply with a setback requirement so long as the difference between the required setback and the actual setback is no more than five percent (5%) of the required setback. The penalties imposed by this section shall be separate and apart and not in lieu of any civil or criminal penalties which may be imposed by G.S. 143-215.114A or G.S. 143-215.114B. The penalties imposed are also in addition to any liability the violator incurs as a result of actions taken by the Department under G.S. 106-947. (1981, c. 1100, s. 2; 1989 (Reg. Sess., 1990), c. 1045, s. 11; 1993, c. 539, s. 835; 1994, Ex. Sess., c. 24, s. 14(c); 2011-145, s. 13.25(w), (x); 2011-394, s. 2(h).)

§ 106-949. Effect on other laws.

This Article shall not be construed as affecting or abridging the lawful authority of local governments to pass ordinances relating to open burning within their boundaries. Nothing in this Article shall relieve any person from compliance with the provisions of Article 21B of Chapter 143 of the General Statutes and regulations adopted thereunder. In the event that permits are required for open burning associated with land clearing under the authority of Article 21B of Chapter 143 of the General Statutes, the authority to issue such permits shall be delegated to forest rangers who are authorized to issue permits under G.S. 106-942(c). (1981, c. 1100, s. 2; 2011-145, s. 13.25(w), (x).)

§ 106-950. Exempt fires; no permit fees.

(a) This Article shall not apply to any fires started, or caused to be started, within 100 feet of an occupied dwelling house if such fire shall be confined (i) within an enclosure from which burning material may not escape or (ii) within a protected area upon which a watch is being maintained and which is provided with adequate fire protection equipment.

(b) No charge shall be made for the granting of any permit required by this Article. (1981, c. 1100, s. 2; 2011-145, s. 13.25(w).)

§ 106-951: Reserved for future codification purposes.

§ 106-952: Reserved for future codification purposes.

§ 106-953: Reserved for future codification purposes.

§ 106-954: Reserved for future codification purposes.

Article 79.

Firefighters on On-Call Status.

§ 106-955. Definitions.

As used in this Article:

(1)   "Firefighter" means an employee of the North Carolina Forest Service of the Department of Agriculture and Consumer Services who engages in fire suppression duties or engages in emergency response duties pursuant to G.S. 166A-19.77.

(2)   "Fire suppression duties" means involvement in on-site fire suppression, participation in Incident Management Team while it is mobilized, Operations Room duty during on-going fires or when required by high readiness plans, mop-up activities to secure fire sites, scouting and detecting forest fires, performance of standby duty, and any other activity that directly contributes to the detection, response to, and control of fires. (1985, c. 757, s. 160(a); 1989, c. 727, s. 218(54); 1997-443, s. 11A.119(a); 2005-386, s. 1.6; 2011-145, s. 13.25(y), (z); 2013-155, s. 14.)

§ 106-956. On-call.

(a)   On-call is time during which a firefighter is required to be available to return to the duty station or respond to an emergency within 30 minutes. The Department of Agriculture and Consumer Services shall provide each firefighter in on-call status with an electronic communication device that makes the wearer accessible to the firefighter's duty station.

(b)   Notwithstanding subsection (a) of this section, after 14 consecutive days that a firefighter is on duty, the Department of Agriculture and Consumer Services shall permit the firefighter to be off duty for two days so long as the firefighter gives the Department of Agriculture and Consumer Services a means of contact where the firefighter can be reached. On the days the firefighter is permitted to be off duty, the Department of Agriculture and Consumer Services may contact the firefighter only when there is a bona fide emergency. (1985, c.

757, s. 160(a); 1989, c. 727, s. 218(55); 1997-443, s. 11A.119(a); 2011-145, s. 13.25(y), (z); 2013-155, s. 14.)

§ 106-957: Reserved for future codification purposes.

§ 106-958: Reserved for future codification purposes.

§ 106-959: Reserved for future codification purposes.

§ 106-960: Reserved for future codification purposes.

§ 106-961: Reserved for future codification purposes.

§ 106-962: Reserved for future codification purposes.

§ 106-963: Reserved for future codification purposes.

§ 106-964: Reserved for future codification purposes.

Article 80.

North Carolina Prescribed Burning Act.

§ 106-965. Legislative findings.

The General Assembly finds that prescribed burning of forestlands is a management tool that is beneficial to North Carolina's public safety, forest and wildlife resources, environment, and economy. The General Assembly finds that the following are benefits that result from prescribed burning of forestlands:

(1)   Prescribed burning reduces the naturally occurring buildup of vegetative fuels on forestlands, thereby reducing the risk and severity of wildfires and lessening the loss of life and property.

(2) The State's ever-increasing population is resulting in urban development directly adjacent to fire-prone forestlands, referred to as a woodland-urban interface area. The use of prescribed burning in these woodland-urban interface areas substantially reduces the risk of wildfires that cause damage.

(3) Many of North Carolina's natural ecosystems require periodic fire for their survival. Prescribed burning is essential to the perpetuation, restoration, and management of many plant and animal communities. Prescribed burning benefits game, nongame, and endangered wildlife species by increasing the growth and yield of plants that provide forage and an area for escape and brooding and that satisfy other habitat needs.

(4) Forestlands are economic, biological, and aesthetic resources of statewide significance. In addition to reducing the frequency and severity of wildfires, prescribed burning of forestlands helps to prepare sites for replanting and natural seeding, to control insects and diseases, and to increase productivity.

(5) Prescribed burning enhances the resources on public use lands, such as State and national forests, wildlife refuges, nature preserves, and game lands. Prescribed burning enhances private lands that are managed for wildlife refuges, nature preserves, and game lands. Prescribed burning enhances private lands that are managed for wildlife, recreation, and other purposes.

As North Carolina's population grows, pressures resulting from liability issues and smoke complaints discourage or limit prescribed burning so that these numerous benefits to forestlands often are not attainable. By recognizing the benefits of prescribed burning and by adopting requirements governing prescribed burning, the General Assembly helps to educate the public, avoid misunderstandings, and reduce complaints about this valuable management tool. (1999-121, s. 1; 2011-145, s. 13.25(aa).)

§ 106-966. Definitions.

As used in this Article:

(1) "Certified prescribed burner" means an individual who has successfully completed a certification program approved by the North Carolina Forest Service of the Department of Agriculture and Consumer Services.

(2) "Prescribed burning" means the planned and controlled application of fire to naturally occurring vegetative fuels under safe weather and safe environmental and other conditions, while following appropriate precautionary measures that will confine the fire to a predetermined area and accomplish the intended management objectives.

(3) "Prescription" means a written plan prepared by a certified prescribed burner for starting, controlling, and extinguishing a prescribed burning. (1999-121, s. 1; 2011-145, s. 13.25(aa), (bb); 2013-155, s. 15.)

§ 106-967. Immunity from liability.

(a) Any prescribed burning conducted in compliance with G.S. 106-968 is in the public interest and does not constitute a public or private nuisance.

(b) A landowner or the landowner's agent who conducts a prescribed burning in compliance with G.S. 106-968 shall not be liable in any civil action for any damage or injury caused by or resulting from smoke.

(c) Notwithstanding subsections (a) and (b), this section does not apply when a nuisance or damage results from a negligently or improperly conducted prescribed burning. (1999-121, s. 1; 2011-145, s. 13.25(aa), (bb).)

§ 106-968. Prescribed burning.

(a) Prior to conducting a prescribed burning, the landowner shall obtain a prescription for the prescribed burning prepared by a certified prescribed burner and filed with the North Carolina Forest Service of the Department of Agriculture and Consumer Services. A copy of the prescription shall be provided to the landowner. A copy of this prescription shall be in the possession of the responsible burner on site throughout the duration of the prescribed burning. The prescription shall include:

(1) The landowner's name and address.

(2) A description of the area to be burned.

(3)   A map of the area to be burned.

(4)   An estimate in tons of the fuel located on the area.

(5)   The objectives of the prescribed burning.

(6)   A list of the acceptable weather conditions and parameters for the prescribed burning sufficient to minimize the likelihood of smoke damage and fire escaping onto adjacent areas.

(7)   The name of the certified prescribed burner responsible for conducting the prescribed burning.

(8)   A summary of the methods that are adequate for the particular circumstances involved to be used to start, control, and extinguish the prescribed burning.

(9)   Provision for reasonable notice of the prescribed burning to be provided to nearby homes and businesses to avoid effects on health and property.

(b)   The prescribed burning shall be conducted by a certified prescribed burner in accordance with a prescription that satisfies subsection (a) of this section. The certified prescribed burner shall be present on the site and shall be in charge of the burning throughout the period of the burning. A landowner may conduct a prescribed burning without being a certified prescribed burner if the landowner is burning a tract of forestland of 50 acres or less owned by that landowner and is following all conditions established in a prescription prepared by a certified prescribed burner.

(c)   Prior to conducting a prescribed burning, the landowner or the landowner's agent shall obtain an open-burning permit under Article 78 of this Chapter from the North Carolina Forest Service of the Department of Agriculture and Consumer Services. This open-burning permit must remain in effect throughout the period of the prescribed burning. The prescribed burning shall be conducted in compliance with all the following:

(1)   The terms and conditions of the open-burning permit under Article 78 of this Chapter.

(2) The State's air pollution control statutes under Article 21 and Article 21B of Chapter 143 of the General Statutes and any rules adopted pursuant to these statutes.

(3) Any applicable local ordinances relating to open burning.

(4) The voluntary smoke management guidelines adopted by the North Carolina Forest Service of the Department of Agriculture and Consumer Services.

(5) Any rules adopted by the North Carolina Forest Service of the Department of Agriculture and Consumer Services, to implement this Article. (1999-121, s. 1; 2011-145, s. 13.25(aa), (bb), (xx); 2013-155, s. 16.)

§ 106-969. Adoption of rules.

The North Carolina Forest Service of the Department of Agriculture and Consumer Services may adopt rules that govern prescribed burning under this Article. (1999-121, s. 1; 2011-145, s. 13.25(aa), (bb); 2013-155, s. 17.)

§ 106-970. Exemption.

This Article does not apply when the Commissioner of Agriculture has cancelled burning permits pursuant to G.S. 106-946 or prohibited all open burning pursuant to G.S. 106-944. (1999-121, s. 1; 2011-145, s. 13.25(aa), (bb).)

§ 106-971: Reserved for future codification purposes.

§ 106-972: Reserved for future codification purposes.

§ 106-973: Reserved for future codification purposes.

§ 106-974: Reserved for future codification purposes.

§ 106-975: Reserved for future codification purposes.

§ 106-976: Reserved for future codification purposes.

§ 106-977: Reserved for future codification purposes.

§ 106-978: Reserved for future codification purposes.

§ 106-979: Reserved for future codification purposes.

Article 81.

Corporations for Protection and Development of Forests.

§ 106-980. Private limited dividend corporations may be formed.

(a)   In this Article, unless the context requires otherwise, "Department" means the Department of Agriculture and Consumer Services, and "Commissioner" means the Commissioner of Agriculture.

(b)   Three or more persons, who associate themselves by an agreement in writing for the purpose, may become a private limited dividend corporation to finance and carry out projects for the protection and development of forests and for such other related purposes as the Secretary shall approve, subject to all the duties, restrictions and liabilities, and possessing all the rights, powers, and privileges, of corporations organized under the general corporation laws of the State of North Carolina, except where such provisions are in conflict with this Article. (1933, c. 178, s. 1; 1973, c. 1262, s. 86; 1977, c. 771, s. 4; 1989, c. 727, s. 80; 1991 (Reg. Sess., 1992), c. 890, s. 4; 1997-443, s. 11A.119(a); 2011-145, s. 13.25(cc), (dd).)

§ 106-981. Manner of organizing.

A corporation formed under this Article shall be organized and incorporated in the manner provided for organization of corporations under the general corporation laws of the State of North Carolina, except where such provisions are in conflict with this Article. The certificate of organization of any such corporation shall contain a statement that it is organized under the provisions of this Article and that it consents to be and shall be at all times subject to the rules and supervision of the Secretary, and shall set forth as or among its purposes the protection and development of forests and the purchase, acquisition, sale, conveyance and other dealing in the same and the products therefrom, subject to the rules from time to time imposed by the Secretary. (1933, c. 178, s. 2; 1973, c. 1262, s. 86; 1977, c. 771, s. 4; 1989, c. 727, s. 81; 2011-145, s. 13.25(cc).)

§ 106-982. Directors.

There shall not be less than three directors, one of whom shall always be a person designated by the Secretary, which one need not be a stockholder. (1933, c. 178, s. 3; 1973, c. 1262, s. 86; 1977, c. 771, s. 4; 1989, c. 727, s. 82; 2011-145, s. 13.25(cc).)

§ 106-983. Duties of supervision by Commissioner.

Corporations formed under this Article shall be regulated by the Commissioner in the manner provided in this Article. Traveling and other expenses incurred by him in the discharge of the duties imposed upon him by this Article shall be charged to, and paid by, the particular corporation or corporations on account of which such expenses are incurred. His general expenses incurred in the discharge of such duties which cannot be fairly charged to any particular corporation or corporations shall be charged to, and paid by, all the corporations then organized and existing under this Article pro rata according to their respective stock capitalizations. The Commissioner shall:

(1) Adopt rules to implement this Article and to protect and develop forests subject to its jurisdiction.

(2) Order all corporations organized under this Article to do such acts as may be necessary to comply with the provisions of law and the rules adopted by the Commissioner, or to refrain from doing any acts in violation thereof.

(3) Keep informed as to the general condition of all such corporations, their capitalization and the manner in which their property is permitted, operated or managed with respect to their compliance with all provisions of law and orders of the Commissioner.

(4) Require every such corporation to file with the Commissioner annual reports and, if the Commissioner shall consider it advisable, other periodic and special reports, setting forth such information as to its affairs as the Commissioner may require. (1933, c. 178, s. 4; 1973, c. 1262, s. 86; 1977, c. 771, s. 4; 1987, c. 827, s. 94; 1989, c. 727, s. 83; 1997-443, s. 11A.119(a); 2011-145, s. 13.25(cc), (dd).)

§ 106-984. Powers of Commissioner.

The Commissioner may:

(1) Examine at any time all books, contracts, records, documents and papers of any such corporation.

(2) In his discretion prescribe uniform methods and forms of keeping accounts, records and books to be observed by such corporation, and prescribe by order accounts in which particular outlays and receipts are to be entered, charged or credited. The Commissioner shall not, however, have authority to require any revaluation of the real property or other fixed assets of such corporations, but he shall allow proper charges for the depletion of timber due to cutting or destruction.

(3) Enforce the provisions of this Article, a rule implementing this Article, or an order issued under this Article by filing a petition for a writ of mandamus or application for an injunction in the superior court of the county in which the respondent corporation has its principal place of business. The final judgment in any such proceeding shall either dismiss the proceeding or direct that a writ of mandamus or an injunction, or both, issue as prayed for in the petition or in such modified or other form as the court may determine will afford appropriate relief. (1933, c. 178, s. 5; 1973, c. 1262, s. 86; 1977, c. 771, s. 4; 1987, c. 827, s. 95; 1989, c. 727, s. 84; 2011-145, s. 13.25(cc), (dd).)

§ 106-985. Provision for appeal by corporations to Governor.

If any corporation organized under this Article is dissatisfied with or aggrieved at any rule or order imposed upon it by the Commissioner, or any valuation or appraisal of any of its property made by the Commissioner, or any failure of or refusal by the Commissioner to approve of or consent to any action which it can take only with such approval or consent, it may appeal to the Governor by filing with him a claim of appeal upon which the decision of the Governor shall be final. Such determination, if other than a dismissal of the appeal, shall be set forth by the Governor in a written mandate to the Commissioner, who shall abide thereby and take such actions as the same may direct. (1933, c. 178, s. 6; 1973, c. 1262, s. 86; 1977, c. 771, s. 4; 1989, c. 727, s. 85; 2011-145, s. 13.25(cc), (dd).)

§ 106-986. Limitations as to dividends.

The shares of stock of corporations organized under this Article shall have a par value and, except as provided in G.S. 106-988 in respect to distributions in kind upon dissolution, no dividend shall be paid thereon at a rate in excess of six per centum (6%) per annum on stock having a preference as to dividends, or eight per centum (8%) per annum on stock not having a preference as to dividends, except that any such dividends may be cumulative without interest. (1933, c. 178, s. 7; 2011-145, s. 13.25(cc), (dd).)

§ 106-987. Issuance of securities restricted.

No such corporation shall issue stock, bonds or other securities except for money, timberlands, or interests therein, located in the State of North Carolina or other property, actually received, or services rendered, for its use and its lawful purposes. Timberlands, or interests therein, and other property or services so accepted therefor, shall be upon a valuation approved by the Commissioner. (1933, c. 178, s. 8; 1973, c. 1262, s. 86; 1977, c. 771, s. 4; 1989, c. 727, s. 86; 2011-145, s. 13.25(cc), (dd).)

§ 106-988. Limitation on bounties to stockholders.

Stockholders shall at no time receive or accept from any such corporation in repayment of their investment in its stock any sums in excess of the par value of the stock together with cumulative dividends at the rate set forth in G.S. 106-986 except that nothing in this section contained shall be construed to prohibit the distribution of the assets of such corporation in kind to its stockholders upon dissolution thereof. (1933, c. 178, s. 9; 2011-145, s. 13.25(cc), (dd).)

§ 106-989. Earnings above dividend requirements payable to State.

Any earnings of such corporation in excess of the amounts necessary to pay dividends to stockholders at the rate set forth in G.S. 106-986 shall be paid over to the State of North Carolina prior to the dissolution of such corporation. Net income or net losses (determined in such manner as the Commissioner shall consider properly to show such income or losses) from the sale of the capital assets of such corporation, whether such sale be upon dissolution or otherwise, shall be considered in determining the earnings of such corporation for the purposes of this section. In determining such earnings unrealized appreciation or depreciation of real estate or other fixed assets shall not be considered. (1933, c. 178, s. 10; 1973, c. 1262, s. 86; 1977, c. 771, s. 4; 1989, c. 727, s. 87; 2011-145, s. 13.25(cc), (dd).)

§ 106-990. Dissolution of corporation.

Any such corporation may be dissolved at any time in the manner provided by and under the provisions of the general corporation laws of the State of North Carolina, except that the court shall dismiss any petition for dissolution of any such corporation filed within 20 years of the date of its organization unless the same is accompanied by a certificate of the Commissioner consenting to such dissolution. (1933, c. 178, s. 11; 1973, c. 1262, s. 86; 1977, c. 771, s. 4; 1989, c. 727, s. 88; 2011-145, s. 13.25(cc), (dd).)

§ 106-991. Cutting and sale of timber.

Any such corporation may cut and sell the timber on its land or permit the cutting thereof, but all such cuttings shall be in accordance with the rules, restrictions and limitations imposed by the Commissioner, who shall impose such rules, restrictions and limitations with respect thereto as may reasonably conform to the accepted custom and usage of good forestry and forest economy, taking into consideration the situation, nature and condition of the tract so cut or to be cut, and the financial needs of such corporation from time to time. (1933, c. 178, s. 12; 1973, c. 1262, s. 86; 1977, c. 771, s. 4; 1989, c. 727, s. 89; 2011-145, s. 13.25(cc), (dd).)

§ 106-992. Corporation may not sell or convey without consent of Commissioner, or pay higher interest rate than 6%.

No such corporation shall do any of the following:

(1)   Sell, assign or convey any real property owned by it or any right, title or interest therein, except upon notice to the Commissioner of the terms of such sale, transfer or assignment, and unless the Commissioner shall consent thereto, and if the Commissioner shall require it, unless the purchaser thereof shall agree that such real estate shall remain subject to the rules and supervision of the Commissioner for such period as the latter may require.

(2)   Pay interest returns on its mortgage indebtedness at a higher rate than six per centum (6%) per annum without the consent of the Commissioner.

(3)   Mortgage any real property without first having obtained the consent of the Commissioner. (1933, c. 178, s. 13; 1973, c. 1262, s. 86; 1977, c. 771, s. 4; 1989, c. 727, s. 90; 2011-145, s. 13.25(cc), (dd).)

§ 106-993. Power to borrow money limited.

Any such corporation formed under this Article may, subject to the approval of the Commissioner, borrow funds and secure their payment thereof by note or notes and mortgage or by the issue of bonds under a trust indenture. The notes or bonds so issued and secured and the mortgage or trust indenture relating thereto may contain such clauses and provisions as shall be approved by the Commissioner, including the right to enter into possession in case of default; but the operations of the mortgagee or receiver entering in such event or of the purchaser of the property upon foreclosure shall be subject to the rules of the Commissioner for such period as the mortgage or trust indenture may specify. (1933, c. 178, s. 14; 1973, c. 1262, s. 86; 1977, c. 771, s. 4; 1989, c. 727, s. 91; 2011-145, s. 13.25(cc), (dd).)

§ 106-994. Commissioner to approve development of forests.

No project for the protection and development of forests proposed by any such corporation shall be undertaken without the approval of the Commissioner, and such approval shall not be given unless:

(1) The Commissioner shall have received a statement duly executed and acknowledged on behalf of the corporation proposing such project, in such adequate detail as the Commissioner shall require of the activities to be included in the project, such statement to set forth the proposals as to

a. Fire prevention and protection,

b. Protection against insects and tree diseases,

c. Protection against damage by livestock and game,

d. Means, methods and rate of, and restrictions upon, cutting and other utilization of the forests, and

e. Planting and spacing of trees.

(2) There shall be submitted to the Commissioner a financial plan satisfactory to him setting forth in detail the amount of money needed to carry out the entire project, and how such sums are to be allocated, with adequate assurances to the Commissioner as to where such funds are to be secured.

(3) The Commissioner shall be satisfied that the project gives reasonable assurance of the operation of the forests involved on a sustained-yield basis except insofar as the Commissioner shall consider the same impracticable.

(4) The corporation proposing such project shall agree that the project shall at all times be subject to the supervision and inspection of the Commissioner, and that it will at all times comply with such rules concerning the project as the Commissioner shall from time to time impose. (1933, c. 178, s. 15; 1973, c. 1262, s. 86; 1977, c. 771, s. 4; 1989, c. 727, s. 92; 2011-145, s. 13.25(cc), (dd).)

§ 106-995. Application of corporate income.

The gross annual income of any such corporation, whether received from sales of timber, timber operations, stumpage permits or other sources, shall be applied as follows: first, to the payment of all fixed charges, and all operating and maintenance charges and expenses including taxes, assessments, insurance, amortization charges in amounts approved by the Commissioner to amortize mortgage or other indebtedness and reserves essential to operation; second, to surplus, and/or to the payment of dividends not exceeding the maximum fixed by this Article; third, the balance, if any, in reduction of debts. (1933, c. 178, s. 16; 1973, c. 1262, s. 86; 1977, c. 771, s. 4; 1989, c. 727, s. 93; 2011-145, s. 13.25(cc), (dd).)

§ 106-996. Reorganization of corporations.

Reorganization of corporations organized under this Article shall be subject to the supervision of the Commissioner and no such reorganization shall be had without the authorization of the Commissioner. (1933, c. 178, s. 17; 1973, c. 1262, s. 86; 1977, c. 771, s. 4; 1989, c. 727, s. 94; 2011-145, s. 13.25(cc), (dd).)

§ 106-997: Reserved for future codification purposes.

§ 106-998: Reserved for future codification purposes.

§ 106-999: Reserved for future codification purposes.

§ 106-1000: Reserved for future codification purposes.

Article 82.

Forestry Services and Advice for Owners and Operators of Forestland.

§ 106-1001. Authority to render scientific forestry services.

(a)   In this Article, unless the context requires otherwise:

(1)   "Commissioner" means the Commissioner of Agriculture.

(2)   "Department" means the Department of Agriculture and Consumer Services.

(b)   The Department is hereby authorized to designate, upon request, forest trees of forest landowners and forest operators for sale or removal, by blazing or otherwise, and to measure or estimate the volume of same under the terms and conditions hereinafter provided. The Department is also authorized to cooperate with landowners of the State and with counties, municipalities and State agencies by making available forestry services consisting of specialized equipment and operators, or by renting such equipment, and to perform such labor and services as may be necessary to carry out approved forestry practices, including site preparation, forest planting, prescribed burning, and other appropriate forestry practices. For such services or rentals, a reasonable fee representing the Commissioner's estimate of not less than the costs of such services or rentals shall be charged, provided however, when the Commissioner deems it in the public interest, said services may be provided without charge, for the purpose of encouraging the use of approved scientific forestry practice on the private or other forestlands within the State, or for the purpose of providing practical demonstrations of said practices. Receipts from these activities and rentals shall be credited to the budget of the Department for the furtherance of these activities. (1947, c. 384, s. 1; 1969, c. 342, s. 3; c. 344; 1973, c. 1262, ss. 28, 86; 1977, c. 771, s. 4; 1989, c. 727, s. 95; 1997-443, s. 11A.119(a); 2011-145, s. 13.25(ee), (ff).)

§ 106-1002. Services under direction of Commissioner; compensation; when services without charge.

(a)   The administration of the provisions of this Article shall be under the direction of the Commissioner. The Commissioner, or his authorized agent, upon receipt of a request from a forest landowner or operator for technical forestry assistance or service, may designate forest trees for removal for lumber, veneer, poles, piling, pulpwood, cordwood, ties, or other forest products by blazing, spotting with paint or otherwise designating in an approved manner; he may measure or estimate the commercial volume contained in the trees designated; he may furnish the landowner or operator with a statement of the volume of the trees so designated and estimated; he may assist in finding a suitable market for the products so designated, and he may offer general forestry advice concerning the management of the forest.

(b) For such designating, measuring or estimating services the Commissioner may make a charge, on behalf of the Department, in an amount not to exceed five percent (5%) of the sale price or fair market value of the stumpage so designated and measured or estimated. Upon receipt from the Commissioner of a statement of such charges, the landowner or operator or his agent shall make payment to the Commissioner within 30 days.

(c) In those cases where the Commissioner deems it desirable to so designate and measure or estimate trees without charge, such services shall be given for the purpose of encouraging the use of approved scientific forestry principles on the private or other forestlands within the State, and to establish practical demonstrations of said principles. (1947, c. 384, s. 2; 1973, c. 1262, s. 86; 1977, c. 771, s. 4; 1989, c. 727, s. 96; 2011-145, s. 13.25(ee), (ff).)

§ 106-1003. Deposit of receipts with State treasury.

All moneys paid to the Secretary for services rendered under the provisions of this Article shall be deposited into the State treasury to the credit of the Department. (1947, c. 384, s. 3; 1973, c. 1262, s. 86; 1977, c. 771, s. 4; 1989, c. 727, s. 97; 2011-145, s. 13.25(ee).)

§ 106-1004: Reserved for future codification purposes.

§ 106-1005: Reserved for future codification purposes.

§ 106-1006: Reserved for future codification purposes.

§ 106-1007: Reserved for future codification purposes.

§ 106-1008: Reserved for future codification purposes.

§ 106-1009: Reserved for future codification purposes.

Article 83.

Forest Development Act.

§ 106-1010. Title.

This Article shall be known as the "Forest Development Act." (1977, c. 562, s. 1; 2011-145, s. 13.25(gg).)

§ 106-1011. Statement of purpose.

(a)   The General Assembly finds that:

(1)   It is in the public interest of the State to encourage the development of the State's forest resources and the protection and improvement of the forest environment.

(2)   Unfavorable environmental impacts, particularly the rapid loss of forest land to urban development, are occurring as a result of population growth. It is in the State's interest that corrective action be developed now to offset forest land losses in the future.

(3)   Regeneration of potentially productive forest land is a high-priority problem requiring prompt attention and action. Private forest land will become more important to meet the needs of the State's population.

(4)   Growing demands on forests and related land resources cannot be met by intensive management of public and industrial forest lands alone.

(b)   The purpose of this Article is to direct the Commissioner of Agriculture to implement a forest development program to:

(1)   Provide financial assistance to eligible landowners to increase the productivity of the privately owned forests of the State through the application of forest renewal practices and other practices that improve tree growth and overall forest health.

(2)   Insure that forest operations in the State are conducted in a manner designed to protect the soil, air, and water resources, including but not limited to streams, lakes and estuaries through actions of landowners on lands for which assistance is sought under provisions in this Article.

(3) Implement a program of voluntary landowner participation through the use of a forest development fund to meet the above goals.

(c) It is the intent of the General Assembly that in implementing the program under this Article, the Commissioner will cause it to be coordinated with other related programs in such a manner as to encourage the utilization of private agencies, firms and individuals furnishing services and materials needed in the application of practices included in the forest development program. (1977, c. 562, s. 2; c. 771, s. 4; 1989, c. 727, s. 218(73); 1989 (Reg. Sess., 1990), c. 1004, s. 19(b); 1997-443, s. 11A.119(a); 2005-126, s. 1; 2011-145, s. 13.25(gg), (hh).)

§ 106-1012. Definitions.

As used in this Article:

(1) "Approved forest management plan" means the forest management plan submitted by the eligible landowner and approved by the Commissioner. Such plan shall include forest management practices to insure both maximum forest productivity and environmental protection of the lands to be treated under the management plan.

(2) "Approved practices" mean those silvicultural practices approved by the Secretary for the purpose of commercially growing timber through the establishment of forest stands, of insuring the proper regeneration of forest stands to commercial production levels following the harvest of mature timber, or of insuring maximum growth potential of forest stands to commercial production levels. Such practices shall include those required to accomplish site preparation, natural and artificial forestation, noncommercial removal of residual stands for silvicultural purposes, cultivation of established young growth of desirable trees for silvicultural purposes, and improvement of immature forest stands for silvicultural purposes. In each case, approved practices will be determined by the needs of the individual forest stand. These practices shall include existing practices and such practices as are developed in the future to insure both maximum forest productivity and environmental protection.

(3) "Commissioner" means the Commissioner of Agriculture.

(4) "Department" means the Department of Agriculture and Consumer Services.

(5) "Eligible land" means land owned by an eligible landowner.

(6) "Eligible landowner" means a private individual, group, association or corporation owning land suitable for forestry purposes. Where forest land is owned jointly by more than one individual, group, association or corporation, as tenants in common, tenants by the entirety, or otherwise, the joint owners shall be considered, for the purpose of this Article, as one eligible landowner and entitled to receive cost-sharing payments as provided herein only once during each fiscal year.

(7) "Forest development assessment" means an assessment on primary forest products from timber severed in North Carolina for the funding of the provisions of this Article, as authorized by the General Assembly.

(8) "Forest development cost-sharing payment" means financial assistance to partially cover the costs of implementing approved practices in such amounts as the Commissioner shall determine, subject to the limitations of this Article.

(9) "Forest development fund" means the Forest Development Fund created by G.S. 106-1018.

(10) "Maintain" means to retain the reforested area as forestland for a 10-year period and to comply with the provisions in the approved forest management plan. (1977, c. 562, s. 3; c. 771, s. 4; 1989, c. 727, s. 218(74); 1989 (Reg. Sess., 1990), c. 1004, s. 19(b); 1997-352, s. 1; 1997-443, s. 11A.119(a); 2005-126, s. 2; 2011-145, s. 13.25(gg), (hh).)

§ 106-1013. Powers and duties.

(a) The Commissioner shall have the powers and duties to administer the provisions of this Article.

(b) The Department shall serve as the disbursing agency for funds to be expended from and deposited to the credit of the Forest Development Fund.

(c) Subject to the limitations set forth in G.S. 106-1018(d), the Commissioner is authorized to employ administrative, clerical and field personnel to support the program created by this Article and to compensate such employees from the Forest Development Fund for services rendered in direct support of the program.

(d) The Commissioner is authorized to purchase equipment for the implementation of this program from the Forest Development Fund subject to the limitations of G.S. 106-1018(e). All equipment purchased with these funds will be assigned to and used only for the forest development program, except for emergency use in forest fire suppression and other activities relating to the protection of life or property. The Forest Development Fund will be reimbursed from other program funds for equipment costs incurred during such emergency use. (1977, c. 562, s. 4; 2011-145, s. 13.25(gg), (hh).)

§ 106-1014. Administration of cost sharing.

The Commissioner shall have authority to administer the cost sharing provisions of this Article, including but not limited to the following:

(1) Prescribe the manner and requirements of making application for cost sharing funds.

(2) Identify those approved forestry practices as defined in G.S. 106-1012(2) which shall be approved for cost sharing under the provisions of this Article.

(3) Review periodically the cost of forest development practices and establish allowable ranges for cost sharing purposes for approved practices under varying conditions throughout the State.

(4) Determine, prior to approving forest development cost sharing payments to any landowner, that all proposed practices are appropriate and are comparable in cost to the prevailing cost of those practices in the general area in which the land is located. Should the Commissioner determine that the submitted cost of any practice is excessive, he shall approve forest development cost sharing payments based upon an allowable cost established under G.S. 106-1014(3).

(5) Determine, prior to approving forest development cost sharing payments, that an approved forest management plan as defined in G.S. 106-1012(1) for the eligible land has been filed with the Commissioner and that the landowner has indicated in writing his intent to comply with the terms of such management plan.

(6) Determine, prior to approving forest development cost sharing payments, that the approved practices for which payment is requested have been completed in a satisfactory manner, conform to the approved forest management plan submitted under G.S. 106-1014(5), and otherwise meet the requirements of this Article.

(7) Disburse from the Forest Development Fund to eligible landowners cost sharing payments for satisfactory completion of practices provided for by this Article and the Commissioner shall, insofar as is practicable, disburse the funds from the State's appropriation on a matching basis with the funds generated by the Primary Forest Product Assessment. (1977, c. 562, s. 5; 2011-145, s. 13.25(gg), (hh).)

§ 106-1015. Cost-share agreements.

(a) In order to receive forest development cost-share payments, an eligible landowner shall enter into a written agreement with the Department describing the eligible land, setting forth the approved practices implemented for the area and covered by the approved forest management plan, and agreeing to maintain those practices for a 10-year period.

(b) In the absence of Vis major or Act of God or other factors beyond the landowner's control, a landowner who fails to maintain the practice or practices for a 10-year period in accordance with the agreement set forth in subsection (a) of this section shall repay to the Fund all cost-sharing funds received for that area.

(c) If the landowner voluntarily relinquishes control or title to the land on which the approved practices have been established, the landowner shall:

(1) Obtain a written statement, or a form approved by the Department, from the new owner or transferee in which the new owner or transferee agrees to maintain the approved practices for the remainder of the 10-year period; or

(2) Repay to the Fund all cost-sharing funds received for implementing the approved practices on the land.

If a written statement is obtained from the new owner or transferee, the original landowner will no longer be responsible for maintaining the approved practices or repaying the cost-sharing funds. The responsibility for maintaining those practices for the remainder of the 10 years shall devolve to the new owner or transferee. (1997-352, s. 2; 2011-145, s. 13.25(gg).)

§ 106-1016. Limitation of payments.

(a) An eligible landowner may receive forest development cost sharing payments for satisfactory completion of approved practices as determined by the Commissioner, except that the Commissioner shall approve no assistance in an amount exceeding the lesser of (i) a sum equal to sixty percent (60%) of the landowner's actual per acre cost incurred in implementing the approved practice or (ii) a sum equal to sixty percent (60%) of the prevailing per acre cost as determined by the Commissioner under G.S. 106-1014(3) for implementing that approved practice.

(b) The maximum amount of forest development cost sharing funds allowed to any landowner in one fiscal year will be the amount required to complete all approved practices on 100 acres of land at the prevailing cost sharing rate established under G.S. 106-1016(a).

(c) Eligible landowners may not use State cost sharing funds if funds from any federal cost sharing program are used on the same acreage for forestry practices during the same fiscal year. (1977, c. 562, s. 6; 2011-145, s. 13.25(gg), (hh).)

§ 106-1017. Participation by government political subdivisions.

No governmental agency, federal, State or local, will be eligible for forest development payments under the provision of this Article. (1977, c. 562, s. 7; 2011-145, s. 13.25(gg).)

§ 106-1018. Forest Development Fund.

(a)   The Forest Development Fund is created in the Department as a special fund. Revenue in the Fund does not revert at the end of a fiscal year, and interest and other investment income earned by the Fund accrues to it. The Fund is created to provide revenue to implement this Article. The Fund consists of the following revenue:

(1)   Assessments on primary forest products collected under Article 81 of Chapter 106 of the General Statutes.

(2)   General Fund appropriations.

(3)   Gifts and grants made to the Fund.

(b),   (c) Repealed by Session Laws 1997-352, s. 3.

(d)   In any fiscal year, no more than five percent (5%) of the available funds generated by the Primary Forest Product Processor Assessment Act may be used for program support under the provisions of G.S. 106-1013(c).

(e)   Funds used for the purchase of equipment under the provisions of G.S. 106-1013(d) shall be limited to appropriations from the General Fund to the Forest Development Fund designated specifically for equipment purchase. (1977, c. 562, s. 8; c. 771, s. 4; 1981, c. 1127, s. 45; 1989, c. 727, s. 218(75); 1997-352, s. 3; 1997-443, s. 11A.119(a); 2011-145, s. 13.25(gg), (hh).)

§ 106-1019: Reserved for future codification purposes.

§ 106-1020: Reserved for future codification purposes.

§ 106-1021: Reserved for future codification purposes.

§ 106-1022: Reserved for future codification purposes.

§ 106-1023: Reserved for future codification purposes.

§ 106-1024: Reserved for future codification purposes.

Article 84.

Primary Forest Product Assessment Act.

§ 106-1025. Short title.

This Article shall be known as the Primary Forest Product Assessment Act. (1977, c. 573, s. 1; 2011-145, s. 13.25(ii).)

§ 106-1026. Statement of purpose.

(a) The purpose of this Article is to create an assessment on primary forest products processed from North Carolina timber to provide a source of funds to finance the forestry operations provided for in the Forest Development Act of 1977.

(b) All assessments levied under the provisions of this Article shall be used only for the purposes specified in G.S. 106-1029(c) and in the Forest Development Act, Article 11 of this Chapter. (1977, c. 573, s. 2; 2011-145, s. 13.25(ii), (jj).)

§ 106-1027. Definitions.

The following words, terms and phrases hereinafter used for the purpose of this Article are defined as follows:

(1) "Primary forest product" shall include those products of the tree after it is severed from the stump and cut to its first roundwood product for further conversion. These products include but are not limited to whole trees for chipping, whole tree logs, sawlogs, pulpwood, veneer bolts, and posts, poles and piling.

(2) "Processor" shall mean the individual, group, association, or corporation that procures primary forest products at their initial point of concentration for conversion to secondary products or for shipment to others for such conversion.

(3) "Forest Development Fund" shall mean the special fund established by G.S. 106-1018.

(4) For the purpose of this Article, the following are not considered "primary forest products":

a. Christmas trees and associated greens;

b. Material harvested from an individual's own land and used on said land for the construction of fences, buildings or other personal use developments;

c. Fuel wood harvested for personal use or use in individual homes. (1977, c. 573, s. 3; 2011-145, s. 13.25(ii), (jj).)

§ 106-1028. Operation of assessment system.

(a) The General Assembly hereby levies an assessment on all primary forest products harvested from lands within the State of North Carolina.

(b) This assessment shall be at the rates as established in G.S. 106-1030(b) and the proceeds of such assessment shall be deposited in the Forest Development Fund. (1977, c. 573, s. 4; 2009-451, s. 13.9; 2011-145, s. 13.25(ii), (jj).)

§ 106-1029. Duties.

(a) The Secretary, Department of Revenue, shall:

(1) Develop the necessary administrative procedures to collect the assessment;

(2) Collect the assessment from the primary forest product processors;

(3) Deposit funds collected from the assessment in the Forest Development Fund;

(4) Audit the records of processors to determine compliance with the provisions of this Article.

(b) The Commissioner of Agriculture shall:

(1) Provide to the Secretary, Department of Revenue, lists of processors subject to the assessment;

(2) Advise the Secretary, Department of Revenue, of the appropriate methods to convert measurements of primary forest products by other systems to those authorized in this Article;

(3) Establish in November prior to those sessions in which the General Assembly considers the State budget, the estimated total assessment that will be collectible in the next budget period and so inform the General Assembly;

(4) Within 30 days of certification of the State budget, notify the Secretary, Department of Revenue, of the need to collect the assessment for those years covered by the approved budget.

(5) By January 15 of each odd-numbered year, report to the General Assembly on the number of acres reforested, type of owners assisted, geographic distribution of funds, the amount of funds encumbered and other matters. The report shall include the information by forestry district and statewide and shall be for the two fiscal years prior to the date of the report.

(c) The Secretary of Revenue shall be reimbursed for those actual expenditures incurred as a cost of collecting the assessment for the Forest Development Fund. This amount shall be transferred from the Forest Development Fund in equal increments at the end of each quarter of the fiscal year to the Department of Revenue. This amount shall not exceed five percent (5%) of the total assessments collected on primary forest products during the preceding fiscal year. (1977, c. 573, s. 5; c. 771, s. 4; 1983, c. 761, s. 120; 1985, c. 526; 1989, c. 727, s. 218(76); 1989 (Reg. Sess., 1990), c. 1004, s. 19(b); 1997-443, s. 11A.119(a); 2006-203, s. 29; 2011-145, s. 13.25(ii), (jj).)

§ 106-1030. Assessment rates.

(a) The assessment rates shall be based on the following standards:

(1) For primary forest products customarily measured in board feet, the "International 1/4 Inch Log Rule" or equivalent will be used;

(2) For primary forest products customarily measured in cords, the standard cord of 128 cubic feet or equivalent will be used;

(3) For any other type of forest product separated from the soil, the Commissioner of Agriculture shall determine a fair unit assessment rate, based on the cubic foot volume of one thousand foot board measure, International 1/4 Inch Log Rule or one standard cord, 128 cubic feet.

(b) The assessment levied on primary forest products shall be at the following rates:

(1) Fifty cents (50¢) per thousand board feet for softwood sawtimber, veneer logs and bolts, and all other softwood products normally measured in board feet;

(2) Forty cents (40¢) per thousand board feet for hardwood and bald cypress sawtimber, veneer, and all other hardwood and bald cypress products normally measured in board feet;

(3) Twenty cents (20¢) per cord for softwood pulpwood and other softwood products normally measured in cords;

(4) Twelve cents (12¢) per cord for hardwood pulpwood and other hardwood and bald cypress products normally measured in cords;

(5) All material harvested within North Carolina for shipment outside the State for primary processing will be assessed at a percentage of the invoice value. This percentage will be established to yield rates equal to those if the material were processed within the State. (1977, c. 573, s. 6; c. 771, s. 4; 1989, c. 727, s. 218(77); 1989 (Reg. Sess., 1990), c. 1004, s. 19(b); 1997-443, s. 11A.119(a); 2011-145, s. 13.25(ii), (jj).)

§ 106-1031. Collection of assessment.

(a) The assessment shall be levied against the processor of the primary forest product.

(b) The assessment shall be submitted on a quarterly basis of the State's fiscal year due and payable the last day of the month following the end of each quarter.

(c) The assessment shall be remitted to the Secretary, Department of Revenue, by check or money order, with such production reports as may be required by said Secretary.

(d) The processor shall maintain for a period of three fiscal years and make available to the Secretary, Department of Revenue, such production records necessary to verify proper reporting and payment of revenue due the Forest Development Fund.

(e) The production reports of the various processors shall be used only for assessment purposes. Production information will not be made a part of the public record on an individual processor basis.

(f) Any official or employee of the State who discloses information obtained from a production report, except as may be necessary for administration and collection of the assessment, or in the performance of official duties, or in administration or judicial proceedings related to the levy or collection of the assessment, shall be guilty of a Class 3 misdemeanor punishable only by a fine not to exceed fifty dollars ($50.00). (1977, c. 573, s. 7; 1987, c. 523; 1993, c. 539, s. 876; 1994, Ex. Sess., c. 24, s. 14(c); 2011-145, s. 13.25(ii).)

§ 106-1032. Enforcement of collection.

The Secretary of Revenue shall enforce collection of the primary forest product assessment in accordance with the remedies and procedures contained in Article 9 of Chapter 105 of the General Statutes. (1977, c. 573, s. 8; 2011-145, s. 13.25(ii).)

Chapter 107.

Agricultural Development Districts.

§§ 107-1 through 107-25. Repealed by Session Laws 1971, c. 780, s. 20.

Chapter 108.

Social Services.

§§ 108-1 through 108-123: Repealed and recodified by Session Laws 1981, c. 275, ss. 1 to 3.

Chapter 108A.

Social Services.

Article 1.

County Administration.

Part 1. County Boards of Social Services.

§ 108A-1. Creation.

Every county shall have a board of social services or a consolidated human services board created pursuant to G.S. 153A-77(b) which shall establish county policies for the programs established by this Chapter in conformity with the rules and regulations of the Social Services Commission and under the supervision of the Department of Health and Human Services. Provided, however, county policies for the program of medical assistance shall be established in conformity with the rules and regulations of the Department of Health and Human Services. (1917, c. 170, s. 1; 1919, c. 46, s. 3; C.S., s. 5014; 1937, c. 319, s. 3; 1941, c. 270, s. 2; 1945, c. 47; 1953, c. 132; 1955, c. 249; 1957, c. 100, s. 1; 1959, c. 1255, s. 1; 1961, c. 186; 1963, c. 139; c. 247, ss. 1, 2; 1969, c. 546, s. 1; 1973, c. 476, s. 138; 1977, 2nd Sess., c. 1219, s. 6; 1981, c. 275, s. 1; 1995 (Reg. Sess., 1996), c. 690, s. 5; 1997-443, s. 11A.118(a).)

§ 108A-2. Size.

The county board of social services of a county shall consist of three members, except that the board of commissioners of any county may increase such number to five members. The decision to increase the size to five members or to reduce a five-member board to three shall be reported immediately in writing by the chairman of the board of commissioners to the Department of Health and Human Services. (1917, c. 170, s. 1; 1919, c. 46, s. 3; C.S., s. 5014; 1937, c. 319, s. 3; 1941, c. 270, s. 2; 1945, c. 47; 1953, c. 132; 1955, c. 249; 1957, c. 100, s. 1; 1959, c. 1255, s. 1; 1961, c. 186; 1963, c. 139; c. 247, ss. 1, 2; 1969, c. 546, s. 1; 1973, c. 476, s. 138; 1981, c. 275, s. 1; 1995 (Reg. Sess., 1996), c. 690, s. 6; 1997-443, s. 11A.118(a).)

§ 108A-3. Method of appointment; residential qualifications; fee or compensation for services; consolidated human services board appointments.

(a) Three-Member Board. - The board of commissioners shall appoint one member who may be a county commissioner or a citizen selected by the board; the Social Services Commission shall appoint one member; and the two members so appointed shall select the third member. In the event the two members so appointed are unable to agree upon selection of the third member, the senior regular resident superior court judge of the county shall make the selection.

(b) Five-Member Board. - The procedure set forth in subsection (a) shall be followed, except that both the board of commissioners and the Social Services Commission shall appoint two members each, and the four so appointed shall select the fifth member by majority vote of the membership. If a majority of the four are unable to agree upon the fifth member, the senior regular superior court judge of the county shall make the selection.

(c) Provided further that each member so appointed under subsection (a) and subsection (b) of this section by the Social Services Commission and by the county board of commissioners or the senior regular resident superior court judge of the county, shall be bona fide residents of the county from which they are appointed to serve, and will receive as their fee or compensation for their services rendered from the Department of Health and Human Services directly or indirectly only the fees and compensation as provided by G.S. 108A-8.

(d) Consolidated Human Services Board. - The board of county commissioners shall be the sole appointing authority for members of a consolidated human services board and shall appoint those members in accordance with G.S. 153A-77(c). (1917, c. 170, s. 1; 1919, c. 46, s. 3; C.S., s.

5014; 1937, c. 319, s. 3; 1941, c. 270, s. 2; 1945, c. 47; 1953, c. 132; 1955, c. 249; 1957, c. 100, s. 1; 1959, c. 1255, s. 1; 1961, c. 186; 1963, c. 139; c. 247, ss. 1, 2; 1969, c. 546, s. 1; 1971, c. 369; 1973, c. 476, s. 138; 1981, c. 275, s. 1; 1995 (Reg. Sess., 1996), c. 690, s. 7; 1997-135, s. 1; 1997-443, s. 11A.118(a).)

§ 108A-4. Term of appointment.

Each member of a county board of social services shall serve for a term of three years. No member may serve more than two consecutive terms.
Notwithstanding the previous sentence, the limitation on consecutive terms does not apply if the member of the social services board was a member of the board of county commissioners at any time during the first two consecutive terms, and is a member of the board of county commissioners at the time of reappointment. (1917, c. 170, s. 1; 1919, c. 46, s. 3; C.S., s. 5014; 1937, c. 319, s. 3; 1941, c. 270, s. 2; 1945, c. 47; 1953, c. 132; 1955, c. 249; 1957, c. 100, s. 1; 1959, c. 1255, s. 1; 1961, c. 186; 1963, c. 139; c. 247, ss. 1, 2; 1969, c. 546, s. 1; 1981, c. 275, s. 1; c. 770.)

§ 108A-5. Order of appointment.

(a) Three-Member Board: The term of the member appointed by the Social Services Commission shall expire on June 30, 1981, and every three years thereafter; the term of the member appointed by the board of commissioners shall expire on June 30, 1983, and every three years thereafter; and the term of the third member shall expire on June 30, 1982, and every three years thereafter.

(b) Five-Member Board: Whenever a board of commissioners of any county decides to expand a three-member board to a five-member board of social services, the Social Services Commission shall appoint an additional member for a term expiring at the same time as the term of the existing member appointed by the board of commissioners, and the board of commissioners shall appoint an additional member for a term expiring at the same time as the term of the existing member appointed by the Social Services Commission. The change to a five-member board shall become effective at the time when the additional members shall have been appointed by both the county board of commissioners and the Social Services Commission. Thereafter all appointments shall be for three-year terms.

(c) Change from Five-Member to Three-Member Board: The change shall become effective on the first day of July following the decision to change by the board of commissioners. On that day, the following two seats on the board of social services shall cease to exist:

(1) The seat held by the member appointed by the Social Services Commission whose term would have expired on June 30, 1983, or triennially thereafter; and

(2) The seat held by the member appointed by the board of commissioners whose term would have expired June 30, 1981, or triennially thereafter. (1917, c. 170, s. 1; 1919, c. 46, s. 3; C.S., s. 5014; 1937, c. 319, s. 3; 1941, c. 270, s. 2; 1945, c. 47; 1953, c. 132; 1955, c. 249; 1957, c. 100, s. 1; 1959, c. 1255, s. 1; 1961, c. 1986; 1963, c. 139; c. 247, ss. 1, 2; 1969, c. 546, s. 1; 1973, c. 476, s. 138; c. 724, s. 1; 1981, c. 275, s. 1.)

§ 108A-6. Vacancies.

Appointments to fill vacancies shall be made in the manner set out in G.S. 108A-3. All such appointments shall be for the remainder of the former member's term of office and shall not constitute a term for the purposes of G.S. 108A-4. (1917, c. 170, s. 1; 1919, c. 46, s. 3; C.S., s. 5014; 1937, c. 319, s. 3; 1941, c. 270, s. 2; 1945, c. 47; 1953, c. 132; 1955, c. 249; 1957, c. 100, s. 1; 1959, c. 1255, s. 1; 1961, c. 186; 1963, c. 139; c. 247, ss. 1, 2; 1969, c. 546, s. 1; 1981, c. 275, s. 1.)

§ 108A-7. Meetings.

The board of social services of a county shall meet at least once per month, or more often if a meeting is called by the chairman. Such board shall elect a chairman from its members at its July meeting each year, and the chairman shall serve a term of one year or until a new chairman is elected by the board. A consolidated county human services board shall meet in accordance with the provisions of G.S. 153A-77. (1917, c. 170, s. 1; 1919, c. 46, s. 4; C.S., s. 5015;

1937, c. 319, s. 4; 1941, c. 270, s. 3; 1947, c. 92; 1959, c. 320; 1961, c. 186; 1969, c. 546, s. 1; 1981, c. 275, s. 1; 1995 (Reg. Sess., 1996), c. 690, s. 8.)

§ 108A-8. Compensation of members.

Members of the county board of social services may receive a per diem in such amount as shall be established by the county board of commissioners. Reimbursement for subsistence and travel shall be in accordance with a policy set by the county board of commissioners. (1917, c. 170, s. 1; 1919, c. 46, s. 4; C.S., s. 5015; 1937, c. 319, s. 4; 1941, c. 270, s. 3; 1947, c. 92; 1959, c. 320; 1961, c. 186; 1969, c. 546, s. 1; 1971, c. 124; 1981, c. 275, s. 1; 1985, c. 418, s. 3.)

§ 108A-9. Duties and responsibilities.

The county board of social services shall have the following duties and responsibilities:

(1) To select the county director of social services according to the merit system rules of the North Carolina Human Resources Commission;

(2) To advise county and municipal authorities in developing policies and plans to improve the social conditions of the community;

(3) To consult with the director of social services about problems relating to his office, and to assist him in planning budgets for the county department of social services;

(4) To transmit or present the budgets of the county department of social services for public assistance, social services, and administration to the board of county commissioners;

(5) To have such other duties and responsibilities as the General Assembly, the Department of Health and Human Services or the Social Services Commission or the board of county commissioners may assign to it. (1917, c. 170, s. 1; 1919, c. 46, s. 3; C.S., s. 5014; 1937, c. 319, s. 3; 1941, c. 270, s. 2; 1945, c. 47; 1953, c. 132; 1955, c. 249; 1957, c. 100, s. 1; 1959, c. 1255, s. 1;

1961, c. 186; 1963, c. 139; c. 247, ss. 1, 2; 1969, c. 546, s. 1; 1973, c. 476, s. 138; 1977, 2nd Sess., c. 1219, s. 7; 1981, c. 275, s. 1; 1997-443, s. 11A.118(a); 2013-382, s. 9.1(c).)

§ 108A-10. Fees.

The county board of social services is authorized to enter into contracts with any governmental or private agency, or with any person, whereby the board of social services agrees to render services to or for such agency or person in exchange for a fee to cover the cost of rendering such service. This authority is to be limited to services voluntarily rendered and voluntarily received, but shall not apply where the charging of a fee for a particular service is specifically prohibited by statute or regulation. The fees to be charged under the authority of this section are to be based upon a plan recommended by the county director of social services and approved by the local board of social services and the board of county commissioners. In no event is the fee charged to exceed the cost to the board of social services. Fee policies may not conflict with rules and regulations adopted by the Social Services Commission or Department of Health and Human Services regarding fees.

The fees collected under the authority of this section are to be deposited to the account of the social services department so that they may be expended for social services purposes in accordance with the provisions of Article 3 of Chapter 159, the Local Government Budget and Fiscal Control Act. No individual employee is to receive any compensation over and above his regular salary as a result of rendering services for which a fee is charged.

The county board of social services shall annually report to the county commissioners receipts received under this section. Fees collected under this section shall not be used to replace any other funds, either State or local, for the program for which the fees were collected. (1981, c. 275, s. 1; 1997-443, s. 11A.118(a).)

§ 108A-11. Inspection of records by members.

Every member of the county board of social services may inspect and examine any record on file in the office of the director relating in any manner to applications for and provision of public assistance and social services authorized by this Chapter. No member shall disclose or make public any information which he may acquire by examining such records. (1917, c. 170, s. 1; 1919, c. 46, s. 3; C.S., s. 5014; 1937, c. 319, s. 3; 1941, c. 270, s. 2; 1945, c. 47; 1953, c. 132; 1955, c. 249; 1957, c. 100, s. 1; 1959, c. 1255, s. 1; 1961, c. 186; 1963, c. 139; c. 247, ss. 1, 2; 1969, c. 546, s. 1; 1981, c. 275, s. 1.)

Part 2. County Director of Social Services.

§ 108A-12. Appointment.

(a)   The board of social services of every county shall appoint a director of social services in accordance with the merit system rules of the North Carolina Human Resources Commission. Any director dismissed by such board shall have the right of appeal under the same rules.

(b)   Two or more boards of social services may jointly employ a director of social services to serve the appointing boards and such boards may also combine any other functions or activities as authorized by Part 1 of Article 20 of Chapter 160A. The boards shall agree on the portion of the director's salary and the portion of expenses for other joint functions and activities that each participating county shall pay. (1917, c. 170, s. 1; 1919, c. 46, ss. 3, 4; C.S., s. 5016; 1921, c. 128; 1929, c. 291, s. 1; 1931, c. 423; 1937, c. 319, s. 5; 1941, c. 270, s. 4; 1957, c. 100, s. 1; 1961, c. 186; 1969, c. 546, s. 1; 1981, c. 275, s. 1; 2013-382, s. 9.1(c).)

§ 108A-13. Salary.

The board of social services of every county, with the approval of the board of county commissioners, shall determine the salary of the director in accordance with the classification plan of the North Carolina Human Resources Commission, and such salary shall be paid by the county from the federal, State and county funds available for this purpose. (1917, c. 170, s. 1; 1919, c. 46, ss. 3, 4; C.S., s. 5016; 1921, c. 128; 1929, c. 291, s. 1; 1931, c. 423; 1937, c. 319, s. 5; 1941, c. 270, s. 4; 1957, c. 100, s. 1; 1961, c. 186; 1969, c. 546, s. 1; 1981, c. 275, s. 1; 2013-382, s. 9.1(c).)

§ 108A-14. Duties and responsibilities.

(a) The director of social services shall have the following duties and responsibilities:

(1) To serve as executive officer of the board of social services and act as its secretary;

(2) To appoint necessary personnel of the county department of social services in accordance with the merit system rules of the North Carolina Human Resources Commission;

(3) To administer the programs of public assistance and social services established by this Chapter under pertinent rules and regulations;

(4) To administer funds provided by the board of commissioners for the care of indigent persons in the county under policies approved by the county board of social services;

(5) To act as agent of the Social Services Commission and Department of Health and Human Services in relation to work required by the Social Services Commission and Department of Health and Human Services in the county;

(6) To investigate cases for adoption and to supervise adoptive placements;

(7) To issue employment certificates to children under the regulations of the State Department of Labor;

(8) To supervise adult care homes under the rules and regulations of the Medical Care Commission;

(9) To assist and cooperate with the Division of Adult Correction of the Department of Public Safety and their representatives;

(10) Repealed by Session Laws 2003-13, s. 7, effective April 17, 2003, and applicable to all petitions for sterilization pending and orders authorizing sterilization that have not been executed as of April 17, 2003.

(11) To assess reports of child abuse and neglect and to take appropriate action to protect such children pursuant to the Child Abuse Reporting Law, Article 3 of Chapter 7B of the General Statutes;

(12) To accept children for placement in foster homes and to supervise placements for so long as such children require foster home care;

(13) To respond by investigation to notification of a proposed adoptive placement pursuant to G.S. 48-3(b) and (c); and

(14) To receive and evaluate reports of abuse, neglect, or exploitation of disabled adults and to take appropriate action as required by the Protection of the Abused, Neglected, or Exploited Disabled Adults Act, Article 6 of this Chapter, to protect these adults.

(15) To receive and evaluate reports of financial exploitation of disabled adults, to investigate credible reports of financial exploitation under Article 6A of this Chapter, and to take appropriate action to protect these adults.

(b) The director may delegate to one or more members of his staff the authority to act as his representative. The director may limit the delegated authority of his representative to specific tasks or areas of expertise. The director may designate, subject to the approval of the Commissioner of Labor, additional personnel outside his staff to issue youth employment certificates. (1917, c. 170, s. 1; 1919, c. 46, s. 3; C.S., s. 5017; 1941, c. 270, s. 5; 1957, c. 100, s. 1; 1961, c. 186; 1969, c. 546, s. 1; 1971, c. 710, s. 5; 1973, c. 476, ss. 133.3, 138; c. 1262, s. 109; c. 1339, s. 2; 1977, 2nd Sess., c. 1219, s. 8; 1981, c. 275, s. 1; 1983, c. 293; 1985, c. 203, ss. 1, 2; 1991, c. 258, s. 1; 1993, c. 553, s. 31; 1995, c. 214, s. 2; c. 535, s. 4; 1997-443, s. 11A.118(a); 1998-202, s. 13(v); 2003-13, s. 7; 2005-55, s. 12; 2005-276, s. 10.42; 2011-145, s. 19.1(h); 2013-337, s. 3; 2013-382, s. 9.1(c).)

§ 108A-15. Social services officials and employees as public guardians.

The director and assistant directors of social services of each county may serve as guardians for adults adjudicated incompetent under the provisions of Chapter 35A, and they shall do so if ordered to serve in that capacity by the clerk of superior court having jurisdiction of a guardianship proceeding brought under either Article. (1977, c. 725, s. 6; 1981, c. 275, s. 1; 1985, c. 361, s. 3; 1987, c. 550, s. 23.)

Part 2A. Consolidated Human Services.

§ 108A-15.1. Consolidated human services board; human services director.

(a) Except as otherwise provided by this section and subject to any limitations that may be imposed by the board of county commissioners under G.S. 153A-77, a consolidated human services board created pursuant to G.S. 153A-77(b) shall have the responsibility and authority to carry out the programs established in this Chapter in conformity with the rules and regulations of the Social Services Commission and under the supervision of the Department of Health and Human Services in the same manner as a county social services board.

(b) In addition to the powers conferred by G.S. 153A-77(d), a consolidated human services board shall have all the powers and duties of a county board of social services as provided by G.S. 108A-9, except that the consolidated human services board may not:

(1) Appoint the human services director.

(2) Transmit or present the budget for social services programs.

(c) In addition to the powers conferred by G.S. 153A-77(e), a human services director shall have all the powers and duties of a director of social services provided by G.S. 108A-14, except that the human services director may:

(1) Serve as the executive officer of the consolidated human services board only to the extent and in the manner authorized by the county manager.

(2) Appoint staff of the consolidated human services agency only upon the approval of the county manager. (1995 (Reg. Sess., 1996), c. 690, s. 9; 1997-443, s. 11A.118(a).)

§§ 108A-15.2 through 108A-15.6. Reserved for future codification purposes.

Part 3. Special County Attorneys for Social Service Matters.

§ 108A-16. Appointment.

With the approval of the board of social services, the board of commissioners of any county may appoint a licensed attorney to serve as a special county attorney for social service matters, or designate the county attorney as special county attorney for social service matters. (1959, c. 1124, s. 1; 1961, c. 186; 1969, c. 546, s. 1; 1981, c. 275, s. 1.)

§ 108A-17. Compensation.

The special county attorney for social service matters shall receive compensation for the performance of his duties and for his expenses in such amount as the board of commissioners may provide. His compensation shall be a proper item in the annual budget of the county department of social services. (1959, c. 1124, s. 1; 1961, c. 186; 1969, c. 546, s. 1; 1981, c. 275, s. 1.)

§ 108A-18. Duties and responsibilities.

(a) The special county attorney shall have the following duties and responsibilities:

(1) To serve as legal advisor to the county director, the county board of social services, and the board of county commissioners on social service matters;

(2) To represent the county, the plaintiff, or the obligee in all proceedings brought under Chapter 52A, the Uniform Reciprocal Enforcement of Support Act and to exercise continuous supervision of compliance with any order entered in any proceeding under that act;

(3) To represent the county board of social services in appeal proceedings and in any litigation relating to appeals;

(4) To assist the district attorney with the preparation and prosecution of criminal cases under Article 40 of Chapter 14, entitled "Protection of the Family";

(5) To assist the district attorney with the preparation and prosecution of proceedings authorized by Chapter 49, entitled "Bastardy";

(6) To perform such other duties as may be assigned to him by the board of county commissioners, the board of social services, or the director of social services.

(b) In performing any of the duties and responsibilities set out in this section, the special county attorney is authorized to call upon any director of social services or the Department of Health and Human Services for any information as he may require to perform his duties, and such director and Department are directed to assist him in performing such duties. (1959, c. 1124, ss. 2, 3; 1969, c. 546, s. 1; 1973, c. 47, s. 2; c. 476, s. 138; 1981, c. 275, s. 1; 1997-443, s. 11A.118(a).)

§§ 108A-19 through 108A-23. Reserved for future codification purposes.

Article 2.

Programs of Public Assistance.

Part 1. In General.

§ 108A-24. Definitions.

As used in Chapter 108A:

(1) "Applicant" is any person who requests assistance or on whose behalf assistance is requested.

(1a) Repealed by Session Laws 2001-424, s. 21.52.

(1b) "Community service" means work exchanged for temporary public assistance.

(1c) "County block grant" means federal and State money appropriated to implement and maintain a county's Work First Program.

(1d) "County department of social services" means a county department of social services, consolidated human services agency, or other local agency designated to administer services pursuant to this Article.

(1e) "County Plan" is the biennial Work First Program plan prepared by each Electing County pursuant to this Article and submitted to the Department for incorporation into the State Plan that also includes the Standard Work First Program.

(2) "Department" is the Department of Health and Human Services, unless the context clearly indicates otherwise.

(3) "Dependent child" is a person 17 years of age or younger or, in the medical assistance program, a person under 19 years of age. A child 18 years of age, if in high school and expected to graduate by his or her 19th birthday, may receive Work First benefits through the month he or she turns 19 years of age or graduates from high school, whichever comes first.

(3a) "Electing County" means a county that elects to develop and is approved to administer a local Work First Program.

(3b) "Employment" means work that requires either a contribution to FICA or the filing of a State N.C. Form D-400, or the equivalent.

(3c) "Family" means a unit consisting of a minor child or children and one or more of their biological parents, adoptive parents, stepparents, or grandparents living together. For purposes of the Work First Program, family also includes a blood or half-blood relative or adoptive relative limited to brother, sister, great-grandparent, great-great-grandparent, uncle, aunt, great-uncle, great-aunt, great-great-uncle, great-great-aunt, nephew, niece, first cousin, stepbrother, and stepsister.

(3d)   "Federal TANF funds" means the Temporary Assistance for Needy Families block grant funds provided for in Title IV-A of the Social Security Act.

(3e)   "FICA" means the taxes imposed by the Federal Insurance Contribution Act, 26 U.S.C. § 3101, et seq.

(3f)   Repealed by Session Laws 2009-489, s. 1, effective August 26, 2009.

(3g)   "Full-time employment" means employment which requires the employee to work a regular schedule of hours per day and days per week established as the standard full-time workweek by the employer, but not less than an average of 30 hours per week.

(4)   Repealed by Session Laws 1983, c. 14, s. 3.

(4a)   "Mutual Responsibility Agreement" ("MRA") is an agreement between a county and a recipient of Work First Program assistance which describes the conditions for eligibility for the assistance and what the county will provide to assist the recipient in moving from assistance to self-sufficiency. A MRA may provide for recipient parental responsibilities and child development goals and what a county or the State will provide to assist the recipient in achieving those child development goals. Improvement in literacy shall be a part of any MRA, but a recipient shall not be penalized if unable to achieve improvement. A MRA is a prerequisite for any Work First Program assistance under this Article.

(4b)   "Parent" means biological parent or adoptive parent, and for Work First purposes, includes a stepparent.

(5)   "Recipient" is a person to whom, or on whose behalf, assistance is granted under this Article.

(6)   "Resident," unless otherwise defined by federal regulation, is a person who is living in North Carolina at the time of application with the intent to remain permanently or for an indefinite period; or who is a person who enters North Carolina seeking employment or with a job commitment.

(7)   "Secretary" is the Secretary of Health and Human Services, unless the context clearly indicates otherwise.

(8)   "Standard Program County" means a county that participates in the Standard Work First Program.

(9)   "Standard Work First Program" means the Work First Program developed by the Department.

(10)   "State Plan" is the biennial Work First Program plan, based upon the aggregate of the Electing County Plans and the Standard Work First Program, prepared by the Department for the State's Work First Program pursuant to this Article, and submitted sequentially to the Budget Director, to the General Assembly, to the Governor, and to the appropriate federal officials for approval.

(11)   "Temporary" is a time period, not to exceed 60 cumulative months, which meets the federal requirement of Title IV-A.

(12)   "Title IV-A" means the Social Security Act, 42 U.S.C. § 601, et seq., as amended by the Personal Responsibility and Work Opportunity Reconciliation Act of 1996, P.L. 104-193, as further amended by the Deficit Reduction Act of 2005, P.L. 109-171 and to other provisions of federal law as may apply to assistance provided in this Article.

(13)   "Work" is lawful activity exchanged for cash, goods, uses, or services.

(14)   "Work First Diversion Assistance" is a short-term cash payment that is intended to substantially reduce the likelihood of a family requiring Work First Family Assistance. Work First Diversion Assistance must be used to address a specific family crisis or episode of need and may not be used for ongoing or recurrent needs. Work First Diversion Assistance is limited to once in a 12-month period.

(15)   "Work First Family Assistance" is a program of time-limited periodic payments to assist in maintaining the children of eligible families while the adult family members engage in activities to prepare for entering and to enter the workplace.

(16)   "Work First Program" is the Temporary Assistance for Needy Families program established in this Article.

(17)   "Work First Program assistance" means the goods or services provided under the Work First Program.

(18)   "Work First Services" are services funded from appropriations made pursuant to this Article and designed to facilitate the purposes of the Work First

Program. (1981, c. 275, s. 1; 1983, c. 14, s. 3; 1997-443, ss. 11A.118(a), 12.2; 2001-424, s. 21.52; 2009-489, s. 1.)

§ 108A-25. Creation of programs.

(a) The following programs of public assistance are established, and shall be administered by the county department of social services or the Department of Health and Human Services under federal regulations or under rules adopted by the Social Services Commission and under the supervision of the Department of Human Resources:

(1) Repealed by S.L. 1997-443, s. 12.3, effective August 28, 1997.

(2) State-county special assistance.

(3) Food and Nutrition Services.

(4) Foster care and adoption assistance payments.

(5) Low income energy assistance program.

(b) The program of medical assistance is established as a program of public assistance and shall be administered by the county departments of social services under rules adopted by the Department of Health and Human Services.

(b1) The Work First Program is established as a program of public assistance and shall be supervised and administered as provided in Part 2 of this Article.

(c) The Department of Health and Human Services may accept all grants-in-aid for programs of public assistance which may be available to the State by the federal government. The provisions of this Article shall be liberally construed in order that the State and its citizens may benefit fully from the federal grants-in-aid.

(d) Each Community Care network organization designated by the Department of Health and Human Services as responsible for coordinating the health care of individuals eligible for medical assistance in a county is hereby deemed to be a public agency that is a local unit of government for the sole and limited purpose of all grants-in-aid, public assistance grant programs, and other funding programs. (1937, c. 135, s. 1; c. 288, ss. 3, 31; 1949, c. 1038, s. 2; 1955, c. 1044, s. 1; 1957, c. 100, s. 1; 1965, c. 1173, s. 1; 1969, c. 546, s. 1; 1973, c. 476, s. 138; 1975, c. 92, s. 4; 1977, 2nd Sess., c. 1219, s. 9; 1979, c. 702, s. 1; 1981, c. 275, s. 1; 1997-443, ss. 11A.118(a), 11A.122, 12.3; 2004-203, s. 41; 2007-97, s. 3; 2010-31, s. 10.19A(b).)

§ 108A-25.1: Repealed by Session Laws 2001-424, s. 21.52.

§ 108A-25.2. Exemption from limitations for individuals convicted of certain drug-related felonies.

Individuals convicted of Class H or I controlled substance felony offenses in this State shall be eligible to participate in the Work First Program and the food and nutrition services program:

(1)   Six months after release from custody if no additional controlled substance felony offense is committed during that period and successful completion of or continuous active participation in a required substance abuse treatment program determined appropriate by the area mental health authority; or

(2)   If not committed to custody, six months after the date of conviction if no additional controlled substance felony offense is committed during that period and successful completion of or continuous active participation in a required substance abuse treatment program determined appropriate by the area mental health authority.

A county department of social services shall require individuals who are eligible for Work First Program assistance and electronic food and nutrition benefits pursuant to this section to undergo substance abuse treatment as a condition for receiving Work First Program or electronic food and nutrition benefits, if funds and programs are available and to the extent allowed by federal law. (1997-443, s. 12.4; 2007-97, s. 4; 2008-187, s. 17.)

§ 108A-25.3. Garnishment of wages to recoup fraudulent public assistance program payment.

(a) The following definitions apply in this section:

(1) Disposable income. - The part of the compensation paid or payable for personal services, whether denominated as wages, salary, commission, bonus, or otherwise which remains after the deduction of any amounts required by law to be withheld.

(2) Fraudulent payment. - Any public assistance program payment made because of a recipient's false statement or representation or failure to disclose a material fact which occurs willfully and knowingly and with intent to deceive.

(3) Garnishee. - The person, firm, association, or corporation owing compensation for personal services, whether denominated as wages, salary, commission, bonus, or otherwise.

(4) Public assistance program. - Any means-tested benefit program administered or supervised by a county department of social services or the Department of Health and Human Services which is funded in whole or in part by federal, State, or county resources.

(b) In any case in which a recipient or former recipient of a public assistance program, who while a recipient, obtained or benefited from a fraudulent payment, a judge of the district court in the county where the recipient or former recipient resides or is found, or in the county where the payment was made, may enter an order of garnishment to recoup a fraudulent payment after 10 days following the entry of a judgment for a sum certain for fraudulent payments pursuant to a petition filed in the action in accordance with subsection (c) of this section. Not more than twenty percent (20%) of the recipient's or former recipient's monthly disposable income may be garnished to recoup payment in cases of fraudulent payment. The order of garnishment shall be subject to all federal and State laws or regulations that may apply to recoupment of fraudulent payments. Garnishment shall not be a remedy under this section when the recipient or former recipient is required to pay restitution for fraudulent public assistance payments pursuant to a criminal court order.

(c) A county department of social services or the Department of Health and Human Services may petition the court for an order of garnishment to recoup a fraudulent public assistance program payment. Garnishment shall be a remedy to recoup payment only after all administrative remedies are exhausted unsuccessfully. The petition shall be verified and provide the court with facts and circumstances of the fraudulent payment to or on behalf of the recipient or former recipient, the name and address of the garnishee, the recipient's or former recipient's monthly disposable income (which may be based on information and belief), and the amount sought to be garnished from the recipient's or former recipient's disposable income. The petition shall be served on both the recipient or former recipient and the garnishee in accordance with the provisions for service of process set forth in G.S. 1A-1, Rule 4. The time period for answering or otherwise responding to process issued pursuant to this section shall be in accordance with the time periods set forth in G.S. 1A-1, Rule 12.

(d)   Upon a hearing held pursuant to this section, the court may enter an order of garnishment. Provided, the court may not enter an order of garnishment if the court finds that the order jeopardizes the recipient's or former recipient's ability to become or remain financially self-sufficient and will result in the likelihood of an increased or recurring dependency on public assistance or an inability to secure basic necessities including, but not limited to, housing, food, health care, and utility costs. If an order of garnishment is entered, a copy of the same shall be served on both the recipient or the former recipient and the garnishee either personally or by certified or registered mail, return receipt requested. The order shall set forth sufficient findings of facts to support the action by the court and the amount to be garnished for each pay period. The amount garnished may be increased by an additional one dollar ($1.00) processing fee to be assessed and retained by the garnishee for each payment under the order. The order shall be subject to review for modification and dissolution upon the filing of a motion in the cause.

(e)   Upon receipt of the order of garnishment, the garnishee shall transmit without delay to the clerk of superior court the amount ordered by the court to be garnished. These funds shall be disbursed to the county department of social services to recoup fraudulent payments subject to the order of garnishment entered pursuant to this section.

(f)   A garnishee who violates the terms of an order of garnishment shall be subject to punishment for contempt.

(g)   The Social Services Commission shall adopt rules to implement this section. The rules shall ensure that a petition for an order of garnishment sought pursuant to this section is consistent with all federal and State laws and regulations. (1997-443, s. 11A.122; 1997-497, s. 1.)

§ 108A-25.4. Use of payments under the Low-Income Energy Assistance Program and Crisis Intervention Program.

(a) The Low-Income Energy Assistance Program Plan developed by the Department of Health and Human Services (Department) and submitted to the U.S. Department of Health and Human Services shall focus the annual energy assistance payments on the elderly population age 60 and above with income up to one hundred thirty percent (130%) of the federal poverty level and disabled persons receiving services through the Division of Aging and Adult Services. The energy assistance payment shall be paid directly to the service provider by the county department of social services. The Plan for Crisis Intervention Program (CIP) shall provide assistance for vulnerable populations who meet income eligibility criteria established by the Department. The CIP payment shall be paid directly to the service provider by the county department of social services and shall not exceed six hundred dollars ($600.00) per household in a fiscal year.

(b) The Department shall submit the Plan for each program to the U.S. Department of Health and Human Services no later than September 1 of each year and implement the Plan no later than October 1 of each year. (2011-145, s. 10.56(a).)

§ 108A-26. Certain financial assistance and in-kind goods not considered in determining assistance paid under Chapters 108A and 111.

Financial assistance and in-kind goods or services received from a governmental agency, or from a civic or charitable organization, shall not be considered in determining the amount of assistance to be paid any person under Chapters 108A and 111 of the General Statutes provided that such financial assistance and in-kind goods and services are incorporated in the rehabilitation plan of such person being assisted by the Division of Vocational Rehabilitation Services or the Division of Services for the Blind of the Department of Health and Human Services, except where such goods and services are required to be considered by federal law or regulations. (1973, c. 716; 1981, c. 275, s. 1; 1997-443, s. 11A.118(a).)

§ 108A-26.1. Information sharing of outstanding arrest warrant of applicant for or recipient of program assistance.

(a)   A county department of social services shall notify an applicant for program assistance under Part 2 or Part 5 of this Article that release of confidential information from the applicant's records may not be protected if there exists an outstanding warrant for arrest against the applicant. A county department of social services shall notify a recipient under a program of public assistance under Part 2 or Part 5 of this Article at the time of renewal of the recipient's application for such program assistance that release of confidential information from the recipient's records may not be protected if there exists an outstanding warrant for arrest against the recipient.

(b)   Notwithstanding G.S. 108A-80, and to the extent otherwise allowed by federal and State law, a county department of social services shall ensure that the criminal history of an applicant, or of a recipient at the time of benefits renewal, is checked in a manner and to the extent necessary to verify whether an applicant for or recipient of program assistance under Part 2 or Part 5 of this Article is (i) fleeing to avoid prosecution, custody, or confinement after conviction under the laws of the place from which the individual flees, for a crime or an attempt to commit a crime, which is a felony under the laws of the place from which the individual flees, or (ii) violating a condition of probation or parole imposed under federal or State law.

A criminal history check utilizing currently accessible databases shall be conducted by the county department of social services, subject to G.S. 114-19.34 and to the extent permitted by allocated county and State resources.

Nothing in this section requires fingerprints to be taken of every applicant for or recipient of a program of public assistance.

Counties are not required to allocate funds to comply with this section but are authorized to make such allocations on a voluntary basis.

(c)   Nothing in this section shall be construed to authorize the disclosure of any information otherwise protected by State or federal law or regulation.

(d) This section applies to applicants for or recipients of program assistance under Part 2 or Part 5 of this Article only.

(e) The Social Services Commission shall adopt any rules necessary to implement this section, including rules addressing the sharing of confidential information between county departments of social services and law enforcement agencies.

(f) The Secretary of the Department of Health and Human Services shall promote cooperation among State and local agencies to perform the functions described in this section. The Department of Health and Human Services shall cooperate and collaborate with the Office of the State Controller, the Administrative Office of the Courts, the Department of Justice, the State Bureau of Investigation, and the Department of Public Safety to develop protocols to implement this section.

(g) Annually on April 1, each county department of social services shall report to the Department of Health and Human Services on the number of individuals who are denied benefits under this section during the preceding calendar year.

(h) Annually on May 1, the Department of Health and Human Services shall report to the Joint Legislative Oversight Committee on Health and Human Services of the General Assembly on the number of individuals who are denied assistance under this section. The report shall include a breakdown by county. (2013-417, s. 1.)

§ 108A-26.2. Fleeing felon or parole or probation violator; eligibility for program assistance; federal approval; review by department.

(a) Subject to subsection (b) of this section, a department of social services shall not grant public assistance under Part 2 or Part 5 of Article 2 of Chapter 108A of the General Statutes if the department receives information described in G.S. 108A-26.1 that the applicant for or recipient of program assistance is subject to arrest under an outstanding warrant arising from a charge of violating conditions of parole or probation or from a felony charge against that applicant or recipient in any jurisdiction. This section does not affect the eligibility for assistance of other members of the applicant's or recipient's household. An applicant or recipient described in this section is eligible for program assistance if all other eligibility criteria of the law are met when the applicant or recipient is no longer subject to arrest under an outstanding warrant as described in this section.

(b)   If federal approval is required in order to prevent the loss of federal reimbursement as a result of the application of this section to an applicant for or recipient of program assistance, the Department of Health and Human Services shall promptly take any action necessary to obtain federal approval. (2013-417, s. 2.)

Part 2. Work First Program.

§ 108A-27. (See editor's note) Authorization and description of Work First Program; Work First Program changes; designation of Electing and Standard Program Counties.

(a)   The Department shall establish, supervise and monitor the Work First Program. The purpose of the Work First Program is to provide eligible families with short-term assistance to facilitate their movement to self-sufficiency through gainful employment, not the mere reduction of the welfare rolls. The Department shall ensure that the Work First Program focuses on this purpose of self-sufficiency. The ultimate goal of the Work First Program is the gradual elimination of generational poverty, and the Department shall ensure that all evaluations of the Work First Program, whether performed at the State or the county level, maintain this purpose and this goal of the Work First Program and effect an ongoing determination of whether the Work First Program is successful in facilitating families to move to self-sufficiency and in gradually eliminating generational poverty.

(b)   The Work First Program in all counties shall include program administration and three categories of assistance to participants:

(1)   Work First Diversion Assistance;

(2)   Work First Family Assistance; and

(3)   Work First Services.

(c) The Department may change the Work First Program when required to comply with federal law. Any changes in federal law that necessitate a change in the Work First Program shall be effected by temporary rule until the next State Plan is approved by the General Assembly. Any change effective by the Department to comply with federal law shall be reported to the Senate Appropriations Committee on Health and Human Services and the House of Representatives Appropriations Subcommittee on Health and Human Services and included in the State Plan submitted during the next session of the General Assembly following the change.

(d) The Department shall allow counties maximum flexibility in the Work First Program while ensuring that the counties comply with federal and State laws and regulations. Subject to any limitations imposed by law, the Department shall allow counties to request to be designated as either Electing Counties or Standard Program Counties in the Work First Program.

(e) All counties shall notify the Department in writing as to whether they desire to be designated as either Electing or Standard Program. A county shall submit in its notification to the Department documentation demonstrating that three-fifths of its county commissioners support its desired designation. Upon receipt of the notification from the county, the Department shall send to the county confirmation of the county's planning designation. A county that desires to be redesignated shall submit a request in writing to the Department at least six months prior to the effective date of the next State Plan. In its request for redesignation, the county shall submit documentation demonstrating that three-fifths of its county commissioners support the redesignation. Upon receipt of the notification from the county, the Department shall send to the county confirmation of the county's planning redesignation. A county's redesignation shall become effective on the effective date of the next State Plan following the redesignation. A county's designation or redesignation shall not be effected except as provided in this Article.

(f) The board of county commissioners in an Electing County shall be responsible for development, administration, and implementation of the Work First Program in that county.

(g) The county department of social services in a Standard Program County shall be responsible for administering and implementing the Standard Work First Program in that county.

(h) The Department and Electing Counties, in developing their respective plans, may distinguish among potential groups of recipients on whatever basis necessary to enhance program purposes and to maximize federal revenues, so long as the rights, including the constitutional rights of equal protection and due process, of individuals are protected. The Department and Electing Counties shall provide Work First Program assistance to qualified immigrants on the same basis as citizens to the extent permitted by federal law. (1981, c. 275, s. 1; 1997-443, s. 12.5; 1998-212, s. 12.27A(a1); 2001-424, s. 21.13(e); 2009-489, s. 2.)

§ 108A-27.01. Income eligibility and payment level for Work First Family Assistance.

The maximum net family annual income eligibility standards for Work First Family Assistance are the same standards of need for eligibility for the categorically needy under the Medicaid Program. The payment level for Work First Family Assistance shall be fifty percent (50%) of the standard of need. (2013-360, s. 12C.8.)

§ 108A-27.1. Time limitations on assistance.

(a) Under the Standard Work First Program, unless an extension or an exemption is provided pursuant to the provisions of the Part or the State Plan, any cash assistance provided to a person or family in the employment program shall only be provided for a cumulative total of 24 months. After having received cash assistance for 24 months, the person or the family may reapply for cash assistance, but not until after 36 months from the last month the person or the family received cash assistance. This subsection shall not apply to child-only cases.

(b) Electing Counties may set any time limitations on assistance it finds appropriate, so long as the time limitations do not conflict with or exceed any federal time limitations. (1997-443, s. 12.6; 1998-212, s. 12.27A(f).)

§ 108A-27.2. General duties of the Department.

The Department shall have the following general duties with respect to the Work First Program:

(1) Ensure that the specifications of the general provisions of the State Plan regarding the procedures required when recipients are sanctioned, prescribed in G.S. 108A-27.9(c), are uniformly developed and implemented across the State;

(1a) Provide technical assistance to Electing Counties developing and implementing and to Standard Counties implementing their County Plans, including providing information concerning applicable federal law and regulations and changes to federal law and regulations that affect the permissible use of federal funds and scope of the Work First Program in a county;

(1b) Reserved for future codification purposes.

(1c) Ensure that all families with work eligible parents and parents with children under the age of 12 months receive Work First benefits in the month after compliance with their Mutual Responsibility Agreement. Failure to comply with their Mutual Responsibility Agreement shall result in no Work First Benefits the following month, unless there is good cause.

(2) Describe authorized federal and State work activities. For up to twenty percent (20%) of Work First recipients, authorized State work activities shall include at least part-time enrollment in a postsecondary education program. In Standard Counties, recipients enrolled on at least a part-time basis in a postsecondary education program and maintaining a 2.5 grade point average or its equivalent shall have their two-year time limit suspended for up to three years.

(3) Define requirements for assignment of child support income and compliance with child support activities;

(4) Establish a schedule for Electing Counties to submit their County Plans to ensure that all Electing County Plans are adopted by Electing Counties by February 1 of each odd-numbered year and review and then recommend a State Plan to the General Assembly;

(5) Ensure that the Electing County Plans comply with federal and State laws, rules, and regulations, are consistent with the overall purposes and goals

of the Work First Program, and maximize federal receipts for the Work First Program;

(6) Prepare the State Plan in accordance with G.S. 108A-27.9 and federal laws and regulations and submit it to the Budget Director for approval;

(7) Submit the State Plan, as approved by the Budget Director, to the General Assembly for approval;

(8) Repealed by Session Laws 2003-284, s. 10.57, effective July 1, 2003.

(9) Develop and implement a system to monitor and evaluate the impact of the Work First Program on children and families, including the impact of the Work First Program on job retention and advancement, child abuse and neglect, caseloads for child protective services and foster care, school attendance, academic and behavioral performance, and other measures of the economic security and health of children and families. The system should be developed to allow monitoring and evaluation of impact based on both aggregated and disaggregated data. State and county agencies shall cooperate in providing information needed to conduct these evaluations, sharing data and information except where prohibited specifically by federal law or regulation;

(10) Monitor the performance of Electing Counties relative to their respective Plans and the overall goals of the Work First Program. Monitor Standard Counties relative to the State Plan and the overall goals of the Standard Work First Program;

(11) Repealed by Session Laws 2003-284, s. 10.57, effective July 1, 2003.

(12) Report to the Senate Appropriations Committee on Health and Human Services and the House of Representatives Appropriations Subcommittee on Health and Human Services the counties which have requested Electing status; provide copies of the proposed Electing County Plans to the Senate Appropriations Committee on Health and Human Services and the House of Representatives Appropriations Subcommittee on Health and Human Services, if requested; and make recommendations to the Senate Appropriations Committee on Health and Human Services and the House of Representatives Appropriations Subcommittee on Health and Human Services on which of the proposed Electing County Plans ensure compliance with federal and State laws, rules, and regulations and are consistent with the overall purposes and goals for the Work First Program; and

(13) Make recommendations to the General Assembly for approval of counties to become Electing Counties which represent, in aggregate, no more than fifteen and one-half percent (15.5%) of the total Work First caseload at September 1 of each year and, for each county submitting a plan, the reasons individual counties were or were not recommended.

(14) Review the county Work First Program of each Electing County and recommend whether the county should continue to be designated an Electing County or whether it should be redesignated as a standard county. In conducting its review and making its recommendation, the Department shall:

a. Examine and consider the results of the Department's monitoring and evaluation of the impact of the Electing County's Work First Program as required under subdivision (9) of this section;

b. Determine whether the Electing County's Work First Program's unique design requires implementation by an Electing County or whether the Work First Program could be implemented by a county designated as a standard county;

c. Determine whether the Electing County's Work First Program and policies are unique and innovative in meeting the purpose of the Work First Program as stated under G.S. 108A-27, and State and federal laws, rules, and regulations, as compared to other standard and Electing County Work First programs.

The Department shall make its recommendation and the reasons therefor to the Senate Appropriations Committee on Health and Human Services and the House of Representatives Appropriations Subcommittee on Health and Human Services not later than three months prior to submitting the State Plan to the Commission for review as required under G.S. 108A-27.9(a). (1997-443, s. 12.6; 1998-212, s. 12.27A(g); 1999-237, s. 7.10(b); 1999-359, ss. 1.2(a), 2(a), (b), 6; 2001-424, s. 21.13(b), (e); 2003-284, s. 10.57; 2009-489, s. 3.)

§ 108A-27.3. Electing Counties - Duties of county boards of commissioners.

(a) The duties of the county boards of commissioners in Electing Counties under the Work First Program are as follows:

(1) Establish county outcome and performance goals based on county economic, educational, and employment factors and adopt criteria for determining the progress of the county in moving persons and families to self-sufficiency;

(2) Establish eligibility criteria for recipients except for those criteria related to sanctioning procedures mandated across the State pursuant to G.S. 108A-27.9(c);

(3) Prescribe the method of calculating benefits for recipients;

(4) Repealed by Session Laws 2009-489, s. 4, effective August 26, 2009.

(5) If made a part of the county's Work First Program, develop and enter into Mutual Responsibility Agreements with Work First Program recipients and ensure that the services and resources that are needed to assist participants to comply with the obligations under their Mutual Responsibility Agreements are available;

(6) Ensure that participants engage in the minimum hours of work activities required by Title IV-A;

(7) Consider providing community service work for any recipient who cannot find employment;

(8) Authorize payments of Work First Diversion Assistance and Work First Family Assistance to recipients having MRAs;

(9) Monitor compliance with Mutual Responsibility Agreements and enforce the agreement provisions;

(10) Repealed by Session Laws 2009-489, s. 4, effective August 26, 2009.

(10a) Ensure that all Work First cases are reviewed no later than three months prior to expiration of time limitations for receiving cash assistance to:

a. Ensure that time limitations on assistance have been computed correctly.

b. Ensure that the family is informed in writing about public assistance benefits, including child care, Medicaid, and food and nutrition services, for which the family is eligible even while cash assistance is no longer available.

c. Provide for an extension of cash assistance benefits if the family qualifies for an extension.

d. Review family status and assist the family in identifying resources and support the family needs to maintain employment and family stability.

(11) Ensure compliance with applicable State and federal laws, rules, and regulations for the Work First Program;

(12) Develop, adopt, and submit to the Department a biennial County Plan;

(13) Repealed by Session Laws 2009-489, s. 4, effective August 26, 2009.

(14) Develop and implement an appeals process for the county's Work First Program that substantially complies with G.S. 108A-79 and comply with the procedures related to sanctioning by the Department for all counties in the State pursuant to G.S. 108A-27.2 and prescribed as general provisions in the State Plan pursuant to G.S. 108A-27.9(c)(1).

(b) The county board of commissioners shall not delegate the responsibilities described in subdivisions (a)(1), (a)(11), and (a)(12) of this section but may delegate other duties to public or private entities. Notwithstanding any delegation of duty, the county board of commissioners shall remain accountable for its duties under the Work First Program.

(c) The county board of commissioners shall appoint a committee of individuals to identify the needs of the population to be served and to review and assist in developing the County Plan to respond to the needs. The committee membership shall include, but is not limited to, representatives of the county board of social services, the board of the area mental health authority, the local public health board, the local school systems, the business community, the board of county commissioners and community-based organizations representative of the population to be served.

(d) The county board of commissioners shall review and approve the County Plan for submission to the Department. (1997-443, s. 12.6; 1998-212, s. 12.27A(h); 1999-359, s. 5(a); 2007-97, s. 5; 2009-489, s. 4.)

§ 108A-27.4. Electing Counties - County Plan.

(a) Each Electing County shall submit to the Department, according to the schedule established by the Department and in compliance with all federal and State laws, rules, and regulations, a biennial County Plan.

(b) An Electing County's County Plan shall have at least the following five parts:

(1) Part I. Conditions Within the County;

(2) Part II. Outcomes and Goals for the County;

(3) Part III. Plans to Achieve and Measure the Outcomes and Goals;

(4) Part IV. Administration; and

(5) Part V. Funding Requirements.

(c) Funding requirements shall, at least, identify the amount of a county block grant for Work First Diversion Assistance, a county block grant for Work First Family Assistance, a county block grant for Work First Services, and the county's maintenance of effort contribution. A county may establish a reserve.

(d) Repealed by Session Laws 2009-489, s. 5, effective August 26, 2009.

(e) Each county shall include in its County Plan the following:

(1) Repealed by Session Laws 2009-489, s. 5, effective August 26, 2009.

(2) A description of the county's plans for serving families who need child care, transportation, substance abuse services, and employment support based on the needs of the community and the availability of services and funding;

(3) Repealed by Session Laws 2009-489, s. 5, effective August 26, 2009.

(4) A description of the county's eligibility criteria, benefit calculation, and any other policies adopted by the county relating to eligibility, terms, and conditions for receiving Work First Program assistance, including sanctions, asset and income requirements, time limits and extensions, rewards, exemptions, and exceptions to requirements. If an Electing County Plan

proposes to change eligibility requirements, benefits levels, or reduce maintenance of effort, the county shall describe the reasons for these changes and how the county intends to utilize the maintenance of effort savings;

(5) A description of how the county plans to utilize public and private resources to assist in moving persons and families to self-sufficiency; and

(6) Any request to the Department for waivers to rules or any proposals for statutory changes to remove any impediments to implementation of the County's Plan.

(7) The process by which the county will review all Work First caseloads no later than three months prior to expiration of time limitations for receiving cash assistance to:

a. Ensure that time limitations on assistance have been computed correctly.

b. Ensure that the family is informed in writing about public assistance benefits, including child care, Medicaid, and food and nutrition services, for which the family is eligible even while cash assistance is no longer available.

c. Provide for an extension of cash assistance benefits if the family qualifies for an extension.

d. Review family status and assist the family in identifying resources and support the family needs to maintain employment and family stability.

(f) Each county shall provide to the general public an opportunity to review and comment upon its County Plan prior to its submission to the Department.

(g) A county may modify its County Plan once each biennium but not at any other time unless the county notifies the Department of the proposed modification and the Department determines that the proposed modification is consistent with State and federal law and the goals for the Work First Program.

(h) Electing Counties shall have an emergency assistance program for Work First eligible families, as defined in the electing county plan. Counties may establish income eligibility for emergency assistance at or below two hundred percent (200%) of the federal poverty level. (1997-443, s. 12.6; 1999-359, s. 5(b), (c); 2007-97, s. 6; 2007-484, s. 38; 2009-489, s. 5.)

§ 108A-27.5. Electing Counties - Duties of the Department.

In addition to the general duties prescribed in G.S. 108A-27.3, the Department shall have the following duties with respect to establishing, supervising, and monitoring the Work First Program in Electing Counties while allowing Electing Counties maximum flexibility in designing and implementing County Plans:

(1) Repealed by Session Laws 2009-489, s. 6, effective August 26, 2009.

(2) At the request of the counties, provide assistance to counties in their activities with private sector individuals and organizations relative to County Plans; and

(3) Establish the baseline for the State maintenance of effort. (1997-443, s. 12.6; 2009-489, s. 6.)

§ 108A-27.6. Standard Program Counties - Duties of county departments of social services and county boards of commissioners.

(a) Except as otherwise provided in this Article, the Standard Work First Program shall be administered by the county departments of social services. The county departments of social services in Standard Program Counties shall:

(1) In consultation with the Department and the county board of commissioners, establish outcome and performance measures for all Standard Program Counties. There exist two goals for the Work First Program: to meet or exceed the federal Work Participation Rate of fifty percent (50%) for all Work Eligible families and ninety percent (90%) for all two-parent families;

(2) Determine eligibility of persons and families for the Work First Program;

(3) Enter into Mutual Responsibility Agreements with participants if required under the State Plan and ensure that the services and resources that are needed to assist participants to comply with their obligations under their Mutual Responsibility Agreements are available;

(4) Comply with State and federal law relating to Work First and Title IV-A;

(5) Repealed by Session Laws 2009-489, s. 7, effective August 26, 2009.

(6) Ensure that participants engage in the minimum hours of work activities required by the State Plan and Title IV-A;

(7) Ensure that the components of the Work First Program are funded solely from authorized sources and that federal TANF funds are used only for purposes and programs authorized by federal and State law; and

(8),(9) Repealed by Session Laws 2009-489, s. 7, effective August 26, 2009.

(10) Ensure that all Work First cases are reviewed no later than three months prior to expiration of time limitations for receiving cash assistance to:

a. Ensure that time limitations on assistance have been computed correctly.

b. Ensure that the family is informed about public assistance benefits, including child care, Medicaid, and food and nutrition services, for which the family is eligible even while cash assistance is no longer available.

c. Provide for an extension of cash assistance benefits if the family qualifies for an extension.

d. Review family status and assist the family in identifying resources and support the family needs to maintain employment and family stability.

(b) In consultation with the Department, a county department of social services may delegate any of its duties under this Article to another public agency or private contractor. Prior to delegating any duty, a county department of social services shall submit its proposed delegation to the Department as the Department may provide. Notwithstanding any delegation of duty, a county department of social services shall remain accountable for its duties under the Work First Program.

(c),(d) Repealed by Session Laws 2009-489, s. 7, effective August 26, 2009. (1997-443, s. 12.6; 1999-359, s. 5(e); 2007-97, s. 7; 2009-489, s. 7.)

§ 108A-27.7. Standard Program County Plan.

Standard counties shall have an emergency assistance program for Work First eligible families, as defined in the standard county plan. Counties may establish income eligibility for emergency assistance at or below two hundred percent (200%) of the federal poverty level. (1997-443, s. 12.6; 1999-359, s. 5(d); 2009-489, s. 8.)

§ 108A-27.8. Standard Program Counties - Duties of Department.

(a) The Department shall establish, develop, supervise, and monitor the Standard Work First Program. In addition to its general duties prescribed in G.S. 108A-27.2, the Department shall have the following duties with respect to the Standard Work First Program and the Standard Program Counties:

(1) Repealed by Session Laws 2009-489, s. 9, effective August 26, 2009.

(2) Advise and assist the Social Services Commission in adopting rules necessary to implement the provisions of this Article;

(3) Supervise disbursement of county block grants to the Standard Program Counties for Work First Services;

(4) Make payments of Work First Family Assistance and Work First Diversion Assistance; and

(5), (6) Repealed by Session Laws 2009-489, s. 9, effective August 26, 2009.

(7) Develop a Mutual Responsibility Agreement for use by Standard Program Counties.

(b) The Secretary, in consultation with the Office of State Budget and Management, may adopt temporary rules when necessary to:

(1) Implement provisions of the State Plan;

(2) Maximize federal revenues to prevent the loss of federal funds;

(3) Enhance the ability of the Department to prevent fraud and abuse in the Work First Program; and

(4) Modify the provisions in the State Plan as necessary to meet changed circumstances after approval of the State Plan.

(c) The Social Services Commission may adopt rules in accordance with G.S. 143B-153 when necessary to implement this Article and subject to delegation by the Secretary of any rule-making authority to implement the provisions of the State Plan. (1997-443, s. 12.6; 2000-140, s. 93.1(a); 2001-424, s. 12.2(b); 2009-489, s. 9.)

§ 108A-27.9. State Plan.

(a) The Department shall prepare and submit to the Director of the Budget a biennial State Plan that proposes the goals and requirements for the State and the terms of the Work First Program for each fiscal year. Prior to submitting a State Plan to the General Assembly, the Department shall:

(1) Consult with local government and private sector organizations regarding the design of the State Plan and allow 45 days to receive comments from those organizations; and

(2) Upon complying with subdivision (1) of this subsection, submit the State Plan to the Senate Appropriations Committee on Health and Human Services and the House of Representatives Appropriations Subcommittee on Health and Human Services for review.

(b) The State Plan shall consist of generally applicable provisions and two separate sections, one proposing the terms of the Work First Program in Electing Counties, and the other proposing the terms for the Standard Work First Program.

(c) The State Plan shall include the following generally applicable provisions:

(1) Provisions to ensure that recipients who are sanctioned are provided a clear explanation of the sanction and that all recipients, including those under sanction or termination for rules infractions, are fully informed of their right to legal counsel and any other representatives they choose at their own cost;

(1a) Provisions to ensure that no Work First Program recipients, required to participate in work activities, shall be employed or assigned when:

a. Any regular employee is on layoff from the same or substantially equivalent job;

b. An employer terminates any regular employee or otherwise causes an involuntary reduction in the employer's workforce in order to hire Work First recipients; or

c. An employer otherwise causes the displacement of any currently employed worker or positions, including partial displacements such as reductions in hours of nonovertime work, wages, or employment benefits, in order to hire Work First recipients;

(1b) Reserved for future codification purposes.

(1c) Provisions to ensure that all work eligible parents and all parents with a child under 12 months of age are subject to pay for performance requirements. Pay for performance requirements means that the family will receive Work First benefits in the month following a month that they comply with their Mutual Responsibility Agreement. Failure to comply with the Mutual Responsibility Agreement without good cause will result in no Work First benefits in the following month.

(2) Provisions to ensure the establishment and maintenance of grievance procedures to resolve complaints by regular employees who allege that the employment or assignment of a Work First Program recipient is in violation of subdivision (1a) of this subsection, and grievance procedures to resolve complaints by Work First Participants made pursuant to subdivision (3) of this subsection;

(3) Provisions to ensure that Work First Program participants, required to participate in work activities, shall be subject to and have the Work First Program employees in similarly situated work activities, including, but not limited to, wage and hour laws, health and safety standards, and nondiscrimination laws, provided that nothing in this subdivision shall be construed to prohibit Work First Program participants from receiving additional State or county services designed to assist Work First Program participants achieve job stability and self-sufficiency;

(4) A description of eligible federal and State work activities. For up to twenty percent (20%) of Work First recipients, authorized State work activities shall include at least part-time enrollment in a postsecondary education program. In Standard Counties, recipients enrolled on at least a part-time basis in a postsecondary education program and maintaining a 2.5 grade point average or its equivalent shall have their two-year time limit suspended for up to three years.

(5) Requirements for assignment of child support income and compliance with child support activities;

(6) Incentives for high-performing counties, contingency plans for counties unable to meet financial commitments during the term of the State Plan, and sanctions against counties failing to meet performance expectations, including allocation of any federal penalties that may be assessed against the State as a result of a county's failure to perform; and

(7) Anything else required by federal or State law, rule, or regulation to be included in the State Plan.

(d) The section of the State Plan proposing the terms of the Work First Program in Electing Counties shall be based upon the aggregate of the Electing County Plans and shall include federal eligibility requirements and a description of the eligibility requirements and benefit calculation in each Electing County.

The Department may modify the section in the State Plan regarding Electing Counties once a biennium or except as necessary to reflect any modifications made by an Electing County. Any changes to the section of the State Plan regarding Electing Counties shall be reported to the Senate Appropriations Committee on Health and Human Services, the House of Representatives Appropriations Subcommittee on Health and Human Services, and the Fiscal Research Division within one month following the changes.

(e) The section of the State Plan describing the Standard Work First Program shall include:

(1) Benefit levels, limitations, and payments and the method for calculating benefit levels and payments;

(2) Eligibility criteria, including asset and income standards;

(3)   Any exceptions or exemptions proposed to work requirements;

(4)   Provisions for when extensions may be granted to a person or family who reaches the time limit for receipt of benefits;

(5)   Provisions for exceptions and exemptions to criteria, time limits, and standards;

(6)   Provisions for sanctions for recipient failure to comply with program requirements; and

(7) through (10) Repealed by Session Laws 2009-489, s. 7, effective August 26, 2009.

(11)   A description of the Department's consultation with local governments and private sector organizations and a summary of any comments received during the 45-day public comment period.

(f)   In addition to those items required to be included pursuant to subsection (e) of this section, the State Plan may include proposals to establish the following as part of the Standard Work First Program:

(1)   Demonstration projects in one or more counties to assess the value of any proposed changes in State policy or to test ways to improve programs; and

(2)   Requirement that recipients shall be required to enter into and comply with Mutual Responsibility Agreements as a condition of receiving benefits. If provided for in the State Plan, the terms and conditions of Mutual Responsibility Agreements shall be consistent with program purposes, federal law, and availability of funds.

(g)   The State Plan may provide for automatic Medicaid eligibility for all Work First Program recipients.

(h)   The State Plan may provide that in cases where benefits are paid only for a child, the case is considered a family case. (1997-443, s. 12.6; 1997-456, s. 55.10; 1998-212, s. 12.27A(b), (b1); 1999-359, ss. 1.2(b), 2(c); 2001-424, s. 21.13(c), (e); 2007-323, s. 10.35A(a); 2009-489, s. 10.)

§ 108A-27.10. Duties of the Director of the Budget/Governor.

(a) The Director of the Budget shall, by May 15 of each odd-numbered year, approve and recommend adoption by the General Assembly of the State Plan.

(b) At the beginning of every fiscal year, the Director of the Budget shall report to the General Assembly the number of permanent State employees who have been Work First Program recipients during the previous calendar year.

(c) After the State Plan has become law, the Governor shall sign it and cause it to be submitted to federal officials in accordance with federal law. (1997-443, s. 12.6; 2007-323, s. 10.35A(b).)

§ 108A-27.11. Work First Program funding.

(a) County block grants, except funds for Work First Family Assistance, shall be computed based on the percentage of each county's total AFDC (including AFDC-EA) and JOBS expenditures, except expenditures for cash assistance, to statewide actual expenditures for those programs in fiscal year 1995-96. The resulting percentage shall be applied to the State's total certified budget enacted by the General Assembly for each fiscal year, except for State funds budgeted for State and county demonstration projects authorized by the General Assembly and for Work First Family Assistance payments.

(b) The following shall apply to funding for Standard Program Counties:

(1) The Department shall make payments of Work First Family Assistance and Work First Diversion Assistance subject to the availability of federal, State, and county funds.

(2) The Department shall reimburse counties for county expenditures under the Work First Program subject to the availability of federal, State, and county funds.

(c) Each Electing County's allocation for Work First Family Assistance shall be computed based on the percentage of each Electing County's total expenditures for cash assistance to statewide actual expenditures for cash assistance in 1995-96. The resulting percentage shall be applied to the federal TANF block grant funds appropriated for cash assistance by the General

Assembly each fiscal year. The Department shall transmit the federal funds contained in the county block grants to Electing Counties as soon as practicable after they become available to the State and in accordance with federal cash management laws and regulations. (1997-443, s. 12.6; 1998-212, s. 12.27A(i); 1999-359, s. 3; 2002-126, s. 10.37; 2003-284, s. 10.50.)

§ 108A-27.12. Maintenance of effort.

(a)   The Department shall define in the State Plan the services that can be provided with TANF federal funds and with State and county maintenance of effort funds. The Department shall work with counties to allow flexibility in the spending of county, State, and federal funds so as to maximize the use of resources while assuring that federal maintenance of effort requirements are met.

(b)   Counties that fail to meet maintenance of effort requirements and that fail to meet the performance indicators for reducing maintenance of effort shall submit a corrective action plan to the Department and shall be subject to G.S. 108A-27.14. The Department may reduce block grant allocations to counties that fail to meet maintenance of effort requirements and performance indicators or may use some of the county's block grant allocation to secure needed services for clients in that county. If a county fails to comply with maintenance of effort requirements, the Director of the Budget may also withhold State funds appropriated to the county pursuant to G.S. 108A-93.

(c)   The Department shall maintain the State's maintenance of effort at one hundred percent (100%) of the State certified budget enacted by the General Assembly for programs under this Part during fiscal year 1996-97. At no time shall the Department reduce or reallocate State funds previously obligated or appropriated for Work First or child welfare services.

(d)   Each standard county shall maintain funding in Work First, child welfare, and related activities as defined by the Department at one hundred percent (100%) of the county funds budgeted in State Fiscal Year 1996-97 for AFDC Administration, JOBS employment and training, and AFDC Emergency Assistance (cash and services). A county may request to reduce its block grant and maintenance of effort if that county can demonstrate that it is meeting all the needs of its clients, as defined by the Department's performance indicators, without spending all of the block grant funds. The needs of clients include child protection, employment services, and related supportive services such as child care. The Department may reallocate any State or federal funds released from a county that reduced its maintenance of effort or from counties not spending their block grants. Funds reallocated to counties will require county match.

(e) During the first year a county operates as an Electing County, the county's maintenance of effort shall be no less than ninety percent (90%) of the amount the county budgeted for programs under this Part during fiscal year 1996-97. If during the first year of operation as Electing the Electing County achieves one hundred percent (100%) of its goals as set forth in its Electing County Plan, then the Electing County may reduce its maintenance of effort to eighty percent (80%) of the amount the county budgeted for programs under this Part during fiscal year 1996-97 for the second year of the Electing County's operation and for all years thereafter that the county maintains Electing Status.

(f) The Department may realign funds if the realignment will assure that maintenance of effort requirements are met while maximizing federal revenues.

(g) The Department of Health and Human Services shall report quarterly on the extent to which the State and counties are meeting federal maintenance of effort requirements under Temporary Assistance of Needy Families and on any realignment of funds. The Department and the counties shall work together to maximize full achievement of the State and county maintenance of effort. The Department shall make its report to members of the House of Representatives Appropriations Subcommittee on Health and Human Services, the Senate Appropriations Committee on Human Resources, and the Joint Legislative Public Assistance Committee, and to the Fiscal Research Division. (1997-443, s. 12.6; 1998-212, s. 12.27A(j); 1999-359, s. 4(a), (c).)

§ 108A-27.13. Performance standards.

(a) The Department, in consultation with the county department of social services and county board of commissioners, shall establish outcome and performance measures for all counties, both Electing and Standard. There exist two goals for the Work First Program: to meet or exceed the federal Work Participation rate of fifty percent (50%) for all Work Eligible families and ninety percent (90%) for all two-parent families. The two goals apply to both Standard and Electing Counties. The Department shall establish monitoring mechanisms and reporting requirements to assess progress toward the goals. The well-being of children and economic factors and conditions within the counties, including the increased numbers of persons employed and increased numbers of hours worked by and wages earned by recipients, shall be considered by the Department.

(b) Repealed by Session Laws 2009-489, s. 11, effective August 26, 2009.

(c) All adult recipients of Work First Program assistance are expected to achieve full-time employment, subject to applicable exceptions. Adult recipients of Work First Program assistance shall comply with the provisions and requirements in their MRAs. (1997-443, s. 12.6; 2009-489, s. 11.)

§ 108A-27.14. Corrective action.

(a) When any county fails to meet acceptable levels of performance, the Department may take one or more of the following actions to assist the county in meeting its Work First goals:

(1) Notify the county of the deficiencies and add additional monitoring and reporting requirements.

(2) Require the county to develop and submit for approval by the Department a corrective action plan.

(b) If any Standard Program County fails to meet acceptable levels of performance for two consecutive years, or fails to comply with a corrective action plan developed pursuant to this section, the Department may assume control of the county's Work First Program, appoint an administrator to administer the county's Work First Program, and exercise the powers assumed to administer the Work First Program either directly or through contract with private or public agencies. County funding shall continue at levels established by the State Plan when the State has assumed control of a county Work First Program. At no time after the State has assumed control of a Work First Program shall a county withdraw funds previously obligated or appropriated to the Work First Program.

(c) If an Electing County fails to achieve its Work First Program goals for two consecutive years, or fails to comply with a corrective action plan developed pursuant to this section, and as a result the federal government imposes a penalty upon the State, then the county shall lose its Electing County status. (1997-443, s. 12.6.)

§ 108A-27.15. Assistance not an entitlement; appeals.

(a) Any assistance programs established under this Part, whether administered by the Department or the counties, are not entitlements, and nothing in this Part shall create any property right.

(b) The Standard Work First Program is a program of temporary public assistance for the purpose of an appeal under G.S. 108A-79. (1997-443, s. 12.6.)

§ 108A-27.16. Repealed by Session Laws 1999-237, s. 6(h).

§§ 108A-28, 108A-28.1: Repealed by Session Laws 1997-443, s. 12.14.

§ 108A-29. Priority for employment services.

(a) Repealed by Session Laws 2009-489, s. 12, effective August 26, 2009.

(b) Individuals seeking to apply or reapply for Work First Program assistance and who are not exempt from work requirements shall register with the Division of Employment Security for employment services. The point of registration shall be at an office of the Division in the county in which the individual resides or at another location designated in a Memorandum of Understanding between the Division and the local department of social services.

(c) Individuals who are not otherwise exempt shall present verification of registration for Work First Program assistance. Unless exempt, the individual shall not be approved for Work First Program assistance until verification is received. Child-only cases are exempt from this requirement.

(d) Once an individual has registered as required in subsection (c) of this section and upon verification of the registration by the agency or contractor providing the Work First Program assistance, the individual's eligibility for Work First Program assistance may be evaluated and the application completed. Continued receipt of Work First Program benefits is contingent upon successful participation in employment services in the Mutual Responsibility Agreement, and lack of cooperation and participation in employment services may result in the termination of benefits to the individual.

(e) Repealed by Session Laws 2009-489, s. 12, effective August 26, 2009.

(f) Each county department of social services shall enter into a cooperative agreement with the local Division to operate the Job Search component on behalf of Work First Program registrants. The cooperative agreement shall include a provision for payment to the Division by the county department of social services for the cost of providing those services, not otherwise available to all clients of the Division, described in this subsection as the same are reflected as a component of the County Plan payable from fund allocations in the county block grant. The county department of social services may also enter into a cooperative agreement with the community college system or any other entity to operate the Job Preparedness component. This cooperative agreement shall include a provision for payment to that entity by the county department of social services for the cost of providing those services, not otherwise available to all clients of the Division, described in this subsection as the same are reflected as a component of the County Plan payable from fund allocations in the county block grant.

(g) The Division shall further assist registrants through job search, job placement, or referral to community service, if contracted to do so.

(h) An individual placed in the Job Search component of the Division or other agency providing Job Search services shall look for work and shall accept any suitable employment. If contracted, the Division shall refer individuals to current job openings and shall make job development contacts for individuals. Individuals so referred shall be required to keep a record of their job search activities on a job search record form provided by the Division, and the Division will monitor these activities. A "job search record" means a written list of dates, times, places, addresses, telephone numbers, names, and circumstances of job interviews. The Job Search component shall include at least one weekly contact with the Division. The Division shall adopt rules to accomplish this subsection.

(i)   The Division of Employment Security shall notify all employers in the State of the "Exclusive No-Fault" Referral Service available through the Division of Employment Security to employers who hire personnel through Job Service referrals.

(j)   All individuals referred to jobs through the Division of Employment Security shall be instructed in the procedures for applying for the Federal Earned Income Credit (FEIC). All individuals referred to jobs through the Division who qualify for the FEIC shall apply for the FEIC by filing a W-5 form with their employers.

(k)   The FEIC shall not be counted as income when eligibility is determined for Work First Program assistance, Medicaid, food and nutrition services, public housing, or Supplemental Security Income.

(l)   The Division of Employment Security shall work with the Department of Labor to develop a relationship with these private employment agencies to utilize their services and make referrals of individuals registered with the Division of Employment Security.

(m)   An individual who has not found a job within 12 weeks of being placed in the Job Search component of the Program may also be placed in the Community Service component at the county's option.

(n)   If after evaluation of an individual the Division of Employment Security believes it necessary, the Division or the county department of social services also may refer an individual to a Job Preparedness provider. The local community college should include General Education Development, Adult Basic Education, or Human Resources Development programs that are already in existence as a part of the Job Preparedness component. Additionally, the Division or the county department of social services may refer an individual to a literacy council. Through a Memorandum of Understanding between the Division of Employment Security, the local department of social services, and other contracted entities, a system shall be established to monitor an individual's progress through close communications with the agencies assisting the individual. The Division of Employment Security or Job Preparedness provider shall adopt rules to accomplish this subsection.

(o)   The Job Preparedness component of the Program shall last a maximum of 12 weeks unless the recipient is registered and is satisfactorily progressing in a program that requires additional time to complete. Every reasonable effort shall be made to place the recipient in part-time employment or part-time community service if the time required exceeds the 12-week maximum. The county department of social services may contract with service providers to provide the services described in this section and shall monitor the provision of the services by the service providers. Registrants may participate in more than one component at a time.

(p)   The Division shall expand its Labor Market Information System. The expansion shall at least include: statistical information on unemployment rates and other labor trends by county; and publications dealing with licensing requirements, economic development, and career projections, and information technology systems which can be used to track participants through the employment and training process.

(q),   (r) Repealed by Session Laws 2009-489, s. 12, effective August 26, 2009.

(s)   Members of families with dependent children and with aggregate family income at or below the level required for eligibility for Work First Family Assistance, regardless of whether or not they have applied for such assistance, shall be given priority in obtaining employment services including training and community service provided by or through State agencies or counties or with funds which are allocated to the State of North Carolina directly or indirectly through prime sponsors or otherwise for the purpose of employment of unemployed persons. (1961, c. 998; 1963, c. 1061; 1965, c. 939, s. 2; 1969, c. 546, s. 1; 1971, c. 283; 1973, c. 476, s. 138; 1977, c. 362; 1981, c. 275, s. 1; 1981 (Reg. Sess., 1982), c. 1282, s. 19; 1989 (Reg. Sess., 1990), c. 966, s. 1; 1997-443, s. 12.7(a); 1998-212, s. 12.27A(l), (m); 1999-340, s. 9; 2001-424, s. 21.13(d), (e); 2007-97, s. 8; 2009-489, s. 12; 2011-401, s. 3.12.)

§ 108A-29.1. (Effective until August 1, 2014) Substance abuse treatment required; drug testing for Work First Program recipients.

(a)   Each applicant or current recipient of Work First Program benefits, determined by a Qualified Professional in Substance Abuse (QPSA) or by a physician certified by the American Society of Addiction Medicine (ASAM) to be addicted to alcohol or drugs and to be in need of professional substance abuse treatment services shall be required, as part of the person's MRA and as a condition to receiving Work First Program benefits, to participate satisfactorily in an individualized plan of treatment in an appropriate treatment program. As a mandatory program component of participation in an addiction treatment program, each applicant or current recipient shall be required to submit to an approved, reliable, and professionally administered regimen of testing for presence of alcohol or drugs, without advance notice, during and after participation, in accordance with the addiction treatment program's individualized plan of treatment, follow-up, and continuing care services for the applicant or current recipient.

(b) An applicant or current recipient who fails to comply with any requirement imposed pursuant to this section shall not be eligible for benefits or shall be subject to the termination of benefits, but shall be considered to be receiving benefits for purposes of determining eligibility for medical assistance.

(c) The children of any applicant or current recipient shall remain eligible for benefits, and these benefits shall be paid to a protective payee pursuant to G.S. 108A-38.

(d) An applicant or current recipient shall not be regarded as failing to comply with the requirements of this section if an appropriate drug or alcohol treatment program is unavailable.

(e) Area mental health authorities organized pursuant to Article 4 of Chapter 122C of the General Statutes shall be responsible for administering the provisions of this section.

(f) The requirements of this section may be waived or modified as necessary in the case of individual applicants or recipients to the degree necessary to comply with Medicaid eligibility provisions. (1997-443, s. 12.8; 2009-489, s. 13.)

§ 108A-29.1. (Effective August 1, 2014) Drug screening and testing for Work First Program applicants and recipients.

(a) The Department shall require a drug test to screen each applicant for or recipient of Work First Program assistance whom the Department reasonably suspects is engaged in the illegal use of controlled substances. The Department shall provide notice of drug testing to each applicant or recipient. The notice shall advise the applicant or recipient that drug screening, and testing if there is reasonable suspicion that an individual is engaged in the illegal use of controlled substances, will be conducted as a condition of receiving Work First Program assistance, and that the results of the drug tests will remain confidential and will not be released to law enforcement. Dependent children under the age of 18 are exempt from the requirements of this section. The Department shall require the following:

(1)   That for two-parent households, both parents comply with the requirements of this section.

(2)   That any teen parent who is emancipated pursuant to Article 35 of Chapter 7B of the General Statutes complies with the requirements of this section.

(3)   That each applicant or recipient be advised before drug testing that he or she may inform the agent administering the test of any prescription or over-the-counter medication he or she is taking.

(4)   That each applicant or recipient being tested signs a written acknowledgement that he or she has received and understood the notice and advice provided under this subsection.

(5)   That each applicant or recipient who fails a drug test understands that he or she has the right to take one or more additional tests at his or her own expense.

(6)   That each applicant or recipient who fails a drug test be provided with information regarding substance abuse, substance abuse counseling, and substance abuse treatment options, including a list of substance abuse treatment programs that may be available to the individual.

(b)   An applicant or recipient who tests positive for controlled substances as a result of a drug test required under this section is ineligible to receive Work First Program assistance for one year from the date of the positive drug test except as provided in subsections (b1) and (b2) of this section. The individual may reapply after one year. However, if the individual has any subsequent positive drug tests, the individual shall be ineligible for benefits for three years from the date of the subsequent positive drug test unless the individual reapplies pursuant to subsection (b1) or (b2) of this section.

(b1) An applicant or recipient deemed ineligible under subsection (b) of this section may reapply for Work First Program assistance after the expiration of 30 days from the date of the positive drug test if the individual can document either the successful completion of or the current satisfactory participation in a substance abuse treatment program offered by a provider under subsection (e) of this section and licensed by the Department. The applicant or recipient who reapplies for Work First Program assistance after successful completion of a substance abuse program shall pass a drug test. The cost of any drug testing and substance abuse program provided under this subsection shall be the responsibility of the individual being tested and receiving treatment. An applicant or recipient who reapplies for Work First Program assistance pursuant to this subsection may reapply one time only.

(b2) An applicant or recipient deemed ineligible under subsection (b) of this section may reapply for Work First Program assistance after the expiration of 30 days from the date of the positive drug test if a qualified professional in substance abuse or a physician certified by the American Society of Addiction Medicine determines a substance abuse program is not appropriate for the individual and that individual has passed a subsequent drug test. The cost of any drug testing provided under this subsection shall be the responsibility of the individual being tested. An applicant or recipient who reapplies for Work First Program assistance pursuant to this subsection may reapply one time only.

(c) The children of any applicant or current recipient shall remain eligible for benefits, and these benefits shall be paid to a protective payee pursuant to G.S. 108A-38.

(d) The Social Services Commission shall adopt rules pertaining to the testing of applicants and recipients under this section. The Social Services Commission shall adopt rules pertaining to the successful completion of, or the satisfactory participation in, a substance abuse treatment program under subsection (b1) of this section, including rules regarding timely reporting of completion of or participation in the substance abuse treatment programs.

(e) Area mental health authorities organized pursuant to Article 4 of Chapter 122C of the General Statutes shall be responsible for administering the provisions of this section.

(f) Repealed by Session Laws 2013-417, s. 4, effective August 1, 2014.

(g)   For the purposes of this section, reasonable suspicion that an applicant for, or recipient of, Work First Program assistance is engaged in the illegal use of controlled substances may be established only by utilizing the following methods:

(1)   A criminal record check conducted under G.S. 114-19.34 that discloses a conviction, arrest, or outstanding warrant relating to illegal controlled substances within the three years prior to the date the criminal record check is conducted.

(2)   A determination by a qualified professional in substance abuse or a physician certified by the American Society of Addiction Medicine that an individual is addicted to illegal controlled substances.

(3)   A screening tool relating to the abuse of illegal controlled substances that yields a result indicating that the applicant or recipient may be engaged in the illegal use of controlled substances.

(4)   Other screening methods, as determined by the Social Services Commission under subsection (d) of this section.

(h)   Child only cases shall be exempt from the requirements of this section. (1997-443, s. 12.8; 2009-489, s. 13; 2013-417, s. 4.)

§ 108A-30: Repealed by Session Laws 1997-443, s. 12.14.

§ 108A-31. Application for assistance.

Any person who believes that the person is eligible to receive Work First Program assistance may apply for assistance to the county department of social services in the county in which the person resides, or, in the case of residents of Electing Counties, to the public or private entity designated by the board of county commissioners. Counties shall record inquiries for and accept applications from all persons requesting to apply for Work First Program assistance. Counties shall process applications in a reasonable and timely manner. (1937, c. 288, ss. 15, 45; 1939, c. 395, s. 1; 1941, c. 232; 1945, c. 615, s. 1; 1947, c. 91, s. 3; 1953, c. 675, s. 12; 1959, c. 179, ss. 1, 2; 1969, c. 546, s. 1; 1973, c. 476, s. 138; c. 742; 1979, c. 702, s. 4; 1981, c. 275, s. 1; 1997-443, s. 12.8A.)

§§ 108A-32 through 108A-35: Repealed by Session Laws 1997-443, s. 12.14.

§ 108A-36. Assistance not assignable; checks payable to decedents.

The assistance granted by this Article shall not be transferable or assignable at law or in equity; and none of the money paid or payable as assistance shall be subject to execution, levy, attachment, garnishment, or other legal processes, or to the operation of any bankruptcy or insolvency law.

In the event of the death of a public assistance recipient during or after the first day of the month for which assistance was previously authorized by the county social services board, or county director if waived, any public assistance check or checks payable to such recipient not endorsed prior to such recipient's death shall be delivered to the clerk of superior court and by him administered under the provisions of G.S. 28A-25-6. (1937, c. 288, ss. 17, 47; 1945, c. 615, s. 1; 1953, c. 213; 1969, c. 546, s. 1; 1971, c. 446, ss. 1, 2; 1977, c. 655, ss. 1, 2; 1981, c. 275, s. 1.)

§ 108A-37. Personal representative for mismanaged public assistance.

(a) Whenever a county director of social services shall determine that a recipient of assistance is unwilling or unable to manage such assistance to the extent that deprivation or hazard to himself or others results, the director shall file a petition before a district court or the clerk of superior court in the county alleging such facts and requesting the appointment of a personal representative to be responsible for receiving such assistance and to use it for the benefit of the recipient.

(b) Upon receipt of such petition, the court shall promptly hold a hearing, provided the recipient shall receive five days' notice in writing of the time and place of such hearing. If the court, sitting without a jury, shall find at the hearing that the facts alleged in the petition are true, it may appoint some responsible person as personal representative. The personal representative shall serve without compensation and be responsible to the court for the faithful performance of his duties. He shall serve until the director of social services or the recipient shows to the court that the personal representative is no longer required or is unsuitable. All costs of court relating to proceedings under this section shall be waived.

(c) Any recipient for whom a personal representative is appointed may appeal such appointment to superior court for a hearing de novo without a jury.

(d) All findings of fact made under the proceedings authorized by this section shall not be competent as evidence in any case or proceeding which concerns any subject matter other than that of appointing a personal representative. (1959, c. 1239, ss. 1, 3; 1961, c. 186; 1969, c. 546, s. 1; 1981, c. 275, s. 1.)

§ 108A-38. Protective and vendor payments.

When necessary to comply with any present or future federal law or regulation in order to obtain federal participation in public assistance payments, the payments may be made direct to vendors to reimburse them for goods and services provided the applicants or recipients, and may be made to protective payees who shall act for the applicant or recipient for receiving and managing assistance. Payments to vendors and protective payees shall be made to the extent provided in, and in accordance with, rules of the Social Services Commission or the Department, which rules shall be subject to applicable federal laws and regulations. (1963, c. 380; 1969, c. 546, s. 1; c. 747; 1973, c. 476, s. 138; 1977, 2nd Sess., c. 1219, s. 20; 1981, c. 275, s. 1; 1997-443, s. 12.9.)

§ 108A-39. Fraudulent misrepresentation.

(a) Any person whether provider or recipient, or person representing himself as such, who willfully and knowingly and with intent to deceive makes a false statement or representation or who fails to disclose a material fact and as a result of making a false statement or representation or failing to disclose a material fact obtains, for himself or another person, attempts to obtain for himself or another person, or continues to receive or enables another person to continue to receive public assistance in the amount of not more than four hundred dollars ($400.00) is guilty of a Class 1 misdemeanor.

(b) Any person, whether provider or recipient, or person representing himself as such who willfully and knowingly with the intent to deceive makes a false statement or representation or fails to disclose a material fact and as a result of making a false statement or representation or failing to disclose a material fact, obtains for himself or another person, attempts to obtain for himself or another person, or continues to receive or enables another person to continue to receive public assistance in an amount of more than four hundred dollars ($400.00) is guilty of a Class I felony.

(c) As used in this section the word "person" means person, association, consortium, corporation, body politic, partnership, or other group, entity, or organization. (1937, c. 288, ss. 27, 57; 1963, cc. 1013, 1024, 1062; 1969, c. 546, s. 1; 1977, c. 604, s. 1; 1979, c. 510, s. 2; c. 907; 1981, c. 275, s. 1; 1993, c. 539, s. 813; 1994, Ex. Sess., c. 24, s. 14(c).)

§ 108A-39.1: Repealed by Session Laws 1997-443, s. 12.14.

§ 108A-39.2: Repealed by Session Laws 1989 (Reg. Sess., 1990), c. 966, s. 3.

Part 3. State-County Special Assistance.

§ 108A-40. Authorization of State-County Special Assistance Program.

The Department is authorized to establish and supervise a State-County Special Assistance Program. This program is to be administered by county departments of social services under rules and regulations of the Social Services Commission. (1981, c. 275, s. 1; 2010-31, s. 10.19A(c).)

§ 108A-41. (See editor's note) Eligibility.

(a) Assistance shall be granted under this Part to all persons in adult care homes for care found to be essential in accordance with the rules and regulations adopted by the Social Services Commission and prescribed by G.S. 108A-42(b). As used in this Part, the term "adult care home" includes a supervised living facility for adults with intellectual and developmental disabilities licensed under Article 2 of Chapter 122C of the General Statutes.

(b) Assistance shall be granted to any person who:

(1) Is 65 years of age and older, is between the ages of 18 and 65, and is permanently and totally disabled or is legally blind pursuant to G.S. 111-11; and

(2) Has insufficient income or other resources to provide a reasonable subsistence compatible with decency and health as determined by the rules and regulations of the Social Services Commission; and

(3) Is one of the following:

a. A resident of North Carolina for at least 90 days immediately prior to receiving this assistance;

b. A person coming to North Carolina to join a close relative who has resided in North Carolina for at least 180 consecutive days immediately prior to the person's application. The close relative shall furnish verification of his or her residency to the local department of social services at the time the applicant applies for special assistance. As used in this sub-subdivision, a close relative is the person's parent, grandparent, brother, sister, spouse, or child; or

c. A person discharged from a State facility who was a patient in the facility as a result of an interstate mental health compact. As used in this sub-subdivision the term State facility is a facility listed under G.S. 122C-181.

(c) When determining whether a person has insufficient resources to provide a reasonable subsistence compatible with decency and health, there shall be excluded from consideration the person's primary place of residence and the land on which it is situated, and in addition there shall be excluded real property contiguous with the person's primary place of residence in which the property tax value is less than twelve thousand dollars ($12,000).

(d) The county shall also have the option of granting assistance to Certain Disabled persons as defined in the rules and regulations adopted by the Social

Services Commission. Nothing in this Part should be interpreted so as to preclude any individual county from operating any program of financial assistance using only county funds. (1949, s. 1038, s. 2; 1961, c. 186; 1969, c. 546, s. 1; 1973, c. 717, s. 1; 1977, 2nd Sess., c. 1252, s. 1; 1979, c. 702, s. 8; 1981, c. 275, s. 1; c. 849, s. 1; 1983, c. 14, s. 2; 1995, c. 535, s. 5; 1997-210, s. 1; 2001-209, s. 3; 2010-31, s. 10.19A(d).)

§ 108A-42. Determination of disability.

(a)   For purposes of G.S. 108A-41(b)(1), a person is permanently and totally disabled if:

(1)   This person was receiving aid to the disabled assistance in December 1973, and continues to be disabled under the definition of disability, having a physical or mental impairment which substantially precludes him from obtaining gainful employment and this impairment appears reasonably certain to continue without substantial improvement throughout his lifetime; or

(2)   This person applied for assistance on or after January 1, 1974, and is disabled under the Social Security standards.

(b)   For purposes of G.S. 108A-41(d), a "Certain Disabled" person is a person in a private living arrangement who is age 18 but less than age 65, having a physical or mental impairment which substantially precludes him from obtaining gainful employment, which impairment appears reasonably certain to continue without substantial improvement throughout his lifetime.

(c)   Disability shall be reviewed by medical consultants employed by the Department. The final decision on the disability shall be made by these medical consultants under rules and regulations adopted by the Social Services Commission. (1979, c. 702, s. 9; 1981, c. 275, s. 1; 1983, c. 14, s. 1.)

§ 108A-43. Application procedure.

(a)   Applications under this Part shall be made to the county director of social services who, with the approval of the county board of social services and in conformity with the rules and regulations of the Social Services Commission, shall determine whether assistance shall be granted and the amount of such assistance; but the county board of social services may delegate to the county director the authority to approve or reject all applications for assistance under this Part, in which event the county director shall not be required to report his actions to the board.

(b)   The amount of assistance which any eligible person may receive shall be determined with regard to the resources and necessary expenditures of the applicant, in accordance with the appropriate rules and regulations of the Social Services Commission. (1949, c. 1038, s. 2; 1961, c. 186; 1969, c. 546, s. 1; 1973, c. 476, s. 138; c. 717, s. 4; 1981, c. 275, s. 1.)

§ 108A-44. State funds to counties.

(a)   Appropriations made under this Part by the General Assembly to the Department, together with grants of the federal government (when such grants are made available to the State) shall be used exclusively for assistance to needy persons eligible under this Part.

(b)   Allotments shall be made annually by the Department to the counties participating in the program established by this Part.

(c)   No allotment shall be used, either directly or indirectly, to replace county appropriations or expenditures. (1949, c. 1038, s. 2; 1955, c. 310, s. 3; 1961, c. 186; 1969, c. 546, s. 1; 1973, c. 717, s. 5; 1975, c. 92, s. 2; 1981, c. 275, s. 1.)

§ 108A-45. Participation.

The State-County Special Assistance Program established by this Part shall be administered by all the county departments of social services under rules and regulations adopted by the Social Services Commission and under the supervision of the Department. Provided that, assistance for certain disabled persons shall be provided solely at the option of the county. (1949, c. 1038, s. 2; 1969, c. 546, s. 1; 1973, c. 476, s. 138; c. 717, s. 6; 1975, c. 92, s. 3; 1977, 2nd Sess., c. 1252, s. 2; 1981, c. 275, s. 1; 2010-31, s. 10.19A(e).)

§ 108A-46: Repealed by Session Laws 2003-284, s. 10.53(a), effective July 1, 2003.

§ 108A-46.1. Transfer of assets for purposes of qualifying for State-county Special Assistance.

Notwithstanding any other provision of law to the contrary, Supplemental Security Income (SSI) policy applicable to transfer of assets and estate recovery, as prescribed by federal law, shall apply to applicants for State-county Special Assistance. (2003-284, s. 10.53(b); 2010-31, s. 10.19A(f).)

§ 108A-47. Limitations on payments.

No payment of assistance under this Part shall be made for the care of any person in a licensed facility that is owned or operated in whole or in part by any of the following:

(1) A member of the Social Services Commission, of any county board of social services, or of any board of county commissioners;

(2) An official or employee of the Department, unless the official or employee has been appointed temporary manager of the facility pursuant to G.S. 131E-237, or of any county department of social services;

(3) A spouse of a person designated in subdivisions (1) and (2). (1979, c. 702, s. 10; 1981, c. 275, s. 1; 1995, c. 298, s. 1; c. 535, s. 6; 2010-31, s. 10.19A(g).)

§ 108A-47.1. Special Assistance in-home payments.

(a) The Department of Health and Human Services may use funds from the existing State-County Special Assistance budget to provide Special Assistance payments to eligible individuals 18 years of age or older in in-home living arrangements. These payments may be made for up to fifteen percent (15%) of the caseload for all State-County Special Assistance. The standard monthly payment to individuals enrolled in the Special Assistance in-home program shall be one hundred percent (100%) of the monthly payment the individual would receive if the individual resided in an adult care home and qualified for Special

Assistance, except if a lesser payment amount is appropriate for the individual as determined by the local case manager. The Department shall implement Special Assistance in-home eligibility policies and procedures to assure that in-home program participants are those individuals who need and, but for the in-home program, would seek placement in an adult care home facility. The Department's policies and procedures shall include the use of a functional assessment.

(b) All county departments of social services shall participate in the State-County Special Assistance in-home program by making Special Assistance in-home slots available to individuals who meet the eligibility requirements established by the Department pursuant to subsection (a) of this section. By February 15, 2013, the Department shall establish a formula to determine the need for additional State-County Special Assistance in-home slots for each county. Beginning July 1, 2014, and each July 1 thereafter, the Department shall review and revise the formula as necessary. (2007-323, s. 10.14(a); 2010-31, s. 10.19A(h); 2012-142, s. 10.23(a).)

Part 4. Foster Care and Adoption Assistance Payments.

§ 108A-48. State Foster Care Benefits Program.

(a) The Department is authorized to establish a State Foster Care Benefits Program with appropriations by the General Assembly for the purpose of providing assistance to children who are placed in foster care facilities by county departments of social services in accordance with the rules and regulations of the Social Services Commission. Such appropriations, together with county contributions for this purpose, shall be expended to provide for the costs of keeping children in foster care facilities.

(b) No benefits provided by this section shall be granted to any individual who has passed his eighteenth birthday unless he is less than 21 years of age and is a full-time student or has been accepted for enrollment as a full-time student for the next school term pursuing a high school diploma or its equivalent; a course of study at the college level; or a course of vocational or technical training designed to fit him for gainful employment. (1981, c. 275, s. 1.)

§ 108A-49. Foster care and adoption assistance payments.

(a) Benefits in the form of foster care assistance shall be granted in accordance with the rules of the Social Services Commission to any dependent child who would have been eligible to receive Aid to Families with Dependent Children (as that program was in effect on June 1, 1995), but for his or her removal from the home of a specified relative for placement in a foster care facility; provided, that the child's placement and care is the responsibility of a county department of social services. A county department of social services shall pay, at a minimum, the monthly graduated foster care assistance payments for eligible children as set by the General Assembly. A county department of social services may make foster care assistance payments in excess of the monthly graduated rates set by the General Assembly.

(b) Adoption assistance payments for certain adoptive children shall be granted in accordance with the rules of the Social Services Commission to adoptive parents who adopt a child eligible to receive foster care maintenance payments or supplemental security income benefits; provided, that the child cannot be returned to his or her parents; and provided, that the child has special needs which create a financial barrier to adoption. A county department of social services shall pay, at a minimum, the monthly graduated adoption assistance payments for eligible children as set by the General Assembly. A county department of social services may make adoption assistance payments in excess of the monthly graduated rates set by the General Assembly.

(c) The Department is authorized to use available federal payments to states under Title IV-E of the Social Security Act for foster care and adoption assistance payments.

(d) Except as otherwise prohibited by federal law, the Department of Health and Human Services, Division of Social Services, shall not require a redetermination of a child's eligibility for vendor payments under any adoption assistance agreement established prior to July 1, 2011. Nothing in this subsection shall make vendor assistance an entitlement. (1981, c. 275, s. 1; 1997-443, s. 12.10; 1999-190, s. 3; 2011-383, s. 1.)

§ 108A-49.1. Foster care and adoption assistance payment rates.

(a) The maximum rates for State participation in the foster care assistance program are established on a graduated scale as follows:

(1) $475.00 per child per month for children from birth through five years of age.

(2) $581.00 per child per month for children six through 12 years of age.

(3) $634.00 per child per month for children 13 through 18 years of age.

(b) The maximum rates for the State adoption assistance program are established consistent with the foster care rates as follows:

(1) $475.00 per child per month for children from birth through five years of age.

(2) $581.00 per child per month for children six through 12 years of age.

(3) $634.00 per child per month for children 13 through 18 years of age.

(c) The maximum rates for the State participation in human immunodeficiency virus (HIV) foster care and adoption assistance are established on a graduated scale as follows:

(1) $800.00 per child per month with indeterminate HIV status.

(2) $1,000 per child per month with confirmed HIV infection, asymptomatic.

(3) $1,200 per child per month with confirmed HIV infection, symptomatic.

(4) $1,600 per child per month when the child is terminally ill with complex care needs.

In addition to providing board payments to foster and adoptive families of HIV-infected children, any additional funds remaining that are appropriated for purposes described in this subsection shall be used to provide medical training in avoiding HIV transmission in the home.

(d) The State and a county participating in foster care and adoption assistance shall each contribute fifty percent (50%) of the nonfederal share of the cost of care for a child placed by a county department of social services or child-placing agency in a family foster home or residential child care facility. A county shall be held harmless from contributing fifty percent (50%) of the nonfederal share of the cost for a child placed in a family foster home or residential child care facility under an agreement with that provider as of October 31, 2008, until the child leaves foster care or experiences a placement change. (2011-145, s. 10.51.)

§ 108A-50. State benefits for certain adoptive children.

(a) The Department is authorized to establish a program of State benefits for certain adoptive children from appropriations made by the General Assembly and from grants available from the federal government to the State. This program shall be used exclusively for the purpose of meeting the needs of adoptive children who are physically or mentally handicapped, older, or otherwise hard to place for adoption.

(b) The purpose of this program is to encourage, within the limits of available funds, the adoption of certain hard-to-place children in order to make it possible for children living in, or likely to be placed in foster homes or institutions, to benefit from the stability and security of permanent homes where such children can receive continuous care, guidance, protection and love to reduce the number of such children who might be placed or remain in foster homes or institutions until they become adults.

(c) Eligibility for an adoptive child to receive assistance shall be determined by the Department under the rules and regulations of the Social Services Commission.

(d) Financial assistance under this program shall not be provided when the needed services are available free of cost to the adoptive child; or are covered by an insurance policy of the adoptive parents; or are available to the child under the Adoption Assistance Program specified in G.S. 108A-49. (1975, c. 953, s. 3; 1981, c. 275, s. 1.)

§ 108A-50.1. Special Needs Adoptions Incentive Fund.

(a)   There is created a Special Needs Adoptions Incentive Fund to provide financial assistance to facilitate the adoption of certain children residing in licensed foster care homes. These funds shall be used to remove financial barriers to the adoption of these children and shall be available to foster care families who adopt children with special needs, as defined by the Social Services Commission. These funds shall be matched by county funds.

(b)   This program shall not constitute an entitlement and is subject to the availability of funds.

(c)   The Social Services Commission shall adopt rules to implement the provisions of this section. (2003-284, s. 10.45.)

§ 108A-50.2. Adoption Promotion Fund.

(a)   Funds appropriated by the General Assembly to the Department of Health and Human Services, Division of Social Services, for the Adoption Promotion Fund shall be used as provided in this section. The Division of Social Services of the Department of Health and Human Services, in consultation with the North Carolina Association of County Directors of Social Services and representatives of licensed private adoption agencies, shall develop guidelines for the awarding of funds to licensed public and private adoption agencies upon the adoption of children described in G.S. 108A-50 and in foster care. Payments received from the Adoption Promotion Fund by participating agencies shall be used exclusively to enhance the adoption services. No local match shall be required as a condition for receipt of these funds. In accordance with State rules for allowable costs, the Adoption Promotion Fund may be used for post-adoption services for families whose income exceeds two hundred percent (200%) of the federal poverty level.

(b)   Of the total funds appropriated for the Adoption Promotion Fund each year, twenty percent (20%) of the total funds available shall be reserved for payment to participating private adoption agencies. If the funds reserved in this subsection for payments to private agencies have not been spent on or before March 31 of each State fiscal year, the Division of Social Services may reallocate those funds, in accordance with this section, to other participating adoption agencies.

(c) The Division of Social Services shall monitor the total expenditures in the Adoption Promotion Fund and redistribute unspent funds to ensure that the funds are used in accordance with the guidelines established in subsection (a) of this section. (2009-451, s. 10.48; 2013-360, s. 12C.10(c).)

Part 5. Food and Nutrition Services.

§ 108A-51. Authorization for Food and Nutrition Services.

The Department is authorized to establish a statewide food and nutrition services program as authorized by the Congress of the United States. The Department of Health and Human Services is designated as the State agency responsible for the supervision of the food and nutrition services program. The boards of county commissioners through the county departments of social services are held responsible for the administration and operation of the food and nutrition services program. (1981, c. 275, s. 1; 1997-443, s. 11A.118(a); 2007-97, s. 9.)

§ 108A-52. Determination of eligibility.

Any person who believes that he or another person is eligible to receive electronic food and nutrition benefits may apply for such assistance to the county department of social services in the county in which the applicant resides. The application shall be made in such form and shall contain such information as the Social Services Commission may require. Upon receipt of an application for electronic food and nutrition benefits, the county department of social services shall make a prompt evaluation or investigation of the facts alleged in the application in order to determine the applicant's eligibility for such assistance and to obtain such other information as the Department may require. Upon the completion of such investigation, the county department of social services shall, within a reasonable period of time, determine eligibility. (1981, c. 275, s. 1; 2007-97, s. 10.)

§ 108A-53. Fraudulent misrepresentation.

(a) Any person, whether provider or recipient or person representing himself as such, who knowingly obtains or attempts to obtain, or aids or abets any person to obtain by means of making a willfully false statement or representation or by impersonation or by failing to disclose material facts or in any manner not authorized by this Part or the regulations issued pursuant thereto, transfers with intent to defraud any electronic food and nutrition benefit to which that person is not entitled in the amount of four hundred dollars ($400.00) or less shall be guilty of a Class 1 misdemeanor. Whoever knowingly obtains or attempts to obtain, or aids or abets any person to obtain by means of making a willfully false statement or representation or by impersonation or by failing to disclose material facts or in any manner not authorized by this Part or the regulations issued pursuant thereto, transfers with intent to defraud any electronic food and nutrition benefit to which he is not entitled in an amount more than four hundred dollars ($400.00) shall be guilty of a Class I felony.

(b) Whoever presents, or causes to be presented, electronic food and nutrition benefits for payment or redemption, knowing the same to have been received, transferred, or used in any manner in violation of the provisions of this Part or the regulations issued pursuant to this Part shall be guilty of a Class 1 misdemeanor.

(c) Whoever receives any electronic food and nutrition benefits for any consumable item knowing that such benefits were procured fraudulently under subsections (a) and/or (b) of this section shall be guilty of a Class 1 misdemeanor.

(d) Whoever receives any electronic food and nutrition benefits for any consumable item whose exchange is prohibited by the United States Department of Agriculture shall be guilty of a Class 1 misdemeanor. (1981, c. 275, s. 1; 1991, c. 523, s. 5; 1993, c. 539, ss. 814, 1299; 1994, Ex. Sess., c. 24, s. 14(c); 1995, c. 507, s. 19.5(n); 1996, 2nd Ex. Sess., c. 18, s. 24.31(a); 2007-97, s. 11; 2008-187, s. 18.)

§ 108A-53.1. Illegal possession or use of electronic food and nutrition benefits.

(a) Any person who knowingly buys, sells, distributes, or possesses with the intent to sell, or distribute electronic food and nutrition benefits or access devices in any manner contrary to that authorized by this Part or the regulations issued pursuant thereto shall be guilty of a Class H felony.

(b) Any person who knowingly uses, transfers, acquires, alters, or possesses electronic food and nutrition benefits or access devices in any manner contrary to that authorized by this Part or the regulations issued pursuant thereto, other than as set forth in subsection (a) of this section, shall be guilty of a Class 1 misdemeanor if the value of such electronic food and nutrition benefits or access devices is less than one hundred dollars ($100.00), or a Class A1 misdemeanor if the value of such electronic food and nutrition benefits or access devices is equal to at least one hundred dollars ($100.00) but less than five hundred dollars ($500.00), or a Class I felony if the value of such electronic food and nutrition benefits or access devices is equal to at least five hundred dollars ($500.00) but less than one thousand dollars ($1,000), or a Class H felony if the value of such electronic food and nutrition benefits or access devices equals or exceeds one thousand dollars ($1,000). (1997-497, s. 2; 2007-97, s. 12.)

Part 6. Medical Assistance Program.

§ 108A-54. Authorization of Medical Assistance Program; administration.

(a) The Department is authorized to establish a Medicaid Program in accordance with Title XIX of the federal Social Security Act. The Department may adopt rules to implement the Program. The State is responsible for the nonfederal share of the costs of medical services provided under the Program. In addition, the State shall pay one hundred percent (100%) of the federal Medicare Part D clawback payments under the Medicare Modernization Act of 2004, P.L. 108-173, as amended. A county is responsible for the county's cost of administering the Program in that county.

(b) Recodified as G.S. 108A-54.1B(a) by Session Laws 2013-360, s. 12H.9(a), effective July 1, 2013.

(c) The Medicaid Program shall be administered and operated in accordance with this Part and the North Carolina Medicaid State Plan and Waivers, as periodically amended by the Department of Health and Human Services in accordance with G.S. 108A-54.1A and approved by the federal government.

(d) The Department of Health and Human Services shall ensure that the North Carolina Families Accessing Services through Technology (NC FAST) information technology system can provide Medicaid eligibility determinations for the federally facilitated Health Benefit Exchange that will operate in North Carolina and shall provide such determinations for the Exchange. (1965, c. 1173, s. 1; 1969, c. 546, s. 1; 1973, c. 476, s. 138; 1977, 2nd Sess., c. 1219, s. 24; 1981, c. 275, s. 1.; 2007-323, s. 31.16.1(c); 2008-107, s. 10.10(c); 2011-399, s. 5; 2012-75, s. 1; 2013-5, s. 2; 2013-360, ss. 12H.3, 12H.9(a); 2013-363, s. 4.9(a).)

§ 108A-54.1: Recodified as G.S. 108A-66.1 by Session Laws 2013-360, s. 12H.10(f), effective July 1, 2013.

§ 108A-54.1A. Amendments to Medicaid State Plan and Medicaid Waivers.

(a) No provision in the Medicaid State Plan or in a Medicaid Waiver may expand or otherwise alter the scope or purpose of the Medicaid program from that authorized by law enacted by the General Assembly. For purposes of this section, the term "amendments to the State Plan" includes State Plan amendments, Waivers, and Waiver amendments.

(b) The Department may submit amendments to the State Plan only as required under any of the following circumstances:

(1) A law enacted by the General Assembly directs the Department to submit an amendment to the State Plan.

(2) A law enacted by the General Assembly makes a change to the Medicaid Program that requires approval by the federal government.

(3) A change in federal law, including regulatory law, or a change in the interpretation of federal law by the federal government requires an amendment to the State Plan.

(4) A change made by the Department to the Medicaid Program requires an amendment to the State Plan, if the change was within the authority granted to the Department by State law.

(5) An amendment to the State Plan is required in response to an order of a court of competent jurisdiction.

(6) An amendment to the State Plan is required to ensure continued federal financial participation.

(c) Amendments to the State Plan submitted to the federal government for approval shall contain only those changes that are allowed by the authority for submitting an amendment to the State Plan in subsection (b) of this section.

(d) No fewer than 10 days prior to submitting an amendment to the State Plan to the federal government, the Department shall post the amendment on its Web site and notify the members of the Joint Legislative Oversight Committee on Health and Human Services and the Fiscal Research Division that the amendment has been posted. This requirement shall not apply to draft or proposed amendments submitted to the federal government for comments but not submitted for approval. If the authority for submitting the amendment to the State Plan is pursuant to subdivision (3), (4), (5), or (6) of subsection (b) of this section, then, prior to submitting an amendment to the federal government, the Department shall submit to the General Assembly members receiving notice under this subsection and to the Fiscal Research Division an explanation of the amendment, the need for the amendment, and the federal time limits required for implementation of the amendment.

(e) The Department shall submit an amendment to the State Plan to the federal government by a date sufficient to provide the federal government adequate time to review and approve the amendment so the amendment may be effective by the date required by the directing authority in subsection (b) of this section. (2013-360, s. 12H.2(a).)

§ 108A-54.1B. Adoption of rules; State Plans, including amendments and waivers to State Plans, have effect of rules.

(a) The Department is expressly authorized to adopt temporary and permanent rules to implement or define the federal laws and regulations, the North Carolina State Plan of Medical Assistance, and the North Carolina State Plan of the Health Insurance Program for Children, the terms and conditions of eligibility for applicants and recipients of the Medical Assistance Program and the Health Insurance Program for Children, audits and program integrity, the services, goods, supplies, or merchandise made available to recipients of the Medical Assistance Program and the Health Insurance Program for Children, and reimbursement for the services, goods, supplies, or merchandise made available to recipients of the Medical Assistance Program and the Health Insurance Program for Children.

(b) Rule-making authority granted under this section for particular circumstances or programs is in addition to any other rule-making authority granted to the Department under Chapter 150B of the General Statutes.

(c) Prior to filing a temporary rule authorized under G.S. 150B-21.1(a)(17) with the Rules Review Commission and the Office of Administrative Hearings, the Department shall consult with the Office of State Budget and Management on the possible fiscal impact of the temporary rule and its effect on State appropriations and local governments.

(d) State Plans, State Plan Amendments, and Waivers approved by the Centers for Medicare and Medicaid Services (CMS) for the North Carolina Medicaid Program and the NC Health Choice program shall have the force and effect of rules adopted pursuant to Article 2A of Chapter 150B of the General Statutes. (2013-360, s. 12H.9(a), (b).)

§ 108A-54.2. Procedures for changing medical policy.

(a) The Department shall adopt rules to develop, amend, and adopt medical coverage policy for Medicaid and NC Health Choice in accordance with this section.

(b) Medical coverage policy is defined as those policies, definitions, or guidelines utilized to evaluate, treat, or support the health or developmental conditions of a recipient so as to determine eligibility, authorization or continued authorization, medical necessity, course of treatment and supports, clinical outcomes, and clinical supports treatment practices for a covered procedure, product, or service. Medical coverage policy is subject to the following:

(1) During the development of new medical coverage policy or amendment to existing medical coverage policy, the Department shall consult with and seek the advice of the Physician Advisory Group and other organizations the Secretary deems appropriate. The Secretary shall also consult with and seek

the advice of officials of the professional societies or associations representing providers who are affected by the new medical coverage policy or amendments to existing medical coverage policy.

(2) At least 45 days prior to the adoption of new or amended medical coverage policy, the Department shall:

a. Publish the proposed new or amended medical coverage policy on the Department's Web site;

b. Notify all Medicaid and NC Health Choice providers of the proposed, new, or amended policy; and

c. Upon request, provide persons copies of the proposed medical coverage policy.

(3) During the 45-day period immediately following publication of the proposed new or amended medical coverage policy, the Department shall accept oral and written comments on the proposed new or amended policy.

(4) If, following the comment period, the proposed new or amended medical coverage policy is modified, then the Department shall, at least 15 days prior to its adoption:

a. Notify all Medicaid and NC Health Choice providers of the proposed policy;

b. Upon request, provide persons notice of amendments to the proposed policy; and

c. Accept additional oral or written comments during this 15-day period.

(c) If the adoption of new or amended medical coverage policies is necessitated by an act of the General Assembly or a change in federal law, then the 45- and 15-day time periods specified in subsection (b) of this section shall instead be 30- and 10-day time periods.

(d) Unless directed to do so by the General Assembly, the Department shall not change medical policy affecting the amount, sufficiency, duration, and scope of health care services and who may provide services until the Division of Medical Assistance has prepared a five-year fiscal analysis documenting the increased cost of the proposed change in medical policy and submitted it for departmental review. Changes to medical policy affecting the amount, sufficiency, duration, and scope of health care services and who may provide services are subject to the following:

(1) If the fiscal impact indicated by the fiscal analysis for any proposed medical policy change exceeds five hundred thousand dollars ($500,000) in total requirements for Medicaid or fifty thousand dollars ($50,000) in total requirements for NC Health Choice for a given fiscal year, then the Department shall submit the proposed medical policy change to the fiscal analysis to the Office of State Budget and Management and the Fiscal Research Division. The Department shall not implement the proposed medical policy change unless the source of State funding is identified and approved by the Office of State Budget and Management.

(2) If the medical policy change meets the requirement thresholds specified in subdivision (1) of this subsection but is required for compliance with federal law, then the Department shall submit the proposed medical policy or policy interpretation change with the five-year fiscal analysis to the Office of State Budget and Management prior to implementing the change.

The Department shall annually report, by November 1 of each year, all medical policy changes with total requirements of less than the amount specified in subdivision (1) of this subsection to the Office of State Budget and Management and the Fiscal Research Division of the Legislative Services Commission. (2006-66, s. 10.4; 2009-451, s. 10.68A(b); 2011-399, s. 4; 2013-360, s. 12H.6(a).)

§ 108A-54.3: Repealed by Session Laws 2013-360, s. 12H.6(b), effective July 26, 2013.

§ 108A-54.4. (Expires December 31, 2017) Income disregard for federal cost-of-living adjustments.

An increase in a Medical Assistance Program recipient's income due solely to a cost-of-living adjustment to federal Social Security and Railroad Retirement payments shall be disregarded when determining income eligibility for the

Medical Assistance Program. This section shall not be deemed to render a recipient eligible for the Medical Assistance Program if all other eligibility requirements are not met. (2012-142, s. 10.6(a).)

§ 108A-55. Payments.

(a) The Department may authorize, within appropriations made for this purpose, payments of all or part of the cost of medical and other remedial care for any eligible person when it is essential to the health and welfare of such person that such care be provided, and when the total resources of such person are not sufficient to provide the necessary care. When determining whether a person has sufficient resources to provide necessary medical care, there shall be excluded from consideration the person's primary place of residence and the land on which it is situated, and in addition there shall be excluded real property contiguous with the person's primary place of residence in which the property tax value is less than twelve thousand dollars ($12,000).

(b) Payments shall be made only to intermediate care facilities, hospitals and nursing homes licensed and approved under the laws of the State of North Carolina or under the laws of another state, or to pharmacies, physicians, dentists, optometrists or other providers of health-related services authorized by the Department. Payments may also be made to such fiscal intermediaries and to the capitation or prepaid health service contractors as may be authorized by the Department. Arrangements under which payments are made to capitation or prepaid health services contracts are not subject to the provisions of Chapter 58 of the General Statutes or of Article 3 of Chapter 143 of the General Statutes. However, the Department shall: (i) submit all proposed contracts for supplies, materials, printing, equipment, and contractual services that exceed one million dollars ($1,000,000) authorized by this subsection to the Attorney General or the Attorney General's designee for review as provided in G.S. 114-8.3; and (ii) include in all agreements or contracts to be awarded by the Department under this subsection a standard clause which provides that the State Auditor and internal auditors of the Department may audit the records of the contractor during and after the term of the contract to verify accounts and data affecting fees and performance. The Department shall not award a cost plus percentage of cost agreement or contract for any purpose.

(c) The Department shall reimburse providers of services, equipment, or supplies under the Medical Assistance Program in the following amounts:

(1) The amount approved by the Health Care Financing Administration of the United States Department of Health and Human Services, if that Administration approves an exact reimbursement amount;

(2) The amount determined by application of a method approved by the Health Care Financing Administration of the United States Department of Health and Human Services, if that Administration approves the method by which a reimbursement amount is determined, and not the exact amount.

The Department shall establish the methods by which reimbursement amounts are determined in accordance with Chapter 150B of the General Statutes. A change in a reimbursement amount becomes effective as of the date for which the change is approved by the Health Care Financing Administration of the United States Department of Health and Human Services. The Department shall report to the Fiscal Research Division of the Legislative Services Office and to the Senate Appropriations Committee on Human Resources and the House of Representatives Appropriations Subcommittee on Human Resources or the Joint Legislative Oversight Committee on Health and Human Services on any change in a reimbursement amount at the same time as it sends out public notice of this change prior to presentation to the Health Care Financing Administration.

(d) No payments shall be made for the care of any person in a nursing home or intermediate care home which is owned or operated in whole or in part by a member of the Social Services Commission, of any county board of social services, or of any board of county commissioners, or by an official or employee of the Department or of any county department of social services or by a spouse of any such person.

(e) Medicaid is a secondary payor of claims. The Department shall apply Medicaid medical policy to recipients who have primary insurance other than Medicare, Medicare Advantage, and Medicaid. For recipients who have primary insurance other than Medicare, Medicare Advantage, or Medicaid, the Department shall pay the lesser of the Medicaid Allowable Amount or an amount up to the actual coinsurance or deductible or both of the primary payor, in accordance with the State Plan, as approved by the Department of Health and Human Services. The Department may disregard application of this policy in cases where application of the policy would adversely affect patient care. (1965, c. 1173, s. 1; 1969, c. 546, s. 1; 1971, c. 435; 1973, c. 476, s. 138; c. 644; 1975, c. 123, ss. 1, 2; 1977, 2nd Sess., c. 1219, c. 25; 1979, c. 702, s. 7;

1981, c. 275, s. 1; c. 849, s. 2; 1991, c. 388, s. 1; 1993, c. 529, s. 7.3; 1998-212, s. 12.12B(c); 2010-194, s. 15; 2011-291, s. 2.22; 2011-326, s. 15(o); 2013-360, s. 12H.4.)

§ 108A-55.1. Medicare enrollment required.

The Department shall require State Medical Assistance Program recipients who qualify for Medicare to enroll in Medicare, in accordance with Title XIX of the Social Security Act, in order to pay medical expenditures that qualify for payment under Medicare Parts B and D, except that enrollment in Part D is not required if the recipient has creditable prescription drug coverage as defined by federal law.

Failure to enroll in Medicare shall result in nonpayment of these expenditures under the State Medical Assistance Program. A provider may seek payment for services from Medicaid enrollees who are eligible for but not enrolled in Medicare Parts B and D. (2003-284, s. 10.27; 2006-66, s. 10.6.)

§ 108A-55.2. Collaboration among agencies to ensure Medicaid-related services payments to eligible students with disabilities in public schools.

The Department shall work with the Department of Public Instruction and local education agencies to develop efficient, effective, and appropriate administrative procedures and guidelines to provide maximum funding for Medicaid-related services for Medicaid-eligible students with disabilities. The procedures and guidelines shall be streamlined to ensure that local education agencies receive Medicaid reimbursement in a timely manner for Medicaid-related services and administrative outreach to Medicaid-eligible students with disabilities. (2003-284, s. 10.29A.)

§ 108A-55.3. Verification of State residency required for medical assistance.

(a) At the time of application for medical assistance benefits, the applicant shall provide satisfactory proof that the applicant is a resident of North Carolina and that the applicant is not maintaining a temporary residence or abode incident to receiving medical assistance under this Part.

(b)   An applicant may meet the requirements of subsection (a) of this section by providing at least two of the following documents:

(1)   A valid North Carolina drivers license or other identification card issued by the North Carolina Division of Motor Vehicles.

(2)   A current North Carolina rent or mortgage payment receipt, or current utility bill in the name of the applicant or the applicant's legal spouse showing a North Carolina address.

(3)   A valid North Carolina motor vehicle registration in the applicant's name and showing the applicant's current address.

(4)   A document showing that the applicant is employed in this State.

(5)   One or more documents proving that the applicant's domicile in the applicant's prior state of domicile has ended, such as closing of a bank account, termination of employment, or sale of a home.

(6)   The tax records of the applicant or the applicant's legal spouse, showing a current North Carolina address.

(7)   A document showing that the applicant has registered with a public or private employment service in this State.

(8)   A document showing that the applicant has enrolled the applicant's children in a public or private school or child care facility located in this State.

(9)   A document showing that the applicant is receiving public assistance or other services requiring proof of domicile, other than medical assistance, in this State.

(10)   Records from a health department or other health care provider located in this State showing the applicant's current North Carolina address.

(11)   A written declaration made under penalty of perjury from a person who has a social, family, or economic relationship with the applicant and who has personal knowledge of the applicant's intent to live in North Carolina

permanently or for an indefinite period of time or that the applicant is residing in North Carolina to seek employment or with a job commitment.

(12)   Current North Carolina voter registration card.

(13)   A document from the U.S. Department of Veterans Affairs, U.S. Department of Defense, or the U.S. Department of Homeland Security verifying the applicant's intent to live in North Carolina permanently or for an indefinite period of time or that the applicant is residing in North Carolina to seek employment or with a job commitment.

(14)   Official North Carolina school records, signed by school officials, or diplomas issued by North Carolina schools, including secondary schools, community colleges, colleges, and universities verifying the applicant's intent to live in North Carolina permanently or for an indefinite period of time or that the applicant is residing in North Carolina to seek employment or with a job commitment.

(15)   A document issued by the Mexican consular or other foreign consulate verifying the applicant's intent to live in North Carolina permanently or for an indefinite period of time or that the applicant is residing in North Carolina to seek employment or with a job commitment.

(c)   For applicants, including those who are homeless or migrant laborers, who declare under penalty of perjury that they do not have two of the verifying documents in subsection (b) of this section, any other evidence that verifies residence may be considered. However, except for applicants of emergency Medicaid, a declaration, affidavit, or other statement from the applicant or another person that the applicant meets the requirements of G.S. 108A-24(6) is insufficient in the absence of other credible evidence. For applicants of emergency Medicaid, a declaration, affidavit, or other statement from the applicant's employer, clergy, or other person with personal knowledge of the applicant's intent to live in North Carolina permanently or for an indefinite period of time or that the applicant is residing in North Carolina to seek employment or with a job commitment satisfies the requirements of this subsection.

(d)   The Division of Medical Assistance shall not provide payment for medical assistance provided to an applicant unless or until the applicant has met the proof of residency requirements of this section.

(e)   Unless otherwise provided for under Title 19 of the Social Security Act, a child under age 18 is a resident of the state where the child's parent or legal guardian is domiciled.

(f)   This section does not apply to an applicant whose eligibility for medical assistance is excepted from State residency requirements under federal law.

(g)   Nothing in this section shall be construed to establish North Carolina residency for a nonqualified alien who is present in North Carolina for a temporary or unspecified period of time unless the applicant is legally admitted for employment purposes. (2005-276, s. 10.21A(a); 2011-183, s. 74.)

§ 108A-55.4. Insurers to provide certain information to Department of Health and Human Services.

(a)   As used in this section, the terms:

(1)   "Applicant" means an applicant or former applicant of medical assistance benefits.

(1a)   "Department" means the Department of Health and Human Services.

(2)   "Division" means the Division of Medical Assistance of the Department of Health and Human Services.

(3)   "Health insurer" includes self-insured plans, group health plans (as defined in section 607(1) of the Employee Retirement Income Security Act of 1974, [29 USC Section 1167(1)]), service benefit plans, managed care organizations, or other parties that are, by statute, contract, or agreement, legally responsible for payment of a claim for a health care item or service as a condition of doing business in the State.

(4)   "Medical assistance" means medical assistance benefits provided under the State Medical Assistance Plan.

(5),   (6) Reserved for future codification.

(7)   "Recipient" means a present or former recipient of medical assistance benefits.

(8) "Request" means any inquiry by the Department or Division for the purpose of determining the existence of insurance where the Department or Division may have expended public assistance benefits.

(9) "Subscriber" means the policyholder or covered person under the insurance policy.

(b) Health insurers, and pharmacy benefit managers regulated as third-party administrators under Article 56 of Chapter 58 of the General Statutes, shall provide, with respect to a subscriber upon request of the Division or its authorized contractor, information to determine during what period the individual or the individual's spouse or dependents may be (or may have been) covered by a health insurer and the nature of the coverage that is or was provided by the health insurer (including the subscriber's name, address, identification number, social security number, date of birth and identifying number of the plan) in a manner prescribed by the Division or its authorized contractor. Notwithstanding any other provision of law, every health insurer shall provide, not more frequently than twelve times in a year and at no cost, to the Department of Health and Human Services, Division of Medical Assistance, or the Department's or Division's authorized contractor, upon its request, information as necessary so that the Division may (i) identify applicants or recipients who may also be subscribers covered under the benefit plans of the health insurer; (ii) determine the period during which the individual, the individual's spouse, or the individual's dependents may be or may have been covered by the health benefit plan; and (iii) determine the nature of the coverage. To facilitate the Division or its authorized contractor in obtaining this and other related information, every health insurer shall:

(1) Cooperate with the Division to determine whether a named individual who is a recipient of medical assistance may be covered under the insurer's health benefit plan and eligible to receive benefits under the health benefit plan for services provided under the State Medical Assistance Plan.

(2) Respond to the request for payment within 90 working days after receipt of written proof of loss or claim for payment for health care services provided to a recipient of medical assistance who is covered by the benefit plan of the health insurer.

(3) Accept the Division's right of recovery and the assignment to the Division of any right of an individual or other entity to payment from the party for

an item or service for which payment has been made under the State Medical Assistance Plan.

(4)   Respond to any inquiry by the Division or its authorized contractor regarding a claim for payment for any health care item or service that is submitted not later than three years after the date of the provision of the health care item or service.

(5)   Notwithstanding subsection (d) of this section, agree not to deny a claim submitted by the Division solely on the basis of the date of submission of the claim, the type of format of the claim form, or a failure to present proper documentation at the point-of-sale that is the basis of the claim, if:

a.   The claim is submitted by the Division within the three-year period beginning on the date on which the item or service was furnished; and

b.   Any action by the Division to enforce its rights with respect to such claim is commenced within six years of the Division's submission of the claim.

(c)   A health insurer that complies with this section shall not be liable on that account in any civil or criminal actions or proceedings.

(d)   A health insurer is obligated to reimburse the Department only if the insurer has a contractual obligation to make payment for the covered service or item. (2006-66, s. 10.8; 2006-221, ss. 9(a)-(c); 2007-442, s. 2.)

§ 108A-56. Acceptance of federal grants.

All of the provisions of the federal Social Security Act providing grants to the states for medical assistance are accepted and adopted, and the provisions of this Part shall be liberally construed in relation to such act so that the intent to comply with it shall be made effectual. Nothing in this Part or the regulations made under its authority shall be construed to deprive a recipient of assistance of the right to choose the licensed provider of the care or service made available under this Part within the provisions of the federal Social Security Act. (1965, c. 1173, s. 1; 1969, c. 546, s. 1; 1981, c. 275, s. 1.)

§ 108A-57. Subrogation rights; withholding of information a misdemeanor.

(a) Notwithstanding any other provisions of the law, to the extent of payments under this Part, the State shall be subrogated to all rights of recovery, contractual or otherwise, of the beneficiary of this assistance, or of the beneficiary's personal representative, heirs, or the administrator or executor of the estate, against any person. A personal injury or wrongful death claim brought by a medical assistance beneficiary against a third party shall include a claim for all medical assistance payments for health care items or services furnished to the medical assistance beneficiary as a result of the injury, hereinafter referred to as the "Medicaid claim." Any personal injury or wrongful death claim brought by a medical assistance beneficiary against a third party that does not state the Medicaid claim shall be deemed to include the Medicaid claim.

(a1) If the amount of the Medicaid claim does not exceed one-third of the medical assistance beneficiary's gross recovery, it is presumed that the gross recovery includes compensation for the full amount of the Medicaid claim. If the amount of the Medicaid claim exceeds one-third of the medical assistance beneficiary's gross recovery, it is presumed that one-third of the gross recovery represents compensation for the Medicaid claim.

(a2) A medical assistance beneficiary may dispute the presumptions established in subsection (a1) of this section by applying to the court in which the medical assistance beneficiary's claim against the third party is pending, or if there is none, then to a court of competent jurisdiction, for a determination of the portion of the beneficiary's gross recovery that represents compensation for the Medicaid claim. An application under this subsection shall be filed with the court and served on the Department pursuant to the Rules of Civil Procedure no later than 30 days after the date that the settlement agreement is executed by all parties and, if required, approved by the court, or in cases in which judgment has been entered, no later than 30 days after the date of entry of judgment. The court shall hold an evidentiary hearing no sooner than 30 days after the date the action was filed. All of the following shall apply to the court's determination under this subsection:

(1) The medical assistance beneficiary has the burden of proving by clear and convincing evidence that the portion of the beneficiary's gross recovery that represents compensation for the Medicaid claim is less than the portion presumed under subsection (a1) of this section.

(2)   The presumption arising under subsection (a1) of this section is not rebutted solely by the fact that the medical assistance beneficiary was not able to recover the full amount of all claims.

(3)   If the beneficiary meets its burden of rebutting the presumption arising under subsection (a1) of this section, then the court shall determine the portion of the recovery that represents compensation for the Medicaid claim and shall order the beneficiary to pay the amount so determined to the Department in accordance with subsection (a5) of this section. In making this determination, the court may consider any factors that it deems just and reasonable.

(4)   If the beneficiary fails to rebut the presumption arising under subsection (a1) of this section, then the court shall order the beneficiary to pay the amount presumed pursuant to subsection (a1) of this section to the Department in accordance with subsection (a5) of this section.

(a3)   Notwithstanding the presumption arising pursuant to subsection (a1) of this section, the medical assistance beneficiary and the Department may reach an agreement on the portion of the recovery that represents compensation for the Medicaid claim. If such an agreement is reached after an application has been filed pursuant to subsection (a2) of this section, a stipulation of dismissal of the application signed by both parties shall be filed with the court.

(a4)   Within 30 days of receipt of the proceeds of a settlement or judgment related to a claim described in subsection (a) of this section, the medical assistance beneficiary or any attorney retained by the beneficiary shall notify the Department of the receipt of the proceeds.

(a5)   The medical assistance beneficiary or any attorney retained by the beneficiary shall, out of the proceeds obtained by or on behalf of the beneficiary by settlement with, judgment against, or otherwise from a third party by reason of injury or death, distribute to the Department the amount due pursuant to this section as follows:

(1)   If, upon the expiration of the time for filing an application pursuant subsection (a2) of this section, no application has been filed, then the amount presumed pursuant to subsection (a1) of this section, as prorated with the claims of all others having medical subrogation rights or medical liens against the amount received or recovered, shall be paid to the Department within 30 days of the beneficiary's receipt of the proceeds, in the absence of an agreement pursuant to subsection (a3) of this section.

(2) If an application has been filed pursuant to subsection (a2) of this section and no agreement has been reached pursuant to subsection (a3) of this section, then the Department shall be paid as follows:

a. If the beneficiary rebuts the presumption arising under subsection (a1) of this section, then the amount determined by the court pursuant to subsection (a2) of this section, as prorated with the claims of all others having medical subrogation rights or medical liens against the amount received or recovered, shall be paid to the Department within 30 days of the entry of the court's order.

b. If the beneficiary fails to rebut the presumption arising under subsection (a1) of this section, then the amount presumed pursuant to subsection (a1) of this section, as prorated with the claims of all others having medical subrogation rights or medical liens against the amount received or recovered, shall be paid to the Department within 30 days of the entry of the court's order.

(3) If an agreement has been reached pursuant to subsection (a3) of this section, then the agreed amount, as prorated with the claims of all others having medical subrogation rights or medical liens against the amount received or recovered, shall be paid to the Department within 30 days of the execution of the agreement by the medical assistance beneficiary and the Department.

(a6) The United States and the State of North Carolina shall be entitled to shares in each net recovery by the Department under this section. Their shares shall be promptly paid under this section and their proportionate parts of such sum shall be determined in accordance with the matching formulas in use during the period for which assistance was paid to the recipient.

(b) It is a Class 1 misdemeanor for any person seeking or having obtained assistance under this Part for himself or another to willfully fail to disclose to the county department of social services or its attorney and to the Department the identity of any person or organization against whom the recipient of assistance has a right of recovery, contractual or otherwise.

(c) This section applies to the administration of and claims payments made by the Department of Health and Human Services under the NC Health Choice Program established under Part 8 of this Article.

(d) As required to ensure compliance with this section, the Department may apply to the court in which the medical assistance beneficiary's claim against the third party is pending, or if there is none, then to a court of competent jurisdiction for enforcement of this section. (1973, c. 476, s. 138; c. 1031, s. 1; 1979, 2nd Sess., c. 1312, ss. 1, 2; 1981, c. 275, s. 1; 1987 (Reg. Sess., 1988), c. 1022; 1993, c. 539, s. 815; 1994, Ex. Sess., c. 24, s. 14(c); 1996, 2nd Ex. Sess., c. 18, s. 24.2(a); 2009-16, s. 4(c); 2013-274, s. 1.)

§ 108A-57.1. Rules governing transfer of medical assistance benefits between counties.

Any recipient of medical assistance who moves from one county to another county of this State shall continue to receive medical assistance if eligible. The county director of social services of the county from which the recipient has moved shall transfer all necessary records relating to the recipient to the county director of social services of the county to which the recipient has moved. The county from which the recipient has moved shall pay the county portion of the nonfederal share of medical assistance payments paid for services provided to the recipient during the month following the recipient's move. Thereafter, the county to which the recipient has moved shall pay the county portion of the nonfederal share of medical assistance payments paid for the services provided to the recipient. (1998-212, s. 12.6.)

§ 108A-58: Repealed by Session Laws 2006-66, s. 10.5(a), effective July 1, 2006.

§ 108A-58.1. Ineligibility for medical assistance based on transferring assets for less than fair market value.

(a) General Rule. - Except as otherwise provided herein, an individual who is otherwise eligible to receive medical assistance under this Part is ineligible for Medicaid coverage and payment for the services specified in subsection (d) during the period specified in subsection (c) if the individual or the individual's spouse transfers an asset for less than fair market value on or after the "lookback date" specified in subsection (b).

(b) Lookback Date. -

-(1) Except as otherwise provided herein, the lookback date is the date specified in 42 U.S.C. § 1396p(c)(1)(B).

(2) Notwithstanding subdivision (1), the lookback date with respect to the medical services specified in subdivision (d)(2) is the date specified in 42 U.S.C. § 1396p(c)(1)(B) or February 1, 2003, whichever is later.

(c) Penalty Period. - The penalty period for the transfer of assets for less than fair market value is the period specified in 42 U.S.C. § 1396p(c)(1)(D), (E), and (H).

(d) Medical Services. -

(1) In the case of an institutionalized individual, the transfer of assets penalty applies with respect to nursing facility services, a level of care in any institution equivalent to that of nursing facility services, and to home- or community-based services furnished under the State's Community Alternatives Program waiver pursuant to 42 U.S.C. § 1396n(c) or (d), and pursuant to the hardship waiver under subsection (k) of this section.

(2) In the case of a noninstitutionalized individual, the transfer of assets penalty applies with respect to home health services and personal care services as defined in 42 U.S.C. § 1396d(a)(7) and (24) and, to the extent permitted by federal law, such other long-term care services specified by rules adopted by the Department of Health and Human Services pursuant to subsection (k) of this section.

(e) Assets. - Assets are the income and resources of an individual or the individual's spouse (including the individual's or spouse's home) as defined in 42 U.S.C. § 1396p(h) and 42 U.S.C. § 1396p(c)(1)(G), (I), and (J).

(f) Fair Market Value and Uncompensated Value. -

(1) The fair market value of an asset is the value (minus any valid and legally enforceable liens, mortgages, and encumbrances against the asset) that would have been received if the asset had been sold for good and valuable consideration at the prevailing market price at the time the asset was transferred. In the case of real or personal property that is taxable under Subchapter II of Chapter 105 of the General Statutes, there is a rebuttable presumption that the fair market value of the property is its most recent value as ascertained under Subchapter II of Chapter 105 of the General Statutes (minus

any valid and legally enforceable liens, mortgages, and encumbrances against the property).

(2) The uncompensated value of an asset is its fair market value minus the amount of good and valuable consideration received in exchange for the asset's transfer.

(g) Individual. - An individual is a person who applies for or is receiving medical assistance under this Part regardless of whether the person was, at the time an asset was transferred, a Medicaid applicant or recipient. The term "individual" also includes an individual's legal representative, anyone acting at the individual's direction or request, and any person, agency, or court acting lawfully on behalf of the individual.

(h) Institutionalized and Noninstitutionalized Individuals. -

(1) An institutionalized individual is an individual who meets the criteria set forth in 42 U.S.C. § 1396p(h)(3), regardless of whether the individual was institutionalized at the time an asset was transferred.

(2) A noninstitutionalized individual is any individual who (i) is not an institutionalized individual, (ii) is an aged, blind, or disabled person who is categorically or medically needy pursuant to 42 C.F.R. § 120 Subpart B, C, or D or a qualified Medicare beneficiary as defined in 42 U.S.C. § 1396d(p)(1), and (iii) is not eligible for medical assistance under this Part based on his or her eligibility for an optional State supplement pursuant to 42 C.F.R. § 435.232.

(i) Exceptions. -

(1) This section does not apply if an individual establishes by the greater weight of the evidence that the transfer was exclusively for some purpose other than establishing or retaining eligibility for medical assistance under this Part.

(2) This section does not apply to any transfer specified in 42 U.S.C. § 1396p(c)(2)(A), (B), (C)(i), or (C)(iii).

(j) Application to Life Estates and Income Producing Real Property. - The Department of Health and Human Services may apply federal transfer of assets policies in accordance with this section to (i) life estates purchased by or on behalf of the recipient, and (ii) to real property excluded as "income producing", tenancy-in-common, or as nonhomesite property made "income producing." The

Department shall exclude from countable resources any life estate in real property that is in the recipient's home and is measured by the recipient's life. Federal transfer of assets policies applied to income producing real property shall become effective not earlier than October 1, 2001. Federal transfer of assets policies applied to real property excluded as tenancy-in-common, or as nonhomesite property made income producing in accordance with this subsection, shall become effective not earlier than October 1, 2005.

(k) Hardship Waiver. - The Department of Health and Human Services shall waive a transfer of assets penalty that has been imposed or is imposable under this section if the Department determines that imposition of the penalty would create an undue hardship.

(l) Rules and Compliance with Federal Law. -

(1) This section shall be interpreted and administered consistently with governing federal law, including 42 U.S.C. § 1396p(c).

(2) The Department of Health and Human Services shall determine and publish at least annually the average monthly cost of nursing facility services for private patients that will be used in determining the length of a penalty period under this section.

(3) The Department of Health and Human Services shall provide for a hardship waiver process in accordance with 42 U.S.C. § 1396p(c)(2)(D).

(4) The Department of Health and Human Services may adopt administrative rules that are necessary and appropriate to implement this section or the requirements of 42 U.S.C. § 1396p(c) or other federal laws governing the transfer of assets and Medicaid eligibility. (2006-66, s. 10.5(b); 2006-221, ss. 8(a)-(c).)

§ 108A-58.2. Waiver of transfer of assets penalty due to undue hardship.

(a) Prior to imposition of a period of ineligibility for long-term care services because of an asset transfer, also known as a penalty period, the county department of social services shall notify the individual of the individual's right to request a waiver of the penalty period because it will cause an undue hardship to the individual. The director of the county department of social services, or the director's designee shall grant a waiver of the penalty period due to undue hardship if the individual meets the conditions set forth in subsection (e) of this section. As used in this section, "long term care services" are those services described in 42 U.S.C. § 1396p(c)(1)(C)(i) and (ii).

(b)   When a Medicaid applicant who is requesting Medicaid to pay for institutional care requests a waiver of a penalty period due to undue hardship, the determination of whether to waive the penalty period shall be processed as part of the Medicaid application and is subject to the application processing standards set forth in 10A NCAC 21B.0203.

(c)   When an ongoing Medicaid recipient applies for institutional care or is receiving Medicaid payment for institutional care receives the notice described in subsection (a) of this section, the recipient has 12 calendar days from the date of the notice to request a waiver of the penalty due to undue hardship. The following are the procedures for processing the waiver request:

(1)   Within five work days of receipt of a request for a waiver of the transfer of assets penalty, the county department of social services shall notify the individual in writing of the information and documentation necessary to determine if the requirements for approving the undue hardship waiver are met.

(2)   The individual shall have 12 calendar days from the date of the notice specified in subdivision (1) of this subsection to provide the necessary information and documentation to establish the undue hardship.

(3)   If at the end of the first 12 calendar day period the necessary information and documentation has not been received by the county department of social services, the county department of social services shall again notify the individual of the necessary information and documentation. The individual shall be given an additional 12 calendar days to provide the information and documentation.

(4)   If the individual fails to request the undue hardship waiver within 12 calendar days from the date of the notice described in subsection (a) of this section, the county department of social services shall impose the transfer of assets penalty in accordance with notice requirements in G.S. 108A-79.

(5)   If by the end of the 12 calendar days from the notice described in subdivision (3) of this subsection, the necessary information and documentation has not been received by the county department of social services, the county

department of social services shall deny the request for waiver of the penalty for undue hardship and notify the individual of the denial in accordance with G.S. 108A-79.

(6) If by the end of the time allowed under subdivisions (2) and (3) of this subsection the county department of social services has received the necessary information and documentation, the county department of social services shall make a determination of whether the imposition of the penalty period would cause an undue hardship to the individual. The county department of social services shall complete the determination and notify the individual, pursuant to subsection (g) of this section, of whether the imposition of the penalty period will be waived due to undue hardship within 12 calendar days of the receipt of the necessary information and documentation.

(7) If as part of the determination described in subdivision (6) of this subsection the county department of social services identifies the need for additional information and documentation, it shall notify the individual in writing of that information and documentation. This notice shall initiate a new period of time for the individual to provide the information and documentation as set forth in subdivisions (2) and (3) of this subsection. Within 12 calendar days of the receipt of the additional information and documentation, the county department of social services shall complete the determination and notify the individual, pursuant to subsection (g) of this section, of whether the imposition of the penalty period will be waived due to undue hardship.

(d) As required by 42 U.S.C. § 1396p(c)(2)(D), the facility in which an institutionalized individual is residing may request an undue hardship waiver on behalf of the institutionalized individual with the written consent of the individual or the personal representative of the individual. A facility applying for a waiver for an individual residing in the facility shall adhere to the requirements of this section but shall not be required to advance the costs of acquiring an attorney to aid the institutionalized individual.

(e) Except as provided for in subsection (f) of this section, undue hardship exists if the imposition of the penalty period would deprive the individual of medical care, such that the individual's health or life would be endangered; or of food, clothing, shelter, or other necessities of life. The individual must provide the information and documentation necessary to demonstrate to the director of the county department of social services or the director's designee that:

(1) The individual currently has no alternative income or resources available to provide the medical care or food, clothing, shelter, or other necessities of life that the individual would be deprived of due to the imposition of the penalty; and

(2) The individual or some other person acting on the individual's behalf is making a good faith effort to pursue all reasonable means to recover the transferred asset or the fair market value of the transferred asset, which may include:

a. Seeking the advice of an attorney and pursuing legal or equitable remedies such as asset freezing, assignment, or injunction; or seeking modification, avoidance, or nullification of a financial instrument, promissory note, loan, mortgage or other property agreement, or other similar transfer agreement; and

b. Cooperating with any attempt to recover the transferred asset or the fair market value of the transferred asset.

(3) The following definitions shall apply to this subsection.

a. "Health or life would be endangered" means a medical doctor with knowledge of the individual's medical condition certifies in writing that in his or her professional opinion, the individual will be in danger of death or the individual's health will suffer irreparable harm if a penalty period is imposed.

b. "Other necessities of life" includes basic, life sustaining utilities, including water, heat, electricity, phone, and other items or activities that without which the individual's health or life would be endangered.

c. "Income" means all income of the individual and the community spouse less a protected amount for the community spouse equal to the minimum monthly maintenance needs allowance as determined under 42 U.S.C. § 1396r-5(d), including in all circumstances the excess shelter allowance described under 42 U.S.C. § 1396r-5(d)(3)(A)(ii), without regard to any adjustment that would be made under 42 U.S.C. § 1396r-5(e), plus fifty percent (50%) of such income in excess of the protected amount.

d. "Resources" means all resources of the individual and of the community spouse except the homesite in which the individual or community spouse has an equity interest not exceeding five hundred thousand dollars ($500,000), a motor vehicle in which the individual or community spouse has an equity interest not exceeding thirty thousand dollars ($30,000), personal property, and, in the case of a community spouse, a portion of such other resources in an amount equal to the community spouse resource allowance as defined by 42 U.S.C. § 1396r-5(f)(2), provided that such amount shall not exceed sixty percent (60%) of the maximum community spouse resource allowance as defined by 42 U.S.C. § 1396r-5(f)(2)(A)(ii). For purposes of this sub-subdivision, "homesite" means the principal place of residence of the individual or the community spouse in which the individual or community spouse has an equity interest.

(f) An undue hardship shall not exist when the application of a transfer of assets penalty merely causes the individual an inconvenience or restricts the individual's lifestyle.

(g) If the director of the county department of social services or the director's designee determines that:

(1) An undue hardship exists, the county department of social services shall waive the penalty period and notify the individual of approval of the waiver of the penalty in accordance with G.S. 108A-79.

(2) An undue hardship does not exist, the county department of social services shall deny the request for the waiver of the penalty and notify the individual of denial of the waiver request in accordance with G.S. 108A-79.

(h) During a penalty period that has been waived because of undue hardship, acquisition by the individual of new or increased income or resources shall be treated as a change in situation and evaluated pursuant to the rules adopted by the Department of Health and Human Services.

(i) While the determination on a request for a waiver of the penalty period due to undue hardship is pending, Medicaid shall not make payments for nursing facility services or intermediate care facility for the mentally retarded services to hold a bed for the individual, as described in 42 U.S.C. § 1396p(c)(2)(D). However, if the individual is institutionalized and receiving Medicaid payment for services, Medicaid will maintain the same level of services until the last day of the month after the latter of the following:

(1) Expiration of the 10 workday period following the notice required by G.S. 108A-79, or

(2) The date of the decision of a local appeal hearing described in G.S. 108A-79 is issued if the individual requests an appeal of the imposition of a transfer of assets penalty period within the 10 workday period described in subdivision (1) of subsection (i) of this section. (2007-442, s. 3(a).)

§ 108A-59. Acceptance of medical assistance constitutes assignment to the State of right to third party benefits; recovery procedure.

(a) Notwithstanding any other provisions of the law, by accepting medical assistance, the recipient shall be deemed to have made an assignment to the State of the right to third party benefits, contractual or otherwise, to which he may be entitled.

It shall be the responsibility of the county attorney of the county from which the medical assistance benefits are received or an attorney retained by that county and/or the State to enforce this subsection, and said attorney shall be compensated for his services in accordance with the attorneys' fee arrangements approved by the Department of Health and Human Services.

(b) The responsible State agency will establish a third party resources collection unit that is adequate to assure maximum collection of third party resources.

(c) Notwithstanding any other law to the contrary, in all actions brought pursuant to subsection (a) of this section to obtain reimbursement for payments for medical services, liability shall be determined on the basis of the same laws and standards, including bases for liability and applicable defenses, as would be applicable if the action were brought by the individual on whose behalf the medical services were rendered. (1977, c. 664; 1979, 2nd Sess., c. 1312, ss. 3-5; 1981, c. 275, s. 1; 1995, c. 508, s. 2; 1997-443, s. 11A.118(a).)

§ 108A-60. Protection of patient property.

(a) It shall be unlawful for any person:

(1) To willfully commingle or cause or solicit the commingling of the personal funds or moneys of a recipient resident of a provider health care facility with the funds or moneys of such facility; or

(2) To willfully embezzle, convert, or appropriate or cause or solicit the embezzlement, conversion or appropriation of recipient personal funds or property to his own use or to the use of any provider or other person or entity.

(b) A violation of subdivision (a)(1) of this section shall be a Class 1 misdemeanor. A violation of subdivision (a)(2) of this section shall be a Class H felony.

(c) For purposes of this section:

(1) "Health care facility" shall include skilled nursing facilities, intermediate care facilities, rest homes, or any other residential health care facility; and

(2) "Person" includes any natural person, association, consortium, corporation, body politic, partnership, or other group, entity or organization; and

(3) "Recipient" shall include current resident recipients, deceased recipients and recipients who no longer reside at such facility. (1979, c. 510, s. 1; 1981, c. 275, s. 1; 1993, c. 539, ss. 816, 1300; 1994, Ex. Sess., c. 24, s. 14(c).)

§ 108A-61: Repealed by Session Laws 1989, c. 701.

§ 108A-61.1. Financial responsibility of a parent for a child under age 21 in a medical institution.

Notwithstanding any other provisions of the law, for the purpose of determining eligibility for medical assistance under Title XIX of the Social Security Act, 42 U.S.C. § 1396 et seq., the income and financial resources of the natural or adoptive parents of a person who is under the age of 21 and who requires Medicaid covered services in a medical institution shall not be counted if the patient's physician certifies, and the Division of Medical Assistance or its agents approve, that continuous care and treatment are expected to exceed 12 months. For purposes of this subsection, "medical institution" means licensed acute care inpatient medical facilities providing medical, surgical, and psychiatric or substance abuse treatment, or facilities providing skilled or intermediate care, including intermediate care for the mentally retarded. (1993, c. 386, s. 1.)

§ 108A-62. Therapeutic leave for medical assistance patients.

Patients at an intermediate care facility or skilled nursing facility may take up to 60 days of therapeutic leave in any one calendar year without the facility losing reimbursement under the medical assistance program, provided, however, no more than 15 consecutive days may be taken without approval of the Department of Health and Human Services, Division of Medical Assistance. Under no circumstances shall the number of Medicaid-covered therapeutic leave days exceed 60 days per patient per calendar year. (1979, c. 925; 1981, c. 275, s. 1; 1985 (Reg. Sess., 1986), c. 1014, s. 120; 1991, c. 126, s. 1; 1997-443, s. 11A.118(a).)

§ 108A-63. Medical assistance provider fraud.

(a) It shall be unlawful for any provider of medical assistance under this Part to knowingly and willfully make or cause to be made any false statement or representation of a material fact:

(1) In any application for payment under this Part, or for use in determining entitlement to such payment; or

(2) With respect to the conditions or operation of a provider or facility in order that such provider or facility may qualify or remain qualified to provide assistance under this Part.

(b) It shall be unlawful for any provider of medical assistance to knowingly and willfully conceal or fail to disclose any fact or event affecting:

(1) His initial or continued entitlement to payment under this Part; or

(2) The amount of payment to which such person is or may be entitled.

(c) Except as otherwise provided in subsection (e) of this section, any person who violates a provision of this section shall be guilty of a Class I felony.

(d) "Provider" shall include any person who provides goods or services under this Part and any other person acting as an employee, representative or agent of such person.

(e) In connection with the delivery of or payment for benefits, items, or services under this Part, it shall be unlawful for any provider of medical assistance under this Part to knowingly and willfully execute, or attempt to execute, a scheme or artifice to:

(1) Defraud the Medical Assistance Program.

(2) Obtain, by means of false or fraudulent pretenses, representations, or promises of material fact, any of the money or property owned by, or under the custody or control of, the Medical Assistance Program.

A violation of this subsection is a Class H felony. A conspiracy to violate this subsection is a Class I felony.

(f) It shall be unlawful for any provider, with the intent to obstruct, delay, or mislead an investigation of a violation of this section by the Attorney General's office, to knowingly and willfully make or cause to be made a false entry in, alter, destroy, or conceal, or make a false statement about a financial, medical, or other record related to the provision of a benefit, item, or service under this Part.

(g) It shall be unlawful for any person to knowingly and willfully solicit or receive any remuneration (including any kickback, bribe, or rebate) directly or indirectly, overtly or covertly, in cash or in-kind:

(1) In return for referring an individual to a person for the furnishing or arranging for the furnishing of any item or service for which payment may be made in whole or in part under this Part.

(2) In return for purchasing, leasing, ordering, or arranging for or recommending purchasing, leasing, or ordering any good, facility, service, or item for which payment may be made in whole or in part under this Part.

(h)   It shall be unlawful for any person to knowingly and willfully offer or pay any remuneration (including any kickback, bribe, or rebate) directly or indirectly, overtly or covertly, in cash or in-kind to any person to induce such person:

(1)   To refer an individual to a person for the furnishing or arranging for the furnishing of any item or service for which payment may be made in whole or in part under this Part.

(2)   To purchase, lease, order, or arrange for or recommend purchasing, leasing, or ordering any good, facility, service, or item for which payment may be made in whole or in part under this Part.

(i)   Subsections (g) and (h) of this section shall not apply to:

(1)   Contracts between the State and a public or private agency where part of the agency's responsibility is referral of a person to a provider.

(2)   Any conduct or activity that is specified in 42 U.S.C. § 1320a-7b(b)(3), as amended, or any federal regulations adopted pursuant thereto.

(j)   Nothing in subsections (g) and (h) of this section shall be interpreted or construed to conflict with 42 U.S.C. § 1320a-7b(b), as amended, or with federal common law or federal agency interpretations of the statute. (1979, c. 510, s. 1; 1981, c. 275, s. 1; 2009-554, s. 3; 2010-185, s. 1.)

§ 108A-63.1. Health care fraud subpoena to produce documents.

(a)   The Attorney General, acting through the Medicaid Investigations Unit of the Department of Justice, may, when engaged in an investigation of an alleged violation of G.S. 108A-63 and prior to the arrest of a suspect, issue in writing and cause to be served a subpoena to produce documents upon any corporation or governmental entity requiring the production of any records, books, papers, electronic media, objects, or other documents which may be relevant to a criminal investigation of a violation of G.S. 108A-63.

(b)   A subpoena under this section may require the custodian of records of the corporation or governmental entity to produce an affidavit certifying that the custodian made a thorough and diligent search for the documents requested and that the documents produced constitute all the records requested to the best of the custodian's knowledge, information, and belief.

(c) A subpoena under this section shall describe the documents required to be produced and prescribe a return date within a reasonable period of time, of no less than 20 days from the date of service, within which the documents can be assembled and made available.

(d) A corporation or governmental entity may comply with a subpoena issued under this section by delivering the documents to the Medicaid Investigations Unit by any of the following methods:

(1) By hand delivery.

(2) By mailing the documents by certified mail.

(3) By making the documents reasonably available for transfer to an agent of the Medicaid Investigations Unit at a place of business of the corporation or governmental entity.

(4) If agreed to by the Medicaid Investigations Unit and the corporation or governmental entity, by any other means.

(e) A corporation or governmental entity may move to quash or modify a subpoena issued under this section if it is oppressive or unreasonable or does not comply with the requirements of this section. The motion must be made before the time specified in the subpoena for production and may be made before a judge of the superior court.

(f) In the case of failure by any corporation or governmental entity without adequate excuse to obey a subpoena issued under this section, the Attorney General may invoke the aid of a judge of the superior court. The court may issue an order requiring the subpoenaed corporation or governmental entity to appear before the Attorney General to produce records. Failure to obey the order of the court may be punished as contempt of court. (2009-554, s. 2.)

§ 108A-64. Medical assistance recipient fraud.

(a) It shall be unlawful for any person to knowingly and willfully and with intent to defraud make or cause to be made a false statement or representation of a material fact in an application for assistance under this Part, or intended for use in determining entitlement to such assistance.

(b) It shall be unlawful for any applicant, recipient or person acting on behalf of such applicant or recipient to knowingly and willfully and with intent to defraud, conceal or fail to disclose any condition, fact or event affecting such applicant's or recipient's initial or continued entitlement to receive assistance under this Part.

(b1) It is unlawful for any person knowingly, willingly, and with intent to defraud, to obtain or attempt to obtain, or to assist, aid, or abet another person, either directly or indirectly, to obtain money, services, or any other thing of value to which the person is not entitled as a recipient under this Part, or otherwise to deliberately misuse a Medicaid identification card. This misuse includes the sale, alteration, or lending of the Medicaid identification card to others for services and the use of the card by someone other than the recipient to receive or attempt to receive Medicaid program coverage for services rendered to that individual.

Proof of intent to defraud does not require proof of intent to defraud any particular person.

(c) (1) A person who violates a provision of this section shall be guilty of a Class I felony if the value of the assistance wrongfully obtained is more than four hundred dollars ($400.00).

(2) A person who violates a provision of this section shall be guilty of a Class 1 misdemeanor if the value of the assistance wrongfully obtained is four hundred dollars ($400.00) or less.

(d) For purposes of this section the word "person" includes any natural person, association, consortium, corporation, body politic, partnership, or other group, entity or organization. (1981, c. 275, s. 1; 1993, c. 539, s. 817; 1994, Ex. Sess., c. 24, s. 14(c); 1995, c. 317, s. 1.)

§ 108A-64.1. Incentives to counties to recover fraudulent Medicaid expenditures.

The Department of Health and Human Services, Division of Medical Assistance, shall provide incentives to counties that successfully recover fraudulently spent Medicaid funds by sharing State savings with counties responsible for the recovery of the fraudulently spent funds. (2013-360, s. 12H.5.)

§ 108A-65. Conflict of interest.

(a) It shall be unlawful for any person who is or has been an officer or employee of State or county government, and as such is or has been responsible for the expenditure of substantial amounts of federal, State or county money under the State medical assistance plan, or any person who is the partner of the present or former officer or employee, to engage in any of the following activities relating to the State medical assistance program:

(1) Knowingly to act as agent or attorney for, or otherwise knowingly to represent, any person other than the United States, the State or a county, in any formal or informal appearance before, or with the intent to influence, make any oral or written communication on behalf of any other person other than the United States, the State or a county to:

a. Any department, agency, court, board, commission, legislature or committee of the United States, the State or a county, or any officer or employee thereof,

b. In connection with any of the following matters in which the United States, the State, or a county is a party or has a direct and substantial interest, such as any judicial or other proceeding, legislation, application, request for a ruling or other determination, contract, claim, controversy, investigation, charge, accusation, arrest, or other particular matter involving a specific party or parties,

c. In which he participated personally and substantially as an officer or an employee through decision, approval, recommendation, the rendering of advice, investigation or otherwise.

(2) Within two years after his employment has ceased, knowingly to act as agent or attorney for, or otherwise knowingly to represent, any other person other than the United States, the State or a county, in any formal or informal appearance before, or, with the intent to influence, make any oral or written

communication on behalf of any other person other than the United States, the State or a county to:

a. Any department, agency, court, board, commission, legislature or committee of the United States, the State, or a county, or any officer or employee thereof,

b. In connection with any of the following matters in which the United States, the State, or a county is a party or has a direct and substantial interest, such as, any judicial or other proceeding, legislation, application, request for a ruling or other determination, contract, claim, controversy, investigation, charge, accusation, arrest, or other particular matter involving a specific party or parties,

c. Which was actually pending under his official responsibility as an officer or employee within a period of one year prior to the termination of responsibility.

(3) Within two years after his employment has ceased, knowingly to aid, counsel, advise, consult or by personal presence represent any other person other than the United States, the State or a county in any formal or informal appearance before:

a. Any department, agency, court, board, commission, legislature or committee of the United States, the State, or the county, or any officer or employee thereof,

b. In connection with any of the following matters in which the United States, the State, or a county is a party or has a direct and substantial interest, such as, any judicial or other proceeding, legislation, application, request for a ruling or other determination, contract, claim, controversy, investigation, charge, accusation, arrest, or other particular matter involving a specific party or parties,

c. Which was actually pending under his official responsibility as an officer or employee within the period of one year prior to the termination of such responsibility.

(4) To participate personally and substantially as an officer or employee, through decision, approval, disapproval, recommendation, rendering of advice, investigation or otherwise, in a judicial or other proceeding legislation, application, request for a ruling or other determination, contract, claim, controversy, charge, accusation, arrest or other particular matter in which, to his knowledge, he, his spouse, minor child, partner, organization in which he is

serving as an officer, director, trustee, partner or employee, or any person or organization with whom he is negotiating or has any arrangement concerning prospective employment, has a financial interest.

(b) Violation of this statute is a Class 1 misdemeanor.

(c) The Department of Health and Human Services shall annually identify and designate by rule or regulation those positions which are filled by State or county officers or employees who are responsible for the expenditure of substantial amounts of moneys under the State medical assistance plan. (1981, c. 679, s. 1; 1993, c. 539, s. 818; 1994, Ex. Sess., c. 24, s. 14(c); 1997-443, s. 11A.118(a).)

§ 108A-66: Repealed by Session Laws 1989, c. 702.

§ 108A-66.1. Medicaid buy-in for workers with disabilities.

(a) Title. - This section may be cited as the Health Coverage for Workers With Disabilities Act. The Department shall implement a Medicaid buy-in eligibility category as permitted under P.L. 106-170, Ticket to Work and Work Incentives Improvement Act of 1999. The Department shall establish rules, policies, and procedures to implement this act in accordance with this section.

(b) Definitions. - As used in this section, unless the context clearly requires otherwise:

(1) "FPG" means the federal poverty guidelines.

(2) "HCWD" means Health Coverage for Workers With Disabilities.

(3) "SSI" means Supplemental Security Income.

(4) "Ticket to Work" means the Ticket to Work and Work Incentives Improvement Act of 1999.

(c) Eligibility. - An individual is eligible for HCWD if:

(1) The individual is at least 16 years of age and is less than 65 years of age;

(2) The individual meets Social Security Disability criteria, or the individual has been enrolled in HCWD and then becomes medically improved as defined in Ticket to Work and as further specified by the Department. An individual shall be determined to be eligible under this section without regard to the individual's ability to engage in, or actual engagement in, substantial gainful activity as defined in section 223 of the Social Security Act (42 U.S.C. § 423(d)(4)). In conducting annual redetermination of eligibility, the Department may not determine that an individual participating in HCWD is no longer disabled based solely on the individual's participation in employment or earned income;

(3) The individual's unearned income does not exceed one hundred fifty percent (150%) of FPG, and countable resources for the individual do not exceed the resource limit for the minimum community spouse resource standard under 42 U.S.C. § 1396r, and as further determined by the Department. In determining an individual's countable income and resources, the Department may not consider income or resources that are disregarded under the State Medical Assistance Plan's financial methodology, including the sixty-five-dollar ($65.00) disregard, impairment-related work expenses, student earned-income exclusions, and other SSI program work incentive income disregards; and

(4) The individual is engaged in a substantial and reasonable work effort (employed) as provided in this subdivision and as further defined by the Department and allowable under federal law. For purposes of this subsection, "engaged in substantial and reasonable work effort" means all of the following:

a. Working in a competitive, inclusive work setting, or self-employed.

b. Earning at least the applicable minimum wage.

c. Having monthly earnings above the SSI basic sixty-five-dollar ($65.00) earned-income disregard.

d. Being able to provide evidence of paying applicable Medicare, Social Security, and State and federal income taxes.

The Department may impose additional earnings requirements in defining "engaged in substantial and reasonable work effort" for individuals who are eligible for HCWD based on medical improvement.

Individuals who participate in HCWD but thereafter become unemployed for involuntary reasons, including health reasons, shall have continued eligibility in HCWD for up to 12 months from the time of involuntary unemployment, so long as the individual (i) maintains a connection with the workforce, as determined by the Department, (ii) meets all other eligibility criteria for HCWD during the period, and (iii) pays applicable fees, premiums, and co-payments.

(d) Fees, Premiums, and Co-Payments. - Individuals who participate in HCWD and have countable income greater than one hundred fifty percent (150%) of FPG shall pay an annual enrollment fee of fifty dollars ($50.00) to their county department of social services. Individuals who participate in HCWD and have countable income greater than or equal to two hundred percent (200%) of FPG shall pay a monthly premium in addition to the annual fee. The Department shall set a sliding scale for premiums, which is consistent with applicable federal law. An individual with countable income equal to or greater than four hundred fifty percent (450%) of FPG shall pay not less than one hundred percent (100%) of the cost of the premium, as determined by the Department. The premium shall be based on the experience of all individuals participating in the Medical Assistance Program. Individuals who participate in HCWD are subject to co-payments equal to those required under the Medical Assistance Program. (2005-276, s. 10.18(a); 2006-66, s. 10.9(a); 2007-144, s. 2; 2009-451, s. 10.69; 2013-360, s. 12H.10(f).)

§ 108A-67. Medicare/Qualified Disabled Working Individuals.

Qualified disabled working individuals are eligible for the payment of the Medicare Part A premium. An individual is qualified for this payment:

(1) If the Social Security Administration determines the individual to be a "Disabled Working Individual";

(2) If the individual's income is less than two hundred percent (200%) of the current federal poverty level, as revised annually; and

(3) If the individual is less than 65 years of age. (1991, c. 127.)

§ 108A-68. Drug Use Review Program; rules.

Notwithstanding the provisions of Chapter 90 of the General Statutes or of any other provision of law, the Division of Medical Assistance, Department of Health and Human Services, shall adopt rules implementing the drug use review provisions of the Omnibus Budget Reconciliation Act of 1990, as amended. (1991 (Reg. Sess., 1992), c. 900, s. 128; 1997-443, s. 11A.118(a).)

§ 108A-68.1. Certain prescription drugs exempt from prior authorization requirements.

Prior authorization shall not be required or utilized for any antihemophilic factor drugs prescribed for the treatment of hemophilia and blood disorders where there is no generically equivalent drug available. Nothing in this section shall prohibit the Secretary from implementing a disease management program. (2003-179, s. 1; 2005-83, s. 1; 2009-210, s. 1.)

§ 108A-69. Employer obligations.

(a)   As used in this section and in G.S. 108A-70:

(1)   "Health benefit plan" means an accident and health insurance policy or certificate; a nonprofit hospital or medical service corporation contract; a health maintenance organization subscriber contract; a plan provided by a multiple employer welfare arrangement; the State Health Plan for Teachers and State Employees under Chapter 135 of the General Statutes; or a plan provided by another benefit arrangement. "Health benefit plan" does not mean a Medicare supplement policy as defined in G.S. 58-54-1(5).

(2)   "Health insurer" means any health insurance company subject to Articles 1 through 63 of Chapter 58 of the General Statutes, including a multiple employee welfare arrangement, and any corporation subject to Articles 65 and 67 of Chapter 58 of the General Statutes; a group health plan, as defined in Section 607(1) of the Employee Retirement Income Security Act of 1974; and the State Health Plan for Teachers and State Employees under Chapter 135 of the General Statutes.

(b) If a parent is required by a court or administrative order to provide health benefit plan coverage for a child, and the parent is eligible for family health benefit plan coverage through an employer, the employer:

(1) Must allow the parent to enroll, under family coverage, the child if the child would be otherwise eligible for coverage without regard to any enrollment season restrictions.

(2) Must enroll the child under family coverage upon application of the child's other parent or upon receipt of notice from the Department of Health and Human Services in connection with its administration of the Medical Assistance or Child Support Enforcement Program if the parent is enrolled but fails to make application to obtain coverage for the child.

(3) May not disenroll or eliminate coverage of the child unless:

a. The employer is provided satisfactory written evidence that:

1. The court or administrative order is no longer in effect; or

2. The child is or will be enrolled in comparable health benefit plan coverage that will take effect not later than the effective date of disenrollment; or

b. The employer has eliminated family health benefit plan coverage for all of its employees.

(4) Must withhold from the employee's compensation the employee's share, if any, of premiums for health benefit plan coverage, not to exceed the maximum amount permitted to be withheld under section 303(b) of the federal Consumer Credit Protection Act, as amended; and must pay this amount to the health insurer; subject to regulations, if any, adopted by the Secretary of the U.S. Department of Health and Human Services. (1993 (Reg. Sess., 1994), c. 644, s. 3; 1995, c. 193, s. 44; 1997-433, s. 3.2; 1997-443, s. 11A.118(a); 1998-17, s. 1; 1999-293, s. 8; 2007-323, s. 28.22A(o); 2007-345, s. 12.)

§ 108A-70. Recoupment of amounts spent on medical care.

(a) The Department may garnish the wages, salary, or other employment income of, and the Secretary of Revenue shall withhold amounts from State tax refunds to, any person who:

(1) Is required by court or administrative order to provide health benefit plan coverage for the cost of health care services to a child eligible for medical assistance under Medicaid; and

(2) Has received payment from a third party for the costs of such services; but

(3) Has not used such payments to reimburse, as appropriate, either the other parent or guardian of the child or the provider of the services;

to the extent necessary to reimburse the Department for expenditures for such costs under this Part; provided, however, claims for current and past due child support shall take priority over any such claims for the costs of such services.

(b) To the extent that payment for covered services has been made under G.S. 108A-55 for health care items or services furnished to an individual, in any case where a third party has a legal liability to make payments, the Department of Health and Human Services is considered to have acquired the rights of the individual to payment by any other party for those health care items or services. (1993 (Reg. Sess., 1994), c. 644, s. 3; 1997-443, s. 11A.118(a).)

§ 108A-70.4. Long-Term Care Partnership Program.

(a) The following definitions apply in this section:

(1) Asset. - Resources and income.

(2) Department. - The Department of Health and Human Services.

(3) Division. - The Division of Medical Assistance.

(4) Estate recovery. - The placing of a statutory claim on the estate of a deceased Medicaid recipient, as provided by G.S. 108A-70.5.

(5) Medicaid. - The federal medical assistance program established under Title XIX of the Social Security Act.

(6) Qualified long-term care partnership policy or qualified policy. - A long-term care insurance policy approved for use in North Carolina and that meets all the requirements of the federal Deficit Reduction Act of 2005, P.L. 109-171.

(7) Resource. - Cash or its equivalent and real or personal property that is available to an applicant or recipient.

(8) Resource disregard. - The amount of resources of an applicant for long-term care Medicaid that is equal to the amount of benefits paid to the applicant under a qualified long-term care partnership policy.

(9) Resource protection. - An amount equal to the resource disregard given to a Medicaid recipient during the long-term care Medicaid eligibility determination process.

(b) There is established the North Carolina Long-Term Care Partnership Program (Partnership Program) to be administered by the Division with assistance from the Department of Insurance. The Partnership Program shall:

(1) Provide a mechanism for individuals to qualify for coverage of the cost of their long-term care needs under Medicaid without first being required to substantially exhaust their resources.

(2) Provide counseling services to individuals planning for their long-term care needs.

(3) Reduce the financial burden on the State medical assistance program by encouraging individuals to obtain private long-term care insurance.

(c) Under the Partnership Program, the Department shall:

(1) Provide resource disregard to an applicant for long-term care Medicaid who has received benefits under a qualified long-term care partnership policy. The amount of the resource disregard shall be equal to the total insurance benefits paid to the individual under a qualified policy after the implementation of the Partnership Program and prior to the individual's first application for long-term care Medicaid.

(2) Provide resource protection by reducing any subsequent recovery by the State under G.S. 108A-70.5 from a deceased recipient's estate for payment of Medicaid paid services by the amount of resource disregard given under subdivision (1) of this subsection.

(d) The Department shall adopt rules and amendments to the State Plan to allow for resource disregard at long-term care Medicaid eligibility determination and resource protection at estate recovery. The Department and the Department of Insurance shall adopt rules to implement the provisions of the Partnership Program and to provide for its administration.

(e) Effective January 1, 2011, or 60 days after approval of the Medicaid State Plan amendment, whichever is later, a qualified long-term care partnership policy shall be accompanied by a Partnership Disclosure Notice detailing in plain language the current law pertaining to the Partnership Program, resource disregard, and resource protection.

(f) The Department may enter into a reciprocal agreement with other states that enter into a national reciprocity agreement to extend the resource disregard and resource protection to residents of the State who purchased, or purchased and used, a qualified long-term care policy in another state.

(g) G.S. 108A-70.5 applies to the estate of an individual who received benefits under a qualified long-term care partnership policy. (2010-68, s. 1.)

§ 108A-70.5. Medicaid Estate Recovery Plan.

(a) There is established in the Department of Health and Human Services, the Medicaid Estate Recovery Plan, as required by the Omnibus Budget Reconciliation Act of 1993, to recover from the estates of recipients of medical assistance an equitable amount of the State and federal shares of the cost paid for the recipient. The Department shall administer the program in accordance with applicable federal law and regulations, including those under Title XIX of the Social Security Act, 42 U.S.C. § 1396(p).

(b) The following definitions apply in this section:

(1) Medical assistance. - Medical care services paid for by the North Carolina Medicaid Program on behalf of the recipient:

a. If the recipient of any age is receiving medical care services as an inpatient in a nursing facility, intermediate care facility for the mentally retarded, or other medical institution, and cannot reasonably be expected to be discharged to return home; or

b. If the recipient is 55 years of age or older and is receiving one or more of the following medical care services:

1. Nursing facility services.

2. Home and community-based services.

3. Hospital care.

3a. Prescription drugs.

4. Personal care services.

5 through 9. Repealed by Session Laws 2007-442, s. 1, effective August 23, 2007.

(2) Estate. - All the real and personal property considered assets of the estate available for the discharge of debt pursuant to G.S. 28A-15-1. The Department has all rights available to estate creditors, including the right to qualify as personal representative or collector of an estate. For individuals who have received benefits under a qualified long-term care partnership policy as described in G.S. 108A-70.4, "estate" also includes any other real and personal property and other assets in which the individual had any legal title or interest at the time of death (to the extent of such interest), including assets conveyed to a survivor, heir, or assign of the deceased individual through joint tenancy, tenancy in common, survivorship, life estate, living trust, or other arrangement.

(3) Repealed by Session Laws 2007-442, s. 1, effective August 23, 2007.

(c) The amount the Department recovers from the estate of any recipient shall not exceed the amount of medical assistance made on behalf of the recipient and shall be recoverable only for medical care services prescribed in subsection (b) of this section. The Department is a sixth-class creditor, as prescribed in G.S. 28A-19-6, for purposes of determining the order of claims against an estate; provided, however, that judgments in favor of other sixth-class creditors docketed and in force before the Department seeks recovery for medical assistance shall be paid prior to recovery by the Department.

(d) The Department of Health and Human Services shall adopt rules pursuant to Chapter 150B of the General Statutes to implement the Plan, including rules to waive whole or partial recovery when this recovery would be inequitable because it would work an undue hardship or because it would not be administratively cost-effective and rules to ensure that all recipients are notified that their estates are subject to recovery at the time they become eligible to receive medical assistance.

(e) Repealed by Session Laws 2007-442, s. 1, effective August 23, 2007. (1993 (Reg. Sess., 1994), c. 769, s. 25.47(a); 1997-443, s. 11A.118(a); 2002-126, s. 10.11(b); 2005-276, s. 10.21C(a); 2005-345, s. 16; 2006-66, s. 10.9B; 2007-145, s. 10; 2007-323, ss. 10.42(a), (b); 2007-442, s. 1(a); 2010-68, s. 2; 2012-18, s. 3.6; 2013-378, s. 2.)

§ 108A-70.6: Repealed by Session Laws 2007-442, s. 1(b), effective August 23, 2007.

§ 108A-70.7: Repealed by Session Laws 2007-442, s. 1(b), effective August 23, 2007.

§ 108A-70.8: Repealed by Session Laws 2007-442, s. 1(b), effective August 23, 2007.

§ 108A-70.9: Repealed by Session Laws 2007-442, s. 1(b), effective August 23, 2007.

Part 6A. Medicaid Recipient Appeals Process.

§ 108A-70.9A. Appeals by Medicaid recipients.

(a) Definitions. - The following definitions apply in this Part, unless the context clearly requires otherwise.

(1) Adverse determination. - A determination by the Department to deny, terminate, suspend, or reduce a Medicaid service or an authorization for a Medicaid service.

(2) OAH. - The Office of Administrative Hearings.

(3) Recipient. - A recipient and the recipient's parent, guardian, or legal representative, unless otherwise specified.

(b) General Rule. - Notwithstanding any provision of State law or rules to the contrary, this section shall govern the process used by a Medicaid recipient to appeal an adverse determination made by the Department.

(c) Notice. - Except as otherwise provided by federal law or regulation, at least 10 days before the effective date of an adverse determination, the Department shall notify the recipient, and the provider, if applicable, in writing of the adverse determination and of the recipient's right to appeal the adverse determination. The Department shall not be required to notify a recipient's parent, guardian, or legal representative unless the recipient's parent, guardian, or legal representative has requested in writing to receive the notice. The notice shall be mailed on the date indicated on the notice as the date of the determination. The notice shall include:

(1) An identification of the recipient whose services are being affected by the adverse determination, including the recipient's full name and Medicaid identification number.

(2) An explanation of what service is being denied, terminated, suspended, or reduced and the reason for the determination.

(3) The specific regulation, statute, or medical policy that supports or requires the adverse determination.

(4) The effective date of the adverse determination.

(5) An explanation of the recipient's right to appeal the Department's adverse determination in an evidentiary hearing before an administrative law judge.

(6) An explanation of how the recipient can request a hearing and a statement that the recipient may represent himself or herself or use legal counsel, a relative, or other spokesperson.

(7) A statement that the recipient will continue to receive Medicaid services at the level provided on the day immediately preceding the Department's adverse determination or the amount requested by the recipient, whichever is less, if the recipient requests a hearing before the effective date of the adverse determination. The services shall continue until the hearing is completed and a final decision is rendered.

(8) The name and telephone number of a contact person at the Department to respond in a timely fashion to the recipient's questions.

(9) The telephone number by which the recipient may contact a Legal Aid/Legal Services office.

(10) The appeal request form described in subsection (e) of this section that the recipient may use to request a hearing.

(d) Appeals. - Except as provided by this section and G.S. 108A-70.9B, a request for a hearing to appeal an adverse determination of the Department under this section is a contested case subject to the provisions of Article 3 of Chapter 150B of the General Statutes. The recipient shall request a hearing within 30 days of the mailing of the notice required by subsection (c) of this section by sending an appeal request form to OAH and the Department. Where a request for hearing concerns the reduction, modification, or termination of Medicaid services, including the failure to act upon a timely request for reauthorization with reasonable promptness, upon the receipt of a timely appeal, the Department shall reinstate the services to the level or manner prior to action by the Department as permitted by federal law or regulation. The Department shall immediately forward a copy of the notice to OAH electronically. The information contained in the notice is confidential unless the recipient appeals. OAH may dispose of the records after one year. The Department may not influence, limit, or interfere with the recipient's decision to request a hearing.

(e) Appeal Request Form. - Along with the notice required by subsection (c) of this section, the Department shall also provide the recipient with an appeal request form which shall be no more than one side of one page. The form shall include the following:

(1) A statement that in order to request an appeal, the recipient must send the form by mail or fax to the address or fax number listed on the form within 30 days of mailing of the notice.

(2) The recipient's name, address, telephone number, and Medicaid identification number.

(3) A preprinted statement that indicates that the recipient would like to appeal the specific adverse determination of which the recipient was notified in the notice.

(4) A statement informing the recipient that he or she may choose to be represented by a lawyer, a relative, a friend, or other spokesperson.

(5) A space for the recipient's signature and date.

(f) Final Decision. - After a hearing before an administrative law judge, the judge shall return the decision to the Department in accordance with G.S. 150B-37. The Department shall notify the recipient of the final decision and of the right to judicial review of the decision pursuant to Article 4 of Chapter 150B of the General Statutes. (2010-31, s. 10.30(a); 2011-398, s. 32.)

§ 108A-70.9B. Contested Medicaid cases.

(a) Application. - This section applies only to contested Medicaid cases commenced by Medicaid recipients under G.S. 108A-70.9A. Except as otherwise provided by G.S. 108A-70.9A and this section governing time lines and procedural steps, a contested Medicaid case commenced by a Medicaid recipient is subject to the provisions of Article 3 of Chapter 150B of the General Statutes. To the extent any provision in this section or G.S. 108A-70.9A conflicts with another provision in Article 3 of Chapter 150B of the General Statutes, this section and G.S. 108A-70.9A control.

(b) Simple Procedures. - Notwithstanding any other provision of Article 3 of Chapter 150B of the General Statutes, the chief administrative law judge may limit and simplify the procedures that apply to a contested Medicaid case involving a Medicaid recipient in order to complete the case as quickly as possible.

(1) To the extent possible, OAH shall schedule and hear contested Medicaid cases within 55 days of submission of a request for appeal.

(2) Hearings shall be conducted telephonically or by video technology with all parties, however the recipient may request that the hearing be conducted in person before the administrative law judge. An in-person hearing shall be conducted in Wake County, however, for good cause shown, the in-person hearing may be conducted in the county of residence of the recipient or a nearby county. Good cause shall include, but is not limited to, the recipient's impairments limiting travel or the unavailability of the recipient's treating professional witnesses. The Department shall provide written notice to the recipient of the use of telephonic hearings, hearings by video conference, and in-person hearings before the administrative law judge, and how to request a hearing in the recipient's county of residence.

(3) The simplified procedure may include requiring that all prehearing motions be considered and ruled on by the administrative law judge in the course of the hearing of the case on the merits. An administrative law judge assigned to a contested Medicaid case shall make reasonable efforts in a case involving a Medicaid recipient who is not represented by an attorney to assure a fair hearing and to maintain a complete record of the hearing.

(4) The administrative law judge may allow brief extensions of the time limits contained in this section for good cause and to ensure that the record is complete. Good cause includes delays resulting from untimely receipt of documentation needed to render a decision and other unavoidable and unforeseen circumstances. Continuances shall only be granted in accordance with rules adopted by OAH and shall not be granted on the day of the hearing, except for good cause shown. If a petitioner fails to make an appearance at a hearing that has been properly noticed via certified mail by OAH, OAH shall immediately dismiss the contested case, unless the recipient moves to show good cause within three business days of the date of dismissal.

(5) The notice of hearing provided by OAH to the recipient shall include the following information:

a. The recipient's right to examine at a reasonable time before the hearing and during the hearing the contents of the recipient's case file and documents to be used by the Department in the hearing before the administrative law judge.

b. The recipient's right to an interpreter during the appeals process.

c. Circumstances in which a medical assessment may be obtained at agency expense and be made part of the record. Qualifying circumstances include those in which (i) a hearing involves medical issues, such as a diagnosis, an examining physician's report, or a medical review team's decision; and (ii) the administrative law judge considers it necessary to have a medical assessment other than that performed by the individual involved in making the original decision.

(c) Mediation. - Upon receipt of an appeal request form as provided by G.S. 108A-70.9A(e) or other clear request for a hearing by a Medicaid recipient, OAH shall immediately notify the Mediation Network of North Carolina, which shall contact the recipient within five days to offer mediation in an attempt to resolve the dispute. If mediation is accepted, the mediation must be completed within 25 days of submission of the request for appeal. Upon completion of the mediation, the mediator shall inform OAH and the Department within 24 hours of the resolution by facsimile or electronic messaging. If the parties have resolved matters in the mediation, OAH shall dismiss the case. OAH shall not conduct a hearing of any contested Medicaid case until it has received notice from the mediator assigned that either: (i) the mediation was unsuccessful, or (ii) the petitioner has rejected the offer of mediation, or (iii) the petitioner has failed to appear at a scheduled mediation. Nothing in this subsection shall restrict the right to a contested case hearing.

(d) Burden of Proof. - The recipient has the burden of proof to show entitlement to a requested benefit or the propriety of requested agency action when the agency has denied the benefit or refused to take the particular action. The agency has the burden of proof when the appeal is from an agency determination to impose a penalty or to reduce, terminate, or suspend a previously granted benefit. The party with the burden of proof on any issue has the burden of going forward, and the administrative law judge shall not make any ruling on the preponderance of evidence until the close of all evidence.

(e) New Evidence. - The recipient shall be permitted to submit evidence regardless of whether obtained prior to or subsequent to the Department's actions and regardless of whether the Department had an opportunity to consider the evidence in making its adverse determination. When the evidence is received, at the request of the Department, the administrative law judge shall continue the hearing for a minimum of 15 days and a maximum of 30 days to allow for the Department's review of the evidence. Subsequent to review of the evidence, if the Department reverses its original decision, it shall immediately inform the administrative law judge.

(f)   Issue for Hearing. - For each adverse determination, the hearing shall determine whether the Department substantially prejudiced the rights of the recipient and if the Department, based upon evidence at the hearing:

(1)   Exceeded its authority or jurisdiction.

(2)   Acted erroneously.

(3)   Failed to use proper procedure.

(4)   Acted arbitrarily or capriciously.

(5)   Failed to act as required by law or rule.

(g)   Decision. - The administrative law judge assigned to a contested Medicaid case shall hear and decide the case without unnecessary delay. The judge shall prepare a written decision and send it to the parties in accordance with G.S. 150B-37. (2010-31, s. 10.30(a); 2011-398, s. 33.)

§ 108A-70.9C. Informal review permitted.

Nothing in this Part shall prevent the Department from engaging in an informal review of a contested Medicaid case with a recipient prior to issuing a notice of adverse determination as provided by G.S. 108A-70.9A(c). (2010-31, s. 10.30(a).)

Part 7. Medical Assistance Provider False Claims Act.

§ 108A-70.10. Short title.

This Part may be cited as the Medical Assistance Provider False Claims Act. (1997-338, s. 1.)

§ 108A-70.11. Definitions.

Definitions. - As used in this Part:

(1)   "Attorney General" means the Attorney General or any Deputy, Assistant, or Associate Attorney General.

(2)   "Claim" means an application for payment or approval or for use in determining entitlement to payment presented to the Medical Assistance Program in any form, including written, electronic, or magnetic, which identifies a service, good, or accommodation as reimbursable under the Medical Assistance Program.

(3)   "Damages" means the difference between what the Medical Assistance Program paid a provider and the amount it would have paid the provider in the absence of a violation of this section and may be established by statistical sampling methods.

(4)   "Knowingly" means that a provider, with respect to the information:

a.   Has actual knowledge of the information;

b.   Acts in deliberate ignorance of the truth or falsity of the information; or

c.   Acts in reckless disregard of the truth or falsity of the information. No proof of specific intent to defraud is required.

(5)   "Medical Assistance Program" means the North Carolina Division of Medical Assistance and its fiscal agent. (1997-338, s. 1.)

§ 108A-70.12. Liability for certain acts; damages; effect of repayment.

(a)   Liability for Certain Acts. - It shall be unlawful for any provider of medical assistance under the Medical Assistance Program to:

(1) Knowingly present, or cause to be presented to the Medical Assistance Program a false or fraudulent claim for payment or approval; or

(2) Knowingly make, use, or cause to be made or used a false record or statement to get a false or fraudulent claim paid or approved by the Medical Assistance Program.

Each claim presented or caused to be presented in violation of this section is a separate violation.

(b) Damages. -

(1) Except as provided in subdivision (2) of this subsection, a court shall assess against any provider of medical assistance under the Medical Assistance Program who violates this section a civil penalty of not less than five thousand dollars ($5,000) and not more than ten thousand dollars ($10,000) plus three times the amount of damages which the Medicaid Assistance Program sustained because of the act of the provider.

(2) A court may assess a penalty of not less than two times the amount of damages which the Medical Assistance Program sustains because of the act of the provider if a court finds that:

a. The provider committing a violation of this section furnished officials of the State responsible for investigating false claims violations with all information known to the provider about the violation within 30 days after the date the provider first obtained the information;

b. The provider fully cooperated with any State investigation of the violation; and

c. At the time the provider furnished the State with the information about the violation, no criminal prosecution, civil action, or administrative action had commenced with respect to the violation, and the provider did not have actual knowledge of the existence of an investigation into the violation.

(3) In addition to the damages and penalty assessed by the court pursuant to subdivision (1) or (2) of this subsection, a provider violating this section shall also be liable for the costs of a civil action brought to recover any penalty or damages, interest on the damages at the maximum legal rate in effect on the date the payment was made to the provider for the period from the date upon

which payment was made to the provider to the date upon which repayment is made by the provider to the Medical Assistance Program, and the costs of the investigation.

(4) As applied to providers that are subject to certification review by the Division of Health Service Regulation, a violation of Medicaid provider certification standards in providing a service, good, or accommodation shall not be considered an independent basis for liability under this Act. However, liability may be imposed if a false or fraudulent claim is presented as set forth in subsection (a) of this section in connection with that service, good, or accommodation.

(c) Effect of Repayment. - Intent to repay or repayment of any amounts obtained by a provider as a result of any acts described in subsection (a) of this section shall not be a defense to or grounds for dismissal of an action brought pursuant to this section. However, a court may consider any repayment in mitigation of the amount of any penalties assessed. (1997-338, s. 1; 2007-182, s. 1.)

§ 108A-70.13. False claims procedure.

(a) The Attorney General shall have the authority to investigate, institute proceedings, compromise and settle any investigation or action, and perform all duties in connection with any civil action to enforce G.S. 108A-70.12.

(b) A civil action under G.S. 108A-70.12 may not be brought more than six years after the date the violation of G.S. 108A-70.12 is committed, or more than three years after the date when facts material to the right of action are known or reasonably should have been known by the official of the State of North Carolina charged with responsibility to act in the circumstances, but in no event more than 10 years after the date on which the violation is committed, whichever occurs last.

(c) In any action brought under G.S. 108A-70.12, the State shall be required to prove all essential elements of the cause of action, including damages, by the greater weight of the evidence.

(d) Notwithstanding any other provision of law or rule, a final judgment rendered in favor of the State in any criminal proceeding charging fraud or false statements, whether upon a verdict after trial or upon a plea of guilty or nolo contendere, shall estop the defendant from denying the essential elements of the offense in any action which involves the same transaction as in the criminal proceeding and which is brought under G.S. 108A-70.12.

(e)   No criminal or administrative action need be brought against any provider as a condition for establishing civil liability under G.S. 108A-70.12. The civil liability under G.S. 108A-70.12 is in addition to any other criminal, civil, and administrative liabilities or penalties that may be prescribed by law. However, treble and double damages and civil penalties provided by G.S. 108A-70.12 shall not be assessed against a provider if treble or double damages or civil penalties have been previously assessed against the provider for the same claims under the federal False Claims Act, 31 U.S.C. § 3729, et seq., or the federal Civil Monetary Penalty Law, 42 U.S.C. § 1320a-7a. In the event that any provider is found liable under the provisions of this Act and is subsequently found liable for the same claim under the federal False Claims Act, or the appropriate sections of the federal Civil Monetary Penalty Law, the State and the Medical Assistance Program shall pay to the federal government on behalf of the provider any amounts, other than restitution, recovered or otherwise obtained by the State under this Act, not to exceed the amount of the federal damages and penalties.

(f)   The amount of damages and number of violations of G.S. 108A-70.12 shall be established by the trial judge or, in the event of a jury trial, by jury verdict. The amount of penalties, treble or double damages, interest, cost of the investigation, and cost of the civil action shall be determined by the trial judge as prescribed in G.S. 108A-70.12(b).

(g)   Venue for any action brought pursuant to G.S. 108A-70.12 shall be in either Wake County or in any county in which claim originated, or in which any statement or record was made, or acts done, or services, goods, or accommodations rendered in connection with any act constituting part of the violation of G.S. 108A-70.12. (1997-338, s. 1.)

§ 108A-70.14. Civil investigative demand.

(a)   If the Attorney General has reasonable cause to believe that a person has information or is in possession, custody, or control of any document or other tangible object relevant to an investigation or that would lead to the discovery of relevant information in an investigation of a violation of G.S. 108A-70.12, the Attorney General may serve upon the person, before bringing an action under G.S. 108A-70.12 or other false claims law, a civil investigative demand to appear and be examined under oath, to answer written interrogatories under oath, and to produce any documents or objects for their inspection and copying.

(b) The civil investigative demand shall:

(1) Be served upon the person in the manner required for service of process in civil actions and may be served by the Attorney General or investigator assigned to the North Carolina Department of Justice;

(2) Describe the nature of the conduct constituting the violation under investigation;

(3) Describe the class or classes of any documents or objects to be produced with sufficient definiteness to permit them to be fairly identified;

(4) Contain a copy of any written interrogatories to be answered;

(5) Prescribe a reasonable date and time at which the person shall appear to testify, answer any written interrogatories, or produce any document or object;

(6) Advise the person that objections to or reasons for not complying with the demand may be filed with the Attorney General on or before that date and time;

(7) Specify a place for the taking of testimony;

(8) Designate a person to whom answers to written interrogatories shall be submitted and to whom any document or object shall be produced; and

(9) Contain a copy of subsections (b) and (c) of this section.

(c) The date within which to answer any written interrogatories and within which any document or object must be produced shall be more than 30 days after the civil investigative demand has been served upon the person. The date within which a person must appear to testify shall be more than 15 days after the demand has been served upon a person who resides out-of-state or more than 10 days after the demand has been served upon a person who resides in-state.

(d)   The person before whom the oral examination is to be taken shall put the person to be examined on oath and shall personally, or by someone acting under the person's direction and in the person's presence, record the testimony of the person to be examined. The Attorney General may exclude from the place where the examination is held all persons except the person giving the testimony, the attorney or other representative of the person giving the testimony, the Attorney General conducting the examination, the investigator assisting the Attorney General, the stenographer, and any other person agreed upon by the Attorney General and the person giving the testimony. When the testimony is transcribed, the person shall have a reasonable opportunity to examine and read the transcript, unless an examination and reading are waived by the person. Any changes in form or substance which the person desires to make shall be entered and identified upon the transcript by the person. The transcript shall then be signed by the person, unless the person in writing waives the signing, is ill, cannot be found, or refuses to sign.

(e)   Each interrogatory in a civil investigative demand served under this section shall be answered separately and fully in writing under oath and shall be submitted under sworn certificate by the person to whom the demand is directed, or in the case of a person other than a natural person, a person having knowledge of the facts and circumstances relating to the production and authorized to act on behalf of the person. If a person objects to any interrogatory, the reasons for the objection shall be stated in the certificate instead of an answer. The certificate shall state that all information required by the demand and in the possession, custody, control, or knowledge of the person to whom the demand is directed has been submitted. To the extent that any information is not furnished, the information shall be identified and reasons set forth with particularity regarding the reasons why the information was not furnished.

(f)   The production of documents and objects in response to a civil investigative demand served under this section shall be made under a sworn certificate by the person to whom the demand is directed, or in the case of a person other than a natural person, a person having knowledge of the facts and circumstances relating to the production and authorized to act on behalf of the person. The certificate shall state that all of the documentary material required by the demand and in the possession, custody, or control of the person to whom the demand is directed has been produced and made available. Upon written agreement between the person served with the civil investigative demand and the Attorney General, the person may substitute copies for originals of all or any part of the documents requested.

(g) No person shall be excused from testifying, answering interrogatories, or producing documents or objects in response to a civil investigative demand on the ground that the testimony, answers, documents, or objects required of the person may tend to incriminate the person. However, no testimony, answers, documents, or objects compelled pursuant to G.S. 108A-70.14 may be used against the person in a criminal action, except a prosecution for perjury or for contempt arising from a failure to comply with an order of the court.

(h) Any person appearing for oral testimony under a civil investigative demand issued pursuant to this section shall be entitled to the same fees and allowances paid to witnesses in the General Court of Justice of the State of North Carolina.

(i) If a person objects to or otherwise fails to comply with a civil investigative demand served upon the person under subsection (a) of this section, the Attorney General may file an action in superior court for an order to enforce the demand. Venue for the action to enforce the demand shall be in either Wake County or the county in which the person resides. Notice of a hearing on the action to enforce the demand and a copy of the action shall be served upon the person in the same manner as prescribed in the Rules for Civil Procedure. If the court finds that the demand is proper, that there is reasonable cause to believe that there may have been a violation of G.S. 108A-70.12, and that the information sought or document or object demanded is relevant to the violation, the court shall order the person to comply with the demand, subject to modifications the court may prescribe.

(j) If the person fails to comply with an order entered pursuant to subsection (i) of this section, the court may:

(1) Adjudge the person to be in contempt of court;

(2) Grant injunctive relief against the person to whom the demand is issued to restrain the conduct which is the subject of the investigation; or

(3) Grant any other relief as the court may deem proper.

(k) Any transcript of oral testimony, answers to written interrogatories, and documents and objects produced pursuant to this section may be used in connection with any civil action brought under G.S. 108A-70.12.

(l) The North Carolina Rules of Civil Procedure shall apply to this section to the extent that the rules are not inconsistent with the provisions of this section. (1997-338, s. 1.)

§ 108A-70.15. Employee remedies.

(a) In the absence of fraud or malice, no person who furnishes information to officials of the State responsible for investigating false claims violations shall be liable for damages in a civil action for any oral or written statement made or any other action that is necessary to supply information required pursuant to this Part.

(b) Any employee of a provider who is discharged, demoted, suspended, threatened, harassed, or in any other manner discriminated against in the terms and conditions of employment by the employee's employer because of lawful acts done by the employee on behalf of the employee or others in furtherance of an action under G.S. 108A-70.12, including investigation for, initiation of, testimony for, or assistance in an action filed or to be filed under G.S. 108A-70.12, shall be entitled to all relief necessary to make the employee whole. Relief shall include reinstatement with the same seniority status as the employee would have had but for the discrimination, two times the amount of back pay, interest on the back pay, and compensation for any special damages sustained as a result of the discrimination, including litigation costs and reasonable attorneys' fees. An employee may bring an action in the appropriate court for the relief provided in this section. (1997-338, s. 1.)

§ 108A-70.16. Uniformity of interpretation.

This Part shall be so interpreted and construed as to be consistent with the federal False Claims Act, 31 U.S.C. § 3729, et seq., and any subsequent amendments to that act. (1997-338, s. 1.)

§ 108A-70.17. Reserved for future codification purposes.

Part 8. Health Insurance Program for Children.

§ 108A-70.18. Definitions.

As used in this Part, unless the context clearly requires otherwise, the term:

(1)   "Comprehensive health coverage" means creditable health coverage as defined under Title XXI.

(2)   "Family income" has the same meaning as used in determining eligibility for the Medical Assistance Program.

(3)   "FPL" or "federal poverty level" means the federal poverty guidelines established by the United States Department of Health and Human Services, as revised each April 1.

(4)   "Medical Assistance Program" means the State Medical Assistance Program established under Part 6 of Article 2 of Chapter 108A of the General Statutes.

(4a)   "Predecessor Plan" means the North Carolina Teachers' and State Employees' Comprehensive Major Medical Plan in effect prior to July 1, 2008.

(5)   "Program" means The Health Insurance Program for Children established in this Part.

(6)   "State Plan" means the State Child Health Plan for the State Children's Health Insurance Program established under Title XXI.

(7)   "Title XXI" means Title XXI of the Social Security Act, as added by Pub. L. 105-33, 111 Stat. 552, codified in scattered sections of 42 U.S.C. (1997).

(8)   "Uninsured" means the applicant for Program benefits is not covered under any private or employer-sponsored comprehensive health insurance plan on the date of enrollment. (1998-1, s. 1; 1998-166, s. 6; 2000-67, s. 11.8(a); 2000-140, s. 90(d); 2001-424, s. 21.22(b); 2008-107, s. 10.13(d).)

§ 108A-70.19. Short title; purpose; no entitlement.

This Part may be cited as "The Health Insurance Program for Children Act of 1998." The purpose of this Part is to provide comprehensive health insurance coverage to uninsured low-income children who are residents of this State. Coverage shall be provided from federal funds received, State funds appropriated, and other nonappropriated funds made available for this purpose. Nothing in this Part shall be construed as obligating the General Assembly to appropriate funds for the Program or as entitling any person to coverage under the Program. (1998-1, s. 1.)

§ 108A-70.20. Program established.

The Health Insurance Program for Children is established. The Program shall be known as North Carolina Health Choice for Children, and it shall be administered by the Department of Health and Human Services in accordance with this Part and as required under Title XXI and related federal rules and regulations. Administration of Program benefits and claims processing shall be as provided under Part 5 of Article 3 of Chapter 135 of the General Statutes. (1998-1, s. 1; 2008-107, s. 10.13(e).)

§ 108A-70.20A. Child health insurance fund.

There is established a Child Health Insurance Fund. All premium receipts or any other receipts, including earnings on investments, occurring or arising in connection with acute medical care benefits provided under the Program shall be deposited into the Child Health Insurance Fund. Disbursements from the Child Health Insurance Fund shall include any and all amounts required to pay the benefits and administrative costs of the Health Insurance Program for Children. (2008-107, s. 10.13(c); 2011-85, s. 2.8.)

§ 108A-70.21. Program eligibility; benefits; enrollment fee and other cost-sharing; coverage from private plans; purchase of extended coverage.

(a) Eligibility. - The Department may enroll eligible children based on availability of funds. Following are eligibility and other requirements for participation in the Program:

(1) Children must:

a. Be between the ages of 6 through 18;

b. Be ineligible for Medicaid, Medicare, or other federal government-sponsored health insurance;

c. Be uninsured;

d. Be in a family whose family income is above one hundred thirty-three percent (133%) through two hundred percent (200%) of the federal poverty level;

e. Be a resident of this State and eligible under federal law; and

f. Have paid the Program enrollment fee required under this Part.

(2) Proof of family income and residency and declaration of uninsured status shall be provided by the applicant at the time of application for Program coverage. The family member who is legally responsible for the children enrolled in the Program has a duty to report any change in the enrollee's status within 60 days of the change of status.

(3) If a responsible parent is under a court order to provide or maintain health insurance for a child and has failed to comply with the court order, then the child is deemed uninsured for purposes of determining eligibility for Program benefits if at the time of application the custodial parent shows proof of agreement to notify and cooperate with the child support enforcement agency in enforcing the order.

If health insurance other than under the Program is provided to the child after enrollment and prior to the expiration of the eligibility period for which the child is enrolled in the Program, then the child is deemed to be insured and ineligible for continued coverage under the Program. The custodial parent has a duty to notify the Department within 10 days of receipt of the other health insurance, and the Department, upon receipt of notice, shall disenroll the child from the Program. As used in this paragraph, the term "responsible parent" means a person who is under a court order to pay child support.

(4) Except as otherwise provided in this section, enrollment shall be continuous for one year. At the end of each year, applicants may reapply for Program benefits.

(b) Benefits. - All health benefits changes of the Program shall meet the coverage requirements set forth in this subsection. Except as otherwise provided for eligibility, fees, deductibles, copayments, and other cost sharing charges, health benefits coverage provided to children eligible under the Program shall be equivalent to coverage provided for dependents under North Carolina Medicaid Program except for the following:

(1) No services for long-term care.

(2) No nonemergency medical transportation.

(3) No EPSDT.

(4) Dental services shall be provided on a restricted basis in accordance with criteria adopted by the Department to implement this subsection.

In addition to the benefits provided under the North Carolina Medicaid Program, the following services and supplies are covered under the Health Insurance Program for Children established under this Part:

(1), (1a) Repealed by Session Laws 2011-145, s. 10.41(b), effective July 1, 2011.

(2) Vision: Scheduled routine eye examinations once every 12 months, eyeglass lenses or contact lenses once every 12 months, routine replacement of eyeglass frames once every 24 months, and optical supplies and solutions when needed. NCHC recipients must obtain optical services, supplies, and solutions from NCHC enrolled, licensed or certified ophthalmologists, optometrists, or opticians. In accordance with G.S. 148-134, NCHC providers must order complete eyeglasses, eyeglass lenses, and ophthalmic frames through Nash Optical Plant. Eyeglass lenses are limited to NCHC-approved single vision, bifocal, trifocal, or other complex lenses necessary for a Plan enrollee's visual welfare. Coverage for oversized lenses and frames, designer frames, photosensitive lenses, tinted contact lenses, blended lenses,

progressive multifocal lenses, coated lenses, and laminated lenses is limited to the coverage for single vision, bifocal, trifocal, or other complex lenses provided by this subsection. Eyeglass frames are limited to NCHC-approved frames made of zylonite, metal, or a combination of zylonite and metal. All visual aids covered by this subsection require prior approval. Requests for medically necessary complete eyeglasses, eyeglass lenses, and ophthalmic frames outside of the NCHC-approved selection require prior approval. Requests for medically necessary fabrication of complete eyeglasses or eyeglass lenses outside of Nash Optical Plant require prior approval. Upon prior approval refractions may be covered more often than once every 12 months.

(3)   Under the North Carolina Health Choice Program for Children, the co-payment for nonemergency visits to the emergency room for children whose family income is at or below one hundred fifty percent (150%) of the federal poverty level is ten dollars ($10.00). The co-payment for children whose family income is between one hundred fifty-one percent (151%) and two hundred percent (200%) of the federal poverty level is twenty-five dollars ($25.00).

(4)   Over the counter medications: Selected over the counter medications provided the medication is covered under the State Medical Assistance Plan. Coverage shall be subject to the same policies and approvals as required under the Medicaid program.

(5)   Routine diagnostic examinations and tests: annual routine diagnostic examinations and tests, including x-rays, blood and blood pressure checks, urine tests, tuberculosis tests, and general health check-ups that are medically necessary for the maintenance and improvement of individual health are covered.

No benefits are to be provided for services and materials under this subsection that do not meet the standards accepted by the American Dental Association.

The Department shall provide services to children enrolled in the NC Health Choice Program through Community Care of North Carolina (CCNC) and shall pay Community Care of North Carolina providers the per member, per month fees as allowed under Medicaid.

(b1)   Payments. - Prescription drug providers shall accept as payment in full, for outpatient prescriptions filled, amounts allowable for prescription drugs under Medicaid. For all other providers, services provided to children enrolled in the

Program shall be provided at rates equivalent to one hundred percent (100%) of Medicaid rates, less any co-payments assessed to enrollees under this Part.

(c)   Annual Enrollment Fee. - There shall be no enrollment fee for Program coverage for enrollees whose family income is at or below one hundred fifty percent (150%) of the federal poverty level. The enrollment fee for Program coverage for enrollees whose family income is above one hundred fifty percent (150%) through two hundred percent (200%) of the federal poverty level shall be fifty dollars ($50.00) per year per child with a maximum annual enrollment fee of one hundred dollars ($100.00) for two or more children. The enrollment fee shall be collected by the county department of social services and retained to cover the cost of determining eligibility for services under the Program. County departments of social services shall establish procedures for the collection of enrollment fees.

(d)   (See note) Cost-Sharing. - There shall be no deductibles, copayments, or other cost-sharing charges for families covered under the Program whose family income is at or below one hundred fifty percent (150%) of the federal poverty level, except that fees for outpatient prescription drugs are applicable and shall be one dollar ($1.00) for each outpatient generic prescription drug, for each outpatient brand-name prescription drug for which there is no generic substitution available, and for each covered over-the-counter medication. The fee for each outpatient brand-name prescription drug for which there is a generic substitution available is three dollars ($3.00). Families covered under the Program whose family income is above one hundred fifty percent (150%) of the federal poverty level shall be responsible for copayments to providers as follows:

(1)   Five dollars ($5.00) per child for each visit to a provider, except that there shall be no copayment required for well-baby, well-child, or age-appropriate immunization services;

(2)   Five dollars ($5.00) per child for each outpatient hospital visit;

(3)   A one dollar ($1.00) fee for each outpatient generic prescription drug, for each outpatient brand-name prescription drug for which there is no generic substitution available, and for each covered over-the-counter medication. The fee for each outpatient brand-name prescription drug for which there is a generic substitution available is ten dollars ($10.00).

(4)   Twenty dollars ($20.00) for each emergency room visit unless:

a. The child is admitted to the hospital, or

b. No other reasonable care was available as determined by the Department.

Copayments required under this subsection for prescription drugs apply only to prescription drugs prescribed on an outpatient basis.

(e) Cost-Sharing Limitations. - The department shall establish maximum annual cost-sharing limits per individual or family, provided that the total annual aggregate cost-sharing, including enrollment fees, with respect to all children in a family receiving benefits under this section shall not exceed five percent (5%) of the family's income for the year involved.

(f) Coverage From Private Plans. - The Department shall, from funds available for the Program, pay the cost for dependent coverage provided under a private insurance plan for persons eligible for coverage under the Program if all of the following conditions are met:

(1) The person eligible for Program coverage requests to obtain dependent coverage from a private insurer in lieu of coverage under the Program and shows proof that coverage under the private plan selected meets the requirements of this subsection;

(2) The dependent coverage under the private plan is actuarially equivalent to the coverage provided under the Program and the private plan does not engage in the exclusive enrollment of children with favorable health care risks;

(3) The cost of dependent coverage under the private plan is the same as or less than the cost of coverage under the Program; and

(4) The total annual aggregate cost-sharing, including fees, paid by the enrollee under the private plan for all dependents covered by the plan, do not exceed five percent (5%) of the enrollee's family income for the year involved.

The Department may reimburse an enrollee for private coverage under this subsection upon a showing of proof that the dependent coverage is in effect for the period for which the enrollee is eligible for the Program.

(g) Purchase of Extended Coverage. - An enrollee in the Program who loses eligibility due to an increase in family income above two hundred percent

(200%) of the federal poverty level and up to and including two hundred twenty-five percent (225%) of the federal poverty level may purchase at full premium cost continued coverage under the Program for a period not to exceed one year beginning on the date the enrollee becomes ineligible under the income requirements for the Program. The benefits, copayments, and other conditions of enrollment under the Program applicable to extended coverage purchased under this subsection shall be the same as those applicable to an NC Kids' Care enrollee whose family income equals two hundred percent (200%) of the federal poverty level.

(h)   No State Funds for Voluntary Participation. - No State or federal funds shall be used to cover, subsidize, or otherwise offset the cost of coverage obtained under subsection (g) of this section.

(i)   No Lifetime Maximum Benefit Limit. - Benefits provided to an enrollee in the Program shall not be subject to a maximum lifetime limit. (1998-1, s. 1; 1999-237, s. 11.9; 2002-126, s. 10.20(a); 2003-284, s. 10.29(a); 2005-276, ss. 10.22(b), 10.22(c), 10.22(d); 2007-323, s. 28.22A(o); 2007-345, s. 12; 2008-107, ss. 10.12(b), (c), 10.13(f), (k); 2008-118, s. 1.6(b), (c); 2009-16, s. 4(d); 2009-451, s. 10.35(a); 2011-145, s. 10.41(b); 2013-360, s. 12H.10(g).)

§ 108A-70.22: Repealed by Session Laws 2008-107, s. 10.13(g), effective July 1, 2008.

§ 108A-70.23: Repealed by Session Laws 2011-145, s. 10.41(c), effective July 1, 2011.

§ 108A-70.24: Repealed by Session Laws 2008-107, s. 10.13(i), effective July 1, 2008.

§ 108A-70.25. State Plan for Health Insurance Program for Children.

(a)   The NC Health Choice program shall be administered and operated in accordance with this Part and the NC Health Choice State Plan, as periodically amended by the Department of Health and Human Services and approved by the federal government.

(b)   The requirements in G.S. 108A-54.1A shall apply to NC Health Choice State Plan amendments in the same manner in which they apply to Medicaid

State Plan amendments. (1998-1, s. 1; 2011-291, s. 2.23; 2013-360, s. 12H.2(b).)

§ 108A-70.26. Application process; outreach efforts; appeals.

(a) Application. - The Department shall use an application form for the Program that is concise, relatively easy for the applicant to comprehend and complete, and only as lengthy as necessary for identifying applicants, determining eligibility for the Program or Medicaid, and providing information to applicants on requirements for application submission and proof of eligibility. Application forms shall be obtainable from public health departments and county departments of social services. Applications shall be processed by the county department of social services and may be submitted by mail. The Department may adopt rules for the submission and processing of applications and for securing the proof of eligibility for benefits under this Part.

The application form for the Program shall have printed on it or attached to it a notice stating substantially: "The Health Insurance Program for Children is a federally and State funded program that may be discontinued if federal funds are not provided for its continuation."

(b) Outreach Efforts. - The Department shall adopt procedures to ensure that the Program is adequately publicized statewide and to comply with federal outreach requirements. The Department shall make information about the Program available through the Internet and shall explore the feasibility of securing a 24-hour toll-free telephone number to facilitate access to Program information. In order to avoid duplication of efforts, in developing outreach procedures the Department shall establish system linkages to ensure the collaboration and coordination of information between and among the Program and such ongoing programs and efforts as:

    WIC Program.

    Maternal and Child Health Block Grant.

    Children's Special Health Services.

    Smart Start.

Head Start.

The Department shall seek private and federal grant funds for outreach activities. The Department shall also seek the participation of the private sector in providing no-cost or low-cost avenues for publicizing the Program in local communities and statewide. The Department may work with the State Health Plan Purchasing Alliance Board to develop programs that utilize the expertise and resources of the Alliances in outreach activities to employees of small businesses.

(c) Appeals. - A person who is dissatisfied with the action of a county department of social services with respect to the determination of eligibility for benefits under the Program may appeal the action in accordance with G.S. 108A-79. (1998-1, s. 1.)

§ 108A-70.27. (See editor's note) Data collection; reporting.

(a) The Department shall ensure that the following data are collected, analyzed, and reported in a manner that will most effectively and expeditiously enable the State to evaluate Program goals, objectives, operations, and health outcomes for children:

(1) Number of applicants for coverage under the Program;

(2) Number of Program applicants deemed eligible for Medicaid;

(3) Number of applicants deemed eligible for the Program, by income level, age, and family size;

(4) Number of applicants deemed ineligible for the Program and the basis for ineligibility;

(5) Number of applications made at county departments of social services, public health departments, and by mail;

(6) Total number of children enrolled in the Program to date and for the immediately preceding fiscal year;

(7) Total number of children enrolled in Medicaid through the Program application process;

(8) Trends showing the Program's impact on hospital utilization, immunization rates, and other indicators of quality of care, and cost-effectiveness and efficiency;

(9) Trends relating to the health status of children;

(10) Other data that would be useful in carrying out the purposes of this Part.

(b) Repealed by Session Laws 2013-360, s. 12A.8(e), effective July 1, 2013.

(c) The Division of Medical Assistance shall provide to the Department data required under this section that are collected by the Plan. Data shall be reported by the Plan in sufficient detail to meet federal reporting requirements under Title XXI. The Plan shall report periodically to the Joint Legislative Oversight Committee on Health and Human Services claims processing data for the Program and any other information the Plan or the Committee deems appropriate and relevant to assist the Committee in its review of the Program. (1998-1, s. 1; 2011-145, s. 10.41(d); 2011-291, ss. 2.24, 2.25; 2013-360, s. 12A.8(e).)

§ 108A-70.28. Fraudulent misrepresentation.

(a) It shall be unlawful for any person to knowingly and willfully, and with intent to defraud, make or cause to be made a false statement or representation of a material fact in an application for coverage under this Part or intended for use in determining eligibility for coverage.

(b) It shall be unlawful for any applicant, recipient, or person acting on behalf of the applicant or recipient to knowingly and willfully, and with intent to defraud, conceal, or fail to disclose any condition, fact, or event affecting the applicant's or recipient's initial or continued eligibility to receive coverage or benefits under this Part.

(c) It is unlawful for any person knowingly, willingly, and with intent to defraud, to obtain or attempt to obtain, or to assist, aid, or abet another person, either directly or indirectly, to obtain money, services, or any other thing of value to which the person is not entitled as a recipient under this Part, or otherwise to deliberately misuse a Program identification card. This misuse includes the sale, alteration, or lending of the Program identification card to others for services and the use of the card by someone other than the recipient to receive or attempt to receive Program coverage for services rendered to that individual.

Proof of intent to defraud does not require proof of intent to defraud any particular person.

(d)   A person who violates a provision of this section shall be guilty of a Class I felony.

(e)   For purposes of this section the word "person" includes any natural person, association, consortium, corporation, body politic, partnership, or other group, entity, or organization. (1998-1, s. 1.)

§ 108A-70.29. Program review process.

(a)   Review of Eligibility and Enrollment Decisions. - Eligibility and enrollment decisions for Program applicants or recipients shall be reviewable pursuant to G.S. 108A-79. Program recipients shall remain enrolled during the review of a decision to terminate or suspend enrollment.

(b)   Review of Health Services Decisions. - In accordance with 42 C.F.R. § 457.1130 and 42 C.F.R. § 457.1150, a Program recipient may seek review of any delay, denial, reduction, suspension, or termination of health services, in whole or in part, including a determination about the type or level of services, through a two-level review process.

(1)   Internal review. - Within 30 days from the date of the decision subject to review under this subsection, a recipient may request a first-level internal review, which shall be conducted by the Clinical Medical Director of the Division of Medical Assistance or the Director's clinical designee.

(2)   External review. - If the recipient is dissatisfied with the first-level review decision, then within 15 days after the internal review decision is rendered the recipient may request a second-level independent external review by the Department of Health and Human Services Hearing Office. The external review

process shall comply with the provisions of 42 C.F.R. § 457.1140. The Department's Hearing Office shall assign the matter to a hearing officer who will preside over the review. The hearing may be in person at the Hearing Office in Raleigh or by telephone. Recipients may:

a. Represent themselves or have representatives of their choosing in the review process.

b. Review, in a timely manner, their files and other applicable information relevant to the review of the decision.

c. Fully participate in the review process, including the opportunity to present supplemental information during the review process.

(3) Time frames. - The hearing officer shall render a written decision within 90 calendar days of the date the recipient requested first-level review, as specified at 42 C.F.R. § 457.1160. If the recipient's physician or health plan determines that operating under the standard 90-day time frame could seriously jeopardize the enrollee's life or health or ability to attain, maintain, or regain maximum function, then each level of review must be completed within 72 hours, except that this expedited time frame may be extended by up to 14 calendar days if the recipient requests an extension.

(4) Coverage of services during review. - When the decision is a reduction, suspension, termination, or denied request for increase of existing services, notwithstanding the request for review, the services shall be covered in accordance with the decision under review, and services which are terminated or suspended services shall not be covered, unless and until the decision is overturned on review.

(c) Review of decisions pursuant to Programmatic changes. - The Program review process set forth in this section shall not apply to instances in which the sole basis for the decision is a provision in the State plan or in Federal or State law requiring an automatic change in eligibility, enrollment, or a change in coverage under the health benefits package that affects all applicants or enrollees or a group of applicants or enrollees without regard to their individual circumstances.

(d) Notice. - A recipient shall receive timely written notice of any decision subject to review under this section in accordance with the requirements of 42 C.F.R. § 457.1180. The notice shall include the reasons for the decision, an explanation of applicable rights to review of that decision, the standard and expedited time frames for review, the manner in which a review can be requested, and the circumstances under which enrollment may continue pending review.

(e) Rule-Making authority. - The Department shall have the authority to adopt rules for the implementation and operation of the Program review process.

(f) Additional Rule-Making Authority. - The Department of Health and Human Services shall have the authority to adopt rules for the transition and operation of the North Carolina Health Choice Program. Notwithstanding G.S. 150B-21.1(a), the Department of Health and Human Services may adopt temporary rules in accordance with Chapter 150B of the General Statutes for enrolling providers to participate in the NC Health Choice Program, for regulating provider participation in the NC Health Choice Program, and for other operational issues regarding the NC Health Choice Program. (2010-70, s. 1; 2010-96, s. 39(a); 2011-145, s. 10.41(e).)

Part 9. Weatherization Assistance Program and Heating/Air Repair and Replacement Program.

§ 108A-70.30: Recodified as Part 33 of Article 7 of Chapter 143B, G.S. 143B-344.46, by Session Laws 2013-360, s. 15.22(h), effective July 1, 2013.

Article 3.

Social Services Programs.

§ 108A-71. Authorization of social services programs.

The Department is hereby authorized to accept all grants-in-aid available for programs of social services under the Social Security Act, other federal laws or regulations, State appropriations and other non-federal sources. The Department is designated as the single State agency responsible for administering or supervising the administration of such programs. It is the intent of this Article that programs of social services be administered so that the State and its citizens may benefit fully from any grants-in-aid. (1981, c. 275, s. 1.)

§ 108A-72. Social services checks payable to decedents.

In the event of the death of a recipient of a cash payment service, any check or checks payable to such recipient but not endorsed prior to such recipient's death shall be returned to the issuing agency, made void, and reissued to the provider of the service. (1981, c. 275, s. 1.)

§ 108A-73. Services appeals and confidentiality of records.

The provisions of Article 4 on public assistance and social services appeals and confidentiality of records shall be applicable to social services programs authorized under this Article. (1981, c. 275, s. 1.)

§ 108A-74. County department failure to provide services; State intervention in or control of service delivery.

(a) Notwithstanding any other provision of law to the contrary, the Secretary of Health and Human Services may take action in accordance with this section to ensure the delivery of child welfare services in accordance with State laws and applicable rules. As used in this section, the terms:

(1) "County department of social services" also means the consolidated human services agency, whichever applies;

(2) "County director of social services" also means the human services director, whichever applies; and

(3) "County board of social services" also means the consolidated human services board, whichever applies.

(b) If the Secretary of Health and Human Services determines that a county department of social services is not providing child protective services, foster care services, or adoption services in accordance with State law and with applicable rules adopted by the Social Services Commission, or fails to demonstrate reasonable efforts to do so, then the Secretary, after providing written notification of intent to the county director of social services, to the chair of the county board of commissioners, and to the chair of the county board of social services, and after providing them with an opportunity to be heard, may intervene in the particular service or services in question. Intervention includes, but is not limited to, the following activities:

(1) Sending staff of the Department of Health and Human Services to the county department of social services to provide technical assistance and to monitor the services being provided;

(2) Establishing a corrective plan of action to correct inappropriate policies and procedures; and

(3) Advising county personnel as to appropriate policies and procedures.

If within 60 days of completion of the intervention activities, the Secretary finds that the county department of social services is not providing in accordance with State laws and applicable rules the particular service or services for which intervention was initiated, or has not demonstrated reasonable efforts to do so, the Secretary shall withhold State and federal child welfare services administrative funds until the particular service or services are provided in accordance with State laws and applicable rules.

(c) If the Secretary determines that a county department of social services is not providing child protective, foster care, or adoption services in accordance with State law and with applicable rules adopted by the Social Services Commission, or fails to demonstrate reasonable efforts to do so, and the failure to provide the services poses a substantial threat to the safety and welfare of children in the county who receive or are eligible to receive the services, then the Secretary, after providing written notification of intent to the chair of the county board of commissioners, to the chair of the county board of social services, and to the county director of social services, and after providing them with an opportunity to be heard, shall withhold funding for the particular service or services in question and shall ensure the provision of these services through contracts with public or private agencies or by direct operation by the Department of Health and Human Services.

(d) In the event that the Secretary assumes control of service delivery pursuant to subsection (c) of this section, the county director of social services shall be divested of all service delivery powers conferred upon the director by G.S. 108A-14 and other applicable State law as the powers pertain to the services in question. Upon assumption of control of service delivery, the Secretary may assign any of the powers and duties of the county director of social services to the Director of the Division of Social Services of the Department of Health and Human Services or to a contractor as the Secretary deems necessary and appropriate to continue the provision of the services in the county.

(e) In the event the Secretary takes action under this section, the Department of Health and Human Services shall, in conjunction with the county board of commissioners, the county board of social services, and the county director of social services develop and implement a corrective plan of action. The Department of Health and Human Services shall also keep the chair of the county board of commissioners, the chair of the county board of social services, and the county director of social services informed of any ongoing concerns or problems with the delivery of the services in question.

(f) Upon the Secretary taking action pursuant to subsection (c) of this section, county funding of the services in question shall continue and at no time during the period of time that the Secretary is taking action shall a county withdraw funds previously obligated or appropriated for the services. Upon the Secretary's assumption of the control of service delivery, the county shall also pay the nonfederal share of any additional cost that may be incurred to operate the services in question at the level necessary to comply fully with State law and Social Services Commission rules.

(g) During the period of time that the Secretary is taking action pursuant to subsection (c) of this section, the Department of Health and Human Services shall work with the county board of commissioners, the county board of social services, and the county director of social services, to enable service delivery to be returned to the county if and when the Secretary has determined that services can be provided by the county in accordance with State law and applicable rules. (1997-390, s. 10; 1997-443, s. 11A.118(a).)

§§ 108A-75 through 108A-78. Reserved for future codification purposes.

Article 4.

Public Assistance and Social Services Appeals and Access to Records.

§ 108A-79. Appeals.

(a)   A public assistance applicant or recipient shall have a right to appeal the decision of the county board of social services, county department of social services, or the board of county commissioners granting, denying, terminating, or modifying assistance, or the failure of the county board of social services or county department of social services to act within a reasonable time under the rules and regulations of the Social Services Commission or the Department. Each applicant or recipient shall be notified in writing of his right to appeal upon denial of his application for assistance and at the time of any subsequent action on his case.

(b)   In cases involving termination or modification of assistance, no action shall become effective until 10 workdays after notice of this action and of the right to appeal is mailed or delivered by hand to the recipient; provided, however, termination or modification of assistance may be effective immediately upon the mailing or delivery of notice in the following circumstances:

(1)   When the modification is beneficial to the recipient; or

(2)   When federal regulations permit immediate termination or modification upon mailing or delivery of notice and the Social Services Commission or the Department of Health and Human Services promulgates regulations adopting said federal law or regulations. When federal and State regulations permit immediate termination or modification, the recipient shall have no right to continued assistance at the present level pending a hearing, as would otherwise be provided by subsection (d) of this section.

(c)   The notice of action and the right to appeal shall comply with all applicable federal and State law and regulations; provided, such notice shall, at a minimum contain a clear statement of:

(1)   The action which was or is to be taken;

(2)   The reasons for which this action was or is to be taken;

(3)   The regulations supporting this action;

(4) The applicant's or recipient's right to both a local and State level hearing, or to a State level hearing in the case of the food and nutrition services program, on the decision to take this action and the method for obtaining these hearings;

(5) The right to be represented at the hearings by a personal representative, including an attorney obtained at the applicant's or recipient's expense;

(6) In cases involving termination or modification of assistance, the recipient's right upon timely request to continue receiving assistance at the present level pending an appeal hearing and decision on that hearing.

An applicant or recipient may give notice of appeal by written or oral statement to the county department of social services, which shall record such notice by completing a form developed by the Department.

Such notice of appeal must be given within 60 days from the date of the action, or 90 days from the date of notification in the case of the food and nutrition services program. Failure to give timely notice of appeal constitutes a waiver of the right to a hearing except that, for good cause shown, the county department of social services may permit an appeal notwithstanding the waiver. The waiver shall not affect the right to reapply for benefits.

(d) If there is such timely appeal in cases not involving disability, in the first instance the hearing shall consist of a local appeal hearing before the county director or a designated representative of the county director, provided whoever hears the local appeal shall not have been involved directly in the initial decision giving rise to the appeal. If there is such timely appeal in cases involving disability, the county director or a designated representative of the county director shall within five days of the request for an appeal forward the request to the Department of Health and Human Services, and the Department shall designate a hearing officer who shall promptly hold a hearing in the county according to the provisions of subsections (i) and (j) of this section. In cases involving termination or modification of assistance (other than cases of immediate termination or modification of assistance pursuant to subsection (b)(2) of this section), the recipient shall continue to receive assistance at the present level pending the decision at the initial hearing, whether that be the local appeal hearing decision or, in cases involving questions of disability, the Department of Health and Human Services hearing decision, provided that in order to continue receiving assistance pending the initial hearing decision the recipient must request a hearing on or before the effective date of the termination or modification of assistance.

(e)   The local appeal hearing shall be held not more than five days after the request for it is received. The recipient may, for good cause shown as defined by rule or regulation of the Social Services Commission or the Department, petition the county department of social services, in writing, for a delay, but in no event shall the local appeal hearing be held more than 15 days after the receipt of the request for hearing. At the local appeal hearing:

(1)   The appellant and the county department may be represented by personal representatives, including attorneys, obtained at their expense.

(2)   The appellant or his personal representative and the county department shall present such sworn evidence and law or regulations as bear upon the case. The hearing need not be recorded or transcribed, but the director or his representative shall summarize in writing the substance of the hearing.

(3)   The appellant or his personal representative and the county department may cross-examine witnesses and present closing arguments summarizing their views of the case and the law.

(4)   Prior to and during the hearing, the appellant or his personal representative shall have adequate opportunity to examine the contents of his case file for the matter pending together with those portions of other public assistance or social services case files which pertain to the appeal, and all documents and records which the county department of social services intends to use at the hearing. Those portions of the public assistance or social services case file which do not pertain to the appeal or which are required by federal statutes or regulations or by State statutes or regulations to be held confidential shall not be released to the appellant or his personal representative. In cases where the appellant has been denied access to the public assistance or social services case file the hearing officer shall certify as part of the official record that the hearing officer has examined the case files and that no portion of those files pertain to the appeal. Such certification may be subject to judicial review as provided in subsection (k) of this section. Nothing in this section is intended to restrict an applicant or recipient access to information if that access is allowed by rules and regulations promulgated pursuant to G.S. 108A-80.

(f)   The director or his designated representative shall make the decision based upon the evidence presented at the hearing and all applicable regulations, and shall prepare a written statement of his decision citing the regulations and evidence to support it. This written statement of the decision will be served by certified mail on the appellant within five days of the local appeal hearing. If the decision terminating or modifying the appellant's benefits is affirmed, the assistance shall be terminated or modified, not earlier than the date the decision is mailed, and any assistance received during the time of the appeal is subject to recovery.

(g)   If the appellant is dissatisfied with the decision of the local appeal hearing, he may within 15 days of the mailing notification of the decision take a further appeal to the Department. However, assistance may not be received pending this further appeal. Failure to give timely notice of further appeal constitutes a waiver of the right to a hearing before an official of the Department except that, for good cause shown, the Department may issue an order permitting a review of the local appeal hearing notwithstanding the waiver. The waiver shall not affect the right to reapply for benefits.

(h)   Subsections (d)-(g) of this section shall not apply to the food and nutrition services program. The first appeal for an electronic food and nutrition benefit recipient or his representative shall be to the Department. Pending hearing, the recipient's assistance shall be continued at the present level upon timely request.

(i)   If there is an appeal from the local appeal hearing decision, or from an electronic food and nutrition benefit recipient or his representative where there is no local hearing, or if there is an appeal of a case involving questions of disability the county director shall notify the Department according to its rules and regulations. The Department shall designate a hearing officer who shall promptly hold a de novo administrative hearing in the county after giving reasonable notice of the time and place of such hearing to the appellant and the county department of social services. Such hearing shall be conducted according to applicable federal law and regulations and Article 3, Chapter 150B, of the General Statutes of North Carolina; provided the Department shall adopt rules and regulations to ensure the following:

(1)   Prior to and during the hearing, the appellant or his personal representative shall have adequate opportunity to examine his case file and all documents and records which the county department of social services intends to use at the hearing together with those portions of other public assistance or social services case files which pertain to the appeal. Those portions of the public assistance or social services case files which do not pertain to the appeal

or which are required by federal statutes or regulations or by State statutes or regulations to be held confidential shall not be released to the appellant or his personal representative. In cases where the appellant has been denied access to portions of the public assistance or social services case file, the hearing officer shall certify as part of the official record that the hearing officer has examined the case files and that no portion of those files pertain to the appeal. Such certification may be subject to judicial review as provided in subsection (k) of this section. Nothing in this section is intended to restrict an applicant or recipient access to information if that access is allowed by rules or regulations promulgated pursuant to G.S. 108A-80.

(2) At the appeal hearing, the appellant and personnel of the county department of social services may present such sworn evidence, law and regulations as bear upon the case.

(3) The appellant and county department shall have the right to be represented by the person of his choice, including an attorney obtained at his own expense.

(4) The appellant and county department shall have the right to cross-examine the other party as well as make a closing argument summarizing his view of the case and the law.

(5) The appeal hearing shall be recorded; however, no transcript will be prepared unless a petition for judicial review is filed pursuant to subsection (k) herein, in which case, the transcript will be made a part of the official record. In the absence of the filing of a petition for a judicial review, the recording of the appeal hearing may be erased or otherwise destroyed 180 days after the final decision is mailed.

(6) Notwithstanding G.S. 150B-28 or any other provision of State law, discovery shall be no more extensive or formal than that required by federal law and regulations applicable to such hearings.

(j) After the administrative hearing, the hearing officer shall prepare a proposal for decision, citing pertinent law, regulations, and evidence, which shall be served upon the appellant and the county department of social services or their personal representatives. The appellant and the county department of social services shall have the opportunity to present oral and written arguments in opposition to or in support of the proposal for decision to the designated official of the Department who is to make the final decision. The final decision shall be based on, conform to, and set forth in detail the relevant evidence, pertinent State and federal law and regulations, and matters officially noticed. The decision shall be rendered not more than 90 days, or 45 days in the case of the food and nutrition services program, from the date of request for the hearing, unless the hearing was delayed at the request of the appellant. If the hearing was delayed at the appellant's request, the decision may only be delayed for the length of time the appellant requested a delay. The final decision shall be served upon the appellant and upon the county department of social services by certified mail, with a copy furnished to either party's attorney of record. In the absence of a petition for judicial review filed pursuant to subsection (k) herein, the final decision shall be binding upon the appellant, the county department of social services, the county board of social services, and the board of county commissioners.

(k) Any applicant or recipient who is dissatisfied with the final decision of the Department may file, within 30 days of the receipt of notice of such decision, a petition for judicial review in superior court of the county from which the case arose. Failure to file a petition within the time stated shall operate as a waiver of the right of such party to review, except that, for good cause shown, a judge of the superior court resident in the district or holding court in the county from which the case arose may issue an order permitting a review of the agency decision under this Chapter notwithstanding such waiver. The hearing shall be conducted according to the provisions of Article 4, Chapter 150B, of the North Carolina General Statutes. The court shall, on request, examine the evidence excluded at the hearing under G.S. 108A-79(e)(4) or G.S. 108A-79(i)(1) and if the evidence was improperly excluded, the court shall consider it. Notwithstanding the foregoing provisions, the court may take testimony and examine into the facts of the case, including excluded evidence, to determine whether the final decision is in error under federal and State law, and under the rules and regulations of the Social Services Commission or the Department of Health and Human Services. Furthermore, the court shall set the matter for hearing within 15 days from the filing of the record under G.S. 150B-47 and after reasonable written notice to the Department of Health and Human Services and the applicant or recipient. Nothing in this subsection shall be construed to abrogate any rights that the county may have under Article 4 of Chapter 150B.

(l) In the event of conflict between federal law or regulations and State law or regulations, the federal law or regulations shall control. (1937, c. 288, ss. 18, 48; 1939, c. 395, s. 1; 1957, c. 100, s. 1; 1969, c. 546, s. 1; cc. 735, 754; 1973, c. 476, s. 138; 1977, 2nd Sess., c. 1219, ss. 14-18; 1979, c. 691; 1981, c. 275,

s. 1; c. 419, ss. 1-3; c. 420, ss. 1-3; 1987, c. 599, ss. 1-3; c. 827, s. 1; 1997-443, s. 11A.118(a); 2007-97, s. 13.)

§ 108A-80. Confidentiality of records.

(a) Except as provided in (b) below, it shall be unlawful for any person to obtain, disclose or use, or to authorize, permit, or acquiesce in the use of any list of names or other information concerning persons applying for or receiving public assistance or social services that may be directly or indirectly derived from the records, files or communications of the Department or the county boards of social services, or county departments of social services or acquired in the course of performing official duties except for the purposes directly connected with the administration of the programs of public assistance and social services in accordance with federal law, rules and regulations, and the rules of the Social Services Commission or the Department.

(b) The Department shall furnish a copy of the recipient check register monthly to each county auditor showing a complete list of all recipients of Work First Family Assistance in Standard Program Counties and State-County Special Assistance, their addresses, and the amounts of the monthly grants. An Electing County whose checks are not being issued by the State shall furnish a copy of the recipient check register monthly to its county auditor showing a complete list of all recipients of Work First Family Assistance in the Electing County, their addresses, and the amounts of the monthly payments. These registers shall be public records open to public inspection during the regular office hours of the county auditor, but the registers or the information contained therein may not be used for any commercial or political purpose. Any violation of this section shall constitute a Class 1 misdemeanor.

(c) Any listing of recipients of benefits under any public assistance or social services program compiled by or used for official purposes by a county board of social services or a county department of social services shall not be used as a mailing list for political purposes. This prohibition shall apply to any list of recipients of benefits of any federal, State, county or mixed public assistance or social services program. Further, this prohibition shall apply to the use of such listing by any person, organization, corporation, or business, including but not limited to public officers or employees of federal, State, county, or other local governments, as a mailing list for political purposes. Any violation of this section shall be punishable as a Class 1 misdemeanor.

(d) The Social Services Commission may adopt rules governing access to case files for social services and public assistance programs, except the Medical Assistance Program. The Secretary of the Department of Health and Human Services shall have the authority to adopt rules governing access to medical assistance case files. (1937, c. 288, ss. 18, 48; 1939, c. 395, s. 1; 1957, c. 100, s. 1; 1969, c. 546, s. 1; cc. 735, 754; 1973, c. 476, s. 138; 1977, 2nd Sess., c. 1219, s. 19; 1981, c. 275, s. 1; c. 419, s. 4; 1993, c. 539, ss. 819, 820; 1994, Ex. Sess., c. 24, s. 14(c); 1997-443, ss. 11A.118(a), 12.12; 2010-31, s. 10.19A(i).)

§§ 108A-81 through 108A-85. Reserved for future codification purposes.

Article 5.

Financing of Programs of Public Assistance and Social Services.

§ 108A-86. Financial transactions between the State and counties.

The Secretary shall have the power to promulgate rules and regulations establishing procedures for the counties to follow in financing programs of public assistance and social services under Article 2 and Article 3. (1981, c. 275, s. 1.)

§ 108A-87. Allocation of nonfederal shares.

(a) The nonfederal share of the annual cost of each public assistance and social services program and related administrative costs may be divided between the State and counties as determined by the General Assembly and in a manner consistent with federal laws and regulations.

(b) The nonfederal share of the annual cost of public assistance and social services programs and related administrative costs provided to Indians living on federal reservations held in trust by the United States on their behalf shall be borne entirely by the State. (1965, c. 708; 1969, c. 546, s. 1; 1973, c. 476, s. 138; 1981, c. 275, s. 1.)

§ 108A-88. Determination of State and county financial participation.

Before February 15 of each year, the Secretary shall notify the county board of commissioners, the county manager, the director of social services, and the director of public health of each county of the amount of State and federal moneys estimated to be available, as best can be determined, to that county for programs of public assistance, social services, public health, and related administrative costs, as well as the percentage of county participation expected to be required for the budget for the succeeding fiscal year. In odd-numbered years, in making such notification, the Secretary shall notify the counties of any changes in funding levels, formulas, or programs relating to public assistance and public health proposed by the Governor to the General Assembly in the proposed budget and budget report submitted under the State Budget Act. Counties shall be notified of additional changes in the proposed budget of the Governor that are made by the General Assembly or the United States Congress subsequent to the February 15 estimates.(1937, c. 288, ss. 9, 21, 39, 51; 1943, c. 505, s. 8; 1969, c.546, s. 1; 1973, c. 476, s. 138; c. 1418, s. 1; 1977, c. 1089,s. 1; 1977, 2nd Sess., c. 1219, s. 21; 1979, 2nd Sess., c. 1198; 1981, c. 275, s. 1; 2001-424, s. 21.16; 2006-203, s. 26.)

§ 108A-89. State Public Assistance Contingency Loan Program.

(a)   The Department is authorized and empowered to establish a program known as the "State Public Assistance Contingency Loan Program." The purpose of this program shall be to make loans available to counties whose actual expenditures, excluding related administrative costs, exceed the estimates for public assistance programs only provided by the Department under G.S. 108A-88.

(b)   Loans shall be made to the counties at any time during the fiscal year by the Department, when satisfied of the county's need for such loan under this Article.

(c)   A loan provided under this section shall be used by a county only to pay the county share of public assistance costs that exceeds the estimate provided by the Department under G.S. 108A-88 in order to sustain an adequate program of public assistance in that county.

(d) Any amount borrowed by a county from the "State Public Assistance Contingency Fund" during one fiscal year shall be repaid to said fund within the next two fiscal years. (1973, c. 1418, s. 2; 1977, c. 1089, s. 2; 1977, 2nd Sess., c. 1219, s. 22; 1981, c. 275, s. 1.)

§ 108A-90. Counties to levy taxes.

(a) Whenever the Secretary or his representative assigns a portion of the nonfederal share of public assistance expenses to the counties under the rules and regulations of the Social Services Commission or the Department, the board of commissioners of each county shall levy and collect the taxes required to meet the county's share of such expenses.

(b) The board of county commissioners may combine any or all of the separate special taxes for each program of public assistance and for the related administrative costs of such programs in place of levying separate special taxes for each item. This consolidated tax shall be sufficient, when combined with other funds available for use for public assistance expenses from any other source of county income and revenue (including borrowing in anticipation of collection of taxes), to meet the financial requirements of public assistance programs, and the related administrative costs of each program. The appropriations and expenditures for each of the several programs and for related administrative costs shall be separately stated and accounted for. (1937, c. 288, ss. 9, 39; 1969, c. 546, s. 1; 1971, c. 780, s. 35; 1973, c. 476, s. 138; c. 1418, s. 4; 1981, c. 275, s. 1.)

§108A-91. Appropriations not to revert.

County appropriations for public assistance expenses or related administrative costs shall not lapse or revert, and the unexpended balances may be considered in making further public assistance or administrative appropriations. At any time during the fiscal year, any county may transfer county funds from one public assistance program to another and between programs of public assistance and administration if such action appears to be both necessary and feasible, provided the county secures the approval of the Secretary or his representative. (1953, c. 891; 1967, c. 554; 1969, c. 546, s. 1; 1973, c. 476, s. 138; c. 1418, s. 5; 1981, c. 275, s. 1.)

§ 108A-92: Repealed by Session Laws 1997-443, s. 12.14.

§ 108A-93. Withholding of State moneys from counties failing to pay public assistance costs.

The Director of the Budget may withhold from any county that does not pay its full share of public assistance costs to the State and has not obtained a loan for repayment under G.S. 108A-89, any State moneys appropriated from the General Fund for public assistance and related administrative costs, or may direct the Secretary of Revenue and State Controller to withhold any tax owed to a county under G.S. 105-113.82, Subchapter VIII of Chapter 105 of the General Statutes, or Chapter 1096 of the Session Laws of 1967. The Director of the Budget shall notify the chair of the board of county commissioners of the proposed action prior to the withholding of funds. (1981, c. 859, s. 16; 1985, c. 114, s. 13; 1995, c. 41, s. 9.)

§§ 108A-94 through 108A-98. Reserved for future codification purposes.

Article 6.

Protection of the Abused, Neglected or Exploited Disabled Adult Act.

§ 108A-99. Short title.

This Article may be cited as the "Protection of the Abused, Neglected, or Exploited Disabled Adult Act." (1973, c. 1378; s. 1; 1975, c. 797; 1981, c. 275, s. 1.)

§ 108A-100. Legislative intent and purpose.

Determined to protect the increasing number of disabled adults in North Carolina who are abused, neglected, or exploited, the General Assembly enacts this Article to provide protective services for such persons. (1973, c. 1378, s. 1; 1975, c. 797; 1981, c. 275, s. 1.)

§ 108A-101. Definitions.

(a) The word "abuse" means the willful infliction of physical pain, injury or mental anguish, unreasonable confinement, or the willful deprivation by a caretaker of services which are necessary to maintain mental and physical health.

(b) The word "caretaker" shall mean an individual who has the responsibility for the care of the disabled adult as a result of family relationship or who has assumed the responsibility for the care of the disabled adult voluntarily or by contract.

(c) The word "director" shall mean the director of the county department of social services in the county in which the person resides or is present, or his representative as authorized in G.S. 108A-14.

(d) The words "disabled adult" shall mean any person 18 years of age or over or any lawfully emancipated minor who is present in the State of North Carolina and who is physically or mentally incapacitated due to mental retardation, cerebral palsy, epilepsy or autism; organic brain damage caused by advanced age or other physical degeneration in connection therewith; or due to conditions incurred at any age which are the result of accident, organic brain damage, mental or physical illness, or continued consumption or absorption of substances.

(e) A "disabled adult" shall be "in need of protective services" if that person, due to his physical or mental incapacity, is unable to perform or obtain for himself essential services and if that person is without able, responsible, and willing persons to perform or obtain for his essential services.

(f) The words "district court" shall mean the judge of that court.

(g) The word "emergency" refers to a situation where (i) the disabled adult is in substantial danger of death or irreparable harm if protective services are not provided immediately, (ii) the disabled adult is unable to consent to services, (iii) no responsible, able, or willing caretaker is available to consent to emergency services, and (iv) there is insufficient time to utilize procedure provided in G.S. 108A-105.

(h)   The words "emergency services" refer to those services necessary to maintain the person's vital functions and without which there is reasonable belief that the person would suffer irreparable harm or death. This may include taking physical custody of the disabled person.

(i)   The words "essential services" shall refer to those social, medical, psychiatric, psychological or legal services necessary to safeguard the disabled adult's rights and resources and to maintain the physical or mental well-being of the individual. These services shall include, but not be limited to, the provision of medical care for physical and mental health needs, assistance in personal hygiene, food, clothing, adequately heated and ventilated shelter, protection from health and safety hazards, protection from physical mistreatment, and protection from exploitation. The words "essential services" shall not include taking the person into physical custody without his consent except as provided for in G.S. 108A-106 and in Chapter 122C of the General Statutes.

(j)   The word "exploitation" means the illegal or improper use of a disabled adult or his resources for another's profit or advantage.

(k)   The word "indigent" shall mean indigent as defined in G.S. 7A-450.

(l)   The words "lacks the capacity to consent" shall mean lacks sufficient understanding or capacity to make or communicate responsible decisions concerning his person, including but not limited to provisions for health or mental health care, food, clothing, or shelter, because of physical or mental incapacity. This may be reasonably determined by the director or he may seek a physician's or psychologist's assistance in making this determination.

(m)   The word "neglect" refers to a disabled adult who is either living alone and not able to provide for himself or herself the services which are necessary to maintain the person's mental or physical health or is not receiving services from the person's caretaker. A person is not receiving services from his caretaker if, among other things and not by way of limitation, the person is a resident of one of the State-owned psychiatric hospitals listed in G.S. 122C-181(a)(1), the State-owned Developmental Centers listed in G.S. 122C-181(a)(2), or the State-owned Neuro-Medical Treatment Centers listed in G.S. 122C-181(a)(3), the person is, in the opinion of the professional staff of that State-owned facility, mentally incompetent to give consent to medical treatment, the person has no legal guardian appointed pursuant to Chapter 35A, or guardian as defined in G.S. 122C-3(15), and the person needs medical treatment.

(n) The words "protective services" shall mean services provided by the State or other government or private organizations or individuals which are necessary to protect the disabled adult from abuse, neglect, or exploitation. They shall consist of evaluation of the need for service and mobilization of essential services on behalf of the disabled adult. (1973, c. 1378, s. 1; 1975, c. 797; 1979, c. 1044, ss. 1-4; 1981, c. 275, s. 1; 1985, c. 589, s. 34; 1987, c. 550, s. 24; 1989, c. 770, s. 29; 1991, c. 258, s. 2; 2007-177, s. 4.)

§ 108A-102. Duty to report; content of report; immunity.

(a) Any person having reasonable cause to believe that a disabled adult is in need of protective services shall report such information to the director.

(b) The report may be made orally or in writing. The report shall include the name and address of the disabled adult; the name and address of the disabled adult's caretaker; the age of the disabled adult; the nature and extent of the disabled adult's injury or condition resulting from abuse or neglect; and other pertinent information.

(c) Anyone who makes a report pursuant to this statute, who testifies in any judicial proceeding arising from the report, or who participates in a required evaluation shall be immune from any civil or criminal liability on account of such report or testimony or participation, unless such person acted in bad faith or with a malicious purpose. (1973, c. 1378, s. 1; 1975, c. 797; 1981, c. 275, s. 1.)

§ 108A-103. Duty of director upon receiving report.

(a) Any director receiving a report that a disabled adult is in need of protective services shall make a prompt and thorough evaluation to determine whether the disabled adult is in need of protective services and what services are needed. The evaluation shall include a visit to the person and consultation with others having knowledge of the facts of the particular case. When necessary for a complete evaluation of the report, the director shall have the authority to review and copy any and all records, or any part of such records, related to the care and treatment of the disabled adult that have been maintained by any individual, facility or agency acting as a caretaker for the disabled adult. This shall include but not be limited to records maintained by facilities licensed by the North Carolina Department of Health and Human Services. Use of information so obtained shall be subject to and governed by the provisions of G.S. 108A-80 and Article 3 of Chapter 122C of the General Statutes. The director shall have the authority to conduct an interview with the disabled adult with no other persons present. After completing the evaluation the director shall make a written report of the case indicating whether he believes protective services are needed and shall notify the individual making the report of his determination as to whether the disabled adult needs protective services.

(b)   The staff and physicians of local health departments, area mental health, developmental disabilities, and substance abuse authorities, and other public or private agencies shall cooperate fully with the director in the performance of his duties. These duties include immediate accessible evaluations and in-home evaluations where the director deems this necessary.

(c)   The director may contract with an agency or private physician for the purpose of providing immediate accessible medical evaluations in the location that the director deems most appropriate.

(d)   The director shall initiate the evaluation described in subsection (a) of this section as follows:

(1)   Immediately upon receipt of the complaint if the complaint alleges a danger of death in an emergency as defined in G.S. 108A-101(g).

(2)   Within 24 hours if the complaint alleges danger of irreparable harm in an emergency as defined by G.S. 108A-101(g).

(3)   Within 72 hours if the complaint does not allege danger of death or irreparable harm in an emergency as defined by G.S. 108A-101(g).

(4)   Repealed by Session Laws 2000, c. 131, s. 1.

The evaluation shall be completed within 30 days for allegations of abuse or neglect and within 45 days for allegations of exploitation. (1973, c. 1378, s. 1; 1975, c. 797; 1981, c. 275, s. 1; 1985, c. 589, s. 35; c. 658, s. 1; 1985 (Reg.

Sess., 1986), c. 863, s. 6; 1991, c. 636, s. 19(c); 1997-443, s. 11A.118(a); 1999-334, s. 1.10; 2000-131, s. 1.)

§ 108A-104. Provision of protective services with the consent of the person; withdrawal of consent; caretaker refusal.

(a)   If the director determines that a disabled adult is in need of protective services, he shall immediately provide or arrange for the provision of protective services, provided that the disabled adult consents.

(b)   When a caretaker of a disabled adult who consents to the receipt of protective services refuses to allow the provision of such services to the disabled adult, the director may petition the district court for an order enjoining the caretaker from interfering with the provision of protective services to the disabled adult. The petition must allege specific facts sufficient to show that the disabled adult is in need of protective services and consents to the receipt of protective services and that the caretaker refuses to allow the provision of such services. If the judge finds by clear, cogent, and convincing evidence that the disabled adult is in need of protective services and consents to the receipt of protective services and that the caretaker refuses to allow the provision of such services, he may issue an order enjoining the caretaker from interfering with the provision of protective services to the disabled adult.

(c)   If a disabled adult does not consent to the receipt of protective services, or if he withdraws his consent, the services shall not be provided. (1973, c. 1378, s. 1; 1975, c. 797; 1981, c. 275, s. 1.)

§ 108A-105. Provision of protective services to disabled adults who lack the capacity to consent; hearing, findings, etc.

(a)   If the director reasonably determines that a disabled adult is being abused, neglected, or exploited and lacks capacity to consent to protective services, then the director may petition the district court for an order authorizing the provision of protective services. The petition must allege specific facts sufficient to show that the disabled adult is in need of protective services and lacks capacity to consent to them.

(b) The court shall set the case for hearing within 14 days after the filing of the petition. The disabled adult must receive at least five days' notice of the hearing. He has the right to be present and represented by counsel at the hearing. If the person, in the determination of the judge, lacks the capacity to waive the right to counsel, then a guardian ad litem shall be appointed pursuant to G.S. 1A-1, Rule 17, and rules adopted by the Office of Indigent Defense Services. If the person is indigent, the cost of representation shall be borne by the State.

(c) If, at the hearing, the judge finds by clear, cogent, and convincing evidence that the disabled adult is in need of protective services and lacks capacity to consent to protective services, he may issue an order authorizing the provision of protective services. This order may include the designation of an individual or organization to be responsible for the performing or obtaining of essential services on behalf of the disabled adult or otherwise consenting to protective services in his behalf. Within 60 days from the appointment of such an individual or organization, the court will conduct a review to determine if a petition should be initiated in accordance with Chapter 35A; for good cause shown, the court may extend the 60 day period for an additional 60 days, at the end of which it shall conduct a review to determine if a petition should be initiated in accordance with Chapter 35A. No disabled adult may be committed to a mental health facility under this Article.

(d) A determination by the court that a person lacks the capacity to consent to protective services under the provisions of this Chapter shall in no way affect incompetency proceedings as set forth in Chapters 33, 35 or 122 of the General Statutes of North Carolina, or any other proceedings, and incompetency proceedings as set forth in Chapters 33, 35, or 122 shall have no conclusive effect upon the question of capacity to consent to protective services as set forth in this Chapter. (1973, c. 1378, s. 1; 1975, c. 797; 1977, c. 725, s. 3, 1979, c. 1044, s. 5; 1981, c. 275, s. 1; 1985, c. 658, s. 2; 1987, c. 550, s. 25; 2000-144, s. 36.)

§ 108A-106. Emergency intervention; findings by court; limitations; contents of petition; notice of petition; court authorized entry of premises; immunity of petitioner.

(a) Upon petition by the director, a court may order the provision of emergency services to a disabled adult after finding that there is reasonable cause to believe that:

(1) A disabled adult lacks capacity to consent and that he is in need of protective service;

(2) An emergency exists; and

(3) No other person authorized by law or order to give consent for the person is available and willing to arrange for emergency services.

(b) The court shall order only such emergency services as are necessary to remove the conditions creating the emergency. In the event that such services will be needed for more than 14 days, the director shall petition the court in accordance with G.S. 108A-105.

(c) The petition for emergency services shall set forth the name, address, and authority of the petitioner; the name, age and residence of the disabled adult; the nature of the emergency; the nature of the disability if determinable; the proposed emergency services; the petitioner's reasonable belief as to the existence of the conditions set forth in subsection (a) above; and facts showing petitioner's attempts to obtain the disabled adult's consent to the services.

(d) Notice of the filing of such petition and other relevant information, including the factual basis of the belief that emergency services are needed and a description of the exact services to be rendered shall be given to the person, to his spouse, or if none, to his adult children or next of kin, to his guardian, if any. Such notice shall be given at least 24 hours prior to the hearing of the petition for emergency intervention; provided, however, that the court may issue immediate emergency order ex parte upon finding as fact (i) that the conditions specified in G.S. 108A-106(a) exist; (ii) that there is likelihood that the disabled adult may suffer irreparable injury or death if such order be delayed; and (iii) that reasonable attempts have been made to locate interested parties and secure from them such services or their consent to petitioner's provision of such service; and such order shall contain a show-cause notice to each person upon whom served directing such person to appear immediately or at any time up to and including the time for the hearing of the petition for emergency services and show cause, if any exists, for the dissolution or modification of the said order. Copies of the said order together with such other appropriate notices as the court may direct shall be issued and served upon all of the interested parties designated in the first sentence of this subsection. Unless dissolved by the court for good cause shown, the emergency order ex parte shall be in effect until the hearing is held on the petition for emergency services. At such hearing, if the court determines that the emergency continues to exist, the court may order the provision of emergency services in accordance with subsections (a) and (b) of this section.

(e)   Where it is necessary to enter a premises without the disabled adult's consent after obtaining a court order in compliance with subsection (a) above, the representative of the petitioner shall do so.

(f)   (1)   Upon petition by the director, a court may order that:

a.   The disabled adult's financial records be made available at a certain day and time for inspection by the director or his designated agent; and

b.   The disabled adult's financial assets be frozen and not withdrawn, spent or transferred without prior order of the court.

(2)   Such an order shall not issue unless the court first finds that there is reasonable cause to believe that:

a.   A disabled adult lacks the capacity to consent and that he is in need of protective services;

b.   The disabled adult is being financially exploited by his caretaker; and

c.   No other person is able or willing to arrange for protective services.

(3)   Provided, before any such inspection is done, the caretaker and every financial institution involved shall be given notice and a reasonable opportunity to appear and show good cause why this inspection should not be done. And, provided further, that any order freezing assets shall expire ten days after such inspection is completed, unless the court for good cause shown, extends it.

(g)   No petitioner shall be held liable in any action brought by the disabled adult if the petitioner acted in good faith. (1975, c. 797; 1981, c. 275, s. 1; 1985, c. 658, s. 3.)

§ 108A-107. Motion in the cause.

Notwithstanding any finding by the court of lack of capacity of the disabled adult to consent, the disabled adult or the individual or organization designated to be responsible for the disabled adult shall have the right to bring a motion in the cause for review of any order issued pursuant to this Article. (1973, c. 1378, s. 1; 1975, c. 797; 1981, c. 275, s. 1.)

§ 108A-108. Payment for essential services.

At the time the director, in accordance with the provisions of G.S. 108A-103 makes an evaluation of the case reported, then it shall be determined, according to regulations set by the Social Services Commission, whether the individual is financially capable of paying for the essential services. If he is, he shall make reimbursement for the costs of providing the needed essential services. If it is determined that he is not financially capable of paying for such essential services, they shall be provided at no cost to the recipient of the services. (1975, c. 797; 1981, c. 275, s. 1.)

§ 108A-109. Reporting abuse.

Upon finding evidence indicating that a person has abused, neglected, or exploited a disabled adult, the director shall notify the district attorney. (1975, c. 797; 1981, c. 275, s. 1.)

§ 108A-110. Funding of protective services.

Any funds appropriated by counties for home health care, boarding home, nursing home, emergency assistance, medical or psychiatric evaluations, and other protective services and for the development and improvement of a system of protective services, including additional staff, may be matched by State and federal funds. Such funds shall be utilized by the county department of social services for the benefit of disabled adults in need of protective services. (1975, c. 797; 1981, c. 275, s. 1.)

§ 108A-111. Adoption of standards.

The Department and the administrative office of the court shall adopt standards and other procedures and guidelines with forms to insure the effective implementation of the provisions of this Article. (1975, c. 797; 1981, c. 275, s. 1.)

Article 6A.

Protection of Disabled and Older Adults From Financial Exploitation.

§ 108A-112. Legislative intent and purpose.

Determined to fight the growing problem of fraud and financial exploitation targeting disabled and older adults in North Carolina, the General Assembly enacts this Article to facilitate the collection of records needed to investigate and prosecute such incidents. (2013-337, s. 4.)

§ 108A-113. Definitions.

As used in this Article, the following definitions apply:

(1) Customer. - A person who is a present or former holder of an account with a financial institution.

(2) Disabled adult. - An individual 18 years of age or older or a lawfully emancipated minor who is present in the State of North Carolina and who is physically or mentally incapacitated as defined in G.S. 108A-101(d).

(3) Financial exploitation. - The illegal or improper use of a disabled adult's or older adult's financial resources for another's profit or pecuniary advantage.

(4) Financial institution. - A banking corporation, trust company, savings and loan association, credit union, or other entity principally engaged in lending money or receiving or soliciting money on deposit.

(5) Financial record. - An original of, a copy of, or information derived from a record held by a financial institution pertaining to a customer's relationship with the financial institution and identified with or identifiable with the customer.

(6) Investigating entity. - A law enforcement agency investigating alleged financial exploitation of a disabled adult or an older adult, or a county department of social services investigating alleged financial exploitation of a disabled adult.

(7) Law enforcement agency. - Any duly accredited State or local government agency possessing authority to enforce the criminal statutes of North Carolina.

(8) Older adult. - An individual 65 years of age or older.

(9) Promptly. - As soon as practicable, with reasonable allowance to be made for the time required to retrieve older data or records that are not readily or immediately retrievable due to their current storage media. (2013-337, s. 4.)

§ 108A-114. Financial institutions encouraged to offer disabled adult and older adult customers the opportunity to submit a list of trusted persons to be contacted in case of financial exploitation.

All financial institutions are encouraged, but not required, to offer to disabled adult and older adult customers the opportunity to submit, and periodically update, a list of persons that the disabled adult or older adult customer would like the financial institution to contact in case of suspected financial exploitation of the disabled adult or older adult customer. No financial institution, or officer or employee thereof, who acts in good faith in offering to its customer the opportunity to submit and update a list of such contact persons may be held liable in any action for doing so. (2013-337, s. 4.)

§ 108A-115. Duty to report suspected fraud; content of report; immunity for reporting.

(a) Any financial institution, or officer or employee thereof, having reasonable cause to believe that a disabled adult or older adult is the victim or target of financial exploitation shall report such information to the following:

(1) Persons on the list provided by the customer under G.S. 108A-114, if such a list has been provided by the customer. The financial institution may choose not to contact persons on the provided list if the financial institution suspects that those persons are financially exploiting the disabled adult or older adult.

(2) The appropriate local law enforcement agency.

(3) The appropriate county department of social services, if the customer is a disabled adult.

(b) The report may be made orally or in writing. The report shall include the name and address of the disabled adult or older adult, the nature of the suspected financial exploitation, and any other pertinent information.

(c) No financial institution, or officer or employee thereof, who acts in good faith in making a report under this section may be held liable in any action for doing so. (2013-337, s. 4.)

§ 108A-116. Production of customers' financial records in cases of suspected financial exploitation; immunity; records may not be used against account owner.

(a) An investigating entity may, under the conditions specified in this section, obtain a subpoena directing a financial institution to provide to the investigating entity the financial records of a disabled adult or older adult customer. The subpoena may be issued by any judge of the superior court, judge of the district court, or magistrate in the county of residence of the disabled adult or older adult customer whose financial records are being subpoenaed, upon finding that all of the following conditions are met:

(1) The investigating entity is investigating, pursuant to the investigating entity's statutory authority, a credible report that the disabled adult or older adult is being or has been financially exploited.

(2) The disabled adult's or older adult's financial records are needed in order to substantiate or evaluate the report.

(3) Time is of the essence in order to prevent further exploitation of that disabled adult or older adult.

(b) Delivery of the subpoena may be effected by hand, via certified mail, return receipt requested, or through a designated delivery service authorized pursuant to 26 U.S.C. § 7502(f)(2) and may be addressed to the financial institution's local branch or office vice president, its local branch or office manager or assistant branch or office manager, or the agent for service of process listed by the financial institution with the North Carolina Secretary of State or, if there is none, with the agent for service of process listed by the financial institution in any state in which it is domiciled.

(c) A financial institution shall promptly provide to the head of an investigating entity, or his or her designated agent, the financial records of a disabled adult or older adult customer upon receipt of a subpoena delivered pursuant to subsection (b) of this section identifying the disabled adult or older adult customer.

(d) All produced copies of the disabled adult's or older adult's financial records, as well as any information obtained pursuant to the duty to report found in G.S. 108A-115, shall be kept confidential by the investigating entity unless required by court rules to be disclosed to a party to a court proceeding or introduced and admitted into evidence in an open court proceeding.

(e) No financial institution or investigating entity, or officer or employee thereof, who acts in good faith in providing, seeking, or obtaining financial records or any other information in accordance with this section, or in providing testimony in any judicial proceeding based upon the contents thereof, may be held liable in any action for doing so.

(f) No customer may be subject to indictment, criminal prosecution, criminal punishment, or criminal penalty by reason of or on account of anything disclosed by a financial institution pursuant to this section, nor may any information obtained through such disclosure be used as evidence against the customer in any criminal or civil proceeding. Notwithstanding the foregoing, information obtained may be used against a person who is a joint account owner accused of financial exploitation of a disabled adult or older adult joint account holder, but solely for criminal or civil proceedings directly related to the alleged financial exploitation of the disabled adult or older adult joint account holder. (2013-337, s. 4.)

§ 108A-117. Notice to customer; delayed notice.

(a) Upon the issuance of a subpoena pursuant to G.S. 108A-116, the investigating entity shall immediately provide the customer with written notice of its action by first-class mail to the customer's last known address, unless an order for delayed notice is obtained pursuant to subsection (b) of this section. The notice shall be sufficient to inform the customer of the name of the investigating entity that has obtained the subpoena, the financial records subject to production pursuant to the subpoena, and the purpose of the investigation.

(b) An investigating entity may include in its application for a subpoena pursuant to G.S. 108A-116 a request for an order delaying the customer notice required pursuant to subsection (a) of this section. The judge or magistrate issuing the subpoena may order a delayed notice in accordance with subsection (c) of this section if it finds, based on affidavit or oral testimony under oath or affirmation before the issuing judge or magistrate, that all of the following conditions are met:

(1) The investigating entity is investigating a credible report that the adult is being or has been financially exploited.

(2) There is reason to believe that the notice will result in at least one of the following:

a. Endangering the life or physical safety of any person.

b. Flight from prosecution.

c. Destruction of or tampering with evidence.

d. Intimidation of potential witnesses.

e. Serious jeopardy to an investigation or official proceeding.

f. Undue delay of a trial or official proceeding.

(c) Upon making the findings required in subsection (b) of this section, the judge or magistrate shall enter an ex parte order granting the requested delay for a period not to exceed 30 days. If the court finds there is reason to believe that the notice may endanger the life or physical safety of any person, the court may order that the delay be for a period not to exceed 180 days. An order delaying notice shall direct that:

(1) The financial institution not disclose to any person the existence of the investigation, of the subpoena, or of the fact that the customer's financial records have been provided to the investigating entity for the duration of the period of delay authorized in the order;

(2) The investigating entity deliver a copy of the order to the financial institution along with the subpoena that is delivered pursuant to G.S. 108-116(b); and

(3) The order be sealed until otherwise ordered by the judge or magistrate.

(d) Upon application by the investigating entity, further extensions of the delay of notice may be granted by order of a judge or magistrate in the county of residence of the disabled adult or older adult customer whose financial records are being subpoenaed, upon a finding of the continued existence of the conditions set forth in subdivisions (1) and (2) of subsection (b) of this section, and subject to the requirements of subsection (c) of this section. If the initial delay was granted for a period not to exceed 30 days, the delay may be extended by additional periods of up to 30 days each and the total delay in notice granted under this section shall not exceed 90 days. If the initial delay was granted for a period not to exceed 180 days, the delay may be extended by additional periods of up to 180 days each and may continue to be extended until the court finds the notice would no longer endanger the life or physical safety of any person.

(e) Upon the expiration of the period of delay of notice granted under this section, including any extensions thereof, the customer shall be served with a copy of the notice required by subsection (a) of this section. (2013-337, s. 4.)

§ 108A-118: Reserved for future codification purposes.

§ 108A-119: Reserved for future codification purposes.

Article 7.

Hospital Provider Assessment Act.

§ 108A-120. Short title and purpose.

This Article shall be known as the "Hospital Provider Assessment Act." The assessments imposed by this Article are to provide revenue to improve funding for payments for hospital services provided to Medicaid and uninsured patients. All assessment proceeds and corresponding matching federal funds must be used to make the payments required under G.S. 108A-124. This Article does not authorize a political subdivision of the State to license a hospital for revenue or impose a tax or assessment on a hospital. (2011-11, s. 1.)

§ 108A-121. Definitions.

The following definitions apply in this Article:

(1) CMS. - Centers for Medicare and Medicaid Services.

(2) Critical access hospital. - Defined in 42 C.F.R. § 400.202.

(3) Department. - The Department of Health and Human Services.

(4) Equity assessment. - The assessment payable under G.S. 108A-123.

(5) Medicaid equity payment. - The amount required to be paid under G.S. 108A-124.

(6) Public hospital. - A hospital that certifies its public expenditures to the Department pursuant to 42 C.F.R. § 433.51(b) during the fiscal year for which the assessment applies.

(7) Secretary. - The Secretary of Health and Human Services.

(8) State's annual Medicaid payment. - For an assessment collected under this Article, an amount equal to twenty-five and nine-tenths percent (25.9%) of the total amount collected under the assessment.

(9) Total hospital costs. - The costs as calculated using the most recent available Hospital Cost Report Information Systems cost report data, available through CMS, or other comparable data.

(10) Upper pay limit (UPL). - The maximum ceiling imposed by federal regulation on hospital Medicaid payments under 42 C.F.R. § 447.272 for inpatient services.

(11) UPL assessment. - The assessment payable under G.S. 108A-123.

(12) UPL gap. - The difference between the UPL attributable to hospital inpatient services and the reasonable costs of inpatient hospital services as defined in Section (f)(2)(A) on page 11 of Attachment 4.19-A of the State Medicaid Plan as approved on December 15, 2005.

(13) UPL payment. - The amount required to be paid under G.S. 108A-124. (2011-11, s. 1; 2013-360, s. 12H.19(a).)

§ 108A-122. Assessment.

(a) Assessment Imposed. - Except as provided in this section, the assessments authorized under this Article are imposed as a percentage of total hospital costs on all licensed North Carolina hospitals. The assessments are due quarterly in the time and manner prescribed by the Secretary. Payment of an assessment is considered delinquent if not paid within seven days of the due date. With respect to any past-due assessment, the Department may withhold the unpaid amount from Medicaid payments otherwise due or impose a late-payment penalty. The Secretary may waive a penalty for good cause shown.

(b) Allowable Cost. - An assessment paid under this Article may be included as allowable costs of a hospital for purposes of any applicable Medicaid reimbursement formula. An assessment imposed under this Article may not be added as a surtax or assessment on a patient's bill.

(c) Full Exemption. - The following hospitals are exempt from both the equity assessment and the UPL assessment:

(1) State-owned and State-operated hospitals.

(2) The primary affiliated teaching hospital for each University of North Carolina medical school.

(3) Critical access hospitals.

(4) Long-term care hospitals.

(5) Freestanding psychiatric hospitals.

(6) Freestanding rehabilitation hospitals.

(d) Partial Exemption. - A public hospital is exempt from the equity assessment. (2011-11, s. 1.)

§ 108A-123. Assessment amount.

(a) Annual Calculation. - The Secretary must annually calculate the equity assessment amount and the UPL assessment amount for each hospital subject to the respective assessment. Each assessment must comply with applicable federal regulations and may be prorated for any partial year. The Secretary must notify each hospital that is assessed the amount of its UPL assessment and, if applicable, its equity assessment. The notice must include all of the following:

(1) The applicable assessment rates.

(2) The hospital costs on which the hospital's assessments are based.

(3) The elements of the calculation of the hospital's UPL.

(b) Equity Assessment. - The equity assessment consists of both inpatient and outpatient components. The equity assessment percentage rate must be calculated to produce an aggregate annual amount equal to the following:

(1) The amount needed to make the Medicaid equity payments under G.S. 108-124.

(2) The applicable portion of the State's annual Medicaid payment, as provided in subsection (d) of this section.

(c) UPL Assessment. - The UPL assessment consists of both inpatient and outpatient components. The UPL assessment percentage rate must be calculated to produce an aggregate annual amount equal to the following:

(1) The amount needed to make the UPL payments under G.S. 108A-124.

(2) The applicable portion of the State's annual Medicaid payment, as provided in subsection (d) of this section.

(d) State's Annual Medicaid Payment. - The first forty-three million dollars ($43,000,000) of the State's annual Medicaid payment must be allocated between the equity assessment and the UPL assessment based on the amount of gross payments received by hospitals under G.S. 108A-124. The remaining portion of the State's annual Medicaid payment must be allocated to the UPL assessment.

(e) Appeal. - A hospital may appeal an assessment determination through a reconsideration review. The pendency of an appeal does not relieve a hospital from its obligation to pay an assessment amount when due. (2011-11, s. 1; 2013-397, s. 10.)

§ 108A-124. Use of assessment proceeds.

(a) Use. - The proceeds of the assessments imposed under this Article and all corresponding matching federal funds must be used to make the State annual Medicaid payment to the State and the Medicaid equity payments and UPL payments to hospitals.

(b) Quarterly Payments. - Within seven business days following the due date for each quarterly assessment imposed under G.S. 108A-123, the Secretary must do the following:

(1) Pay to each hospital that has paid its equity assessment for the respective quarter twenty-five percent (25%) of its Medicaid equity payment amount. A hospital's Medicaid equity payment amount is the sum of the hospital's Medicaid inpatient and outpatient deficits after calculating all other Medicaid payments, excluding disproportionate share hospital payments and the UPL payment remitted to the hospital under subdivision (2) of this subsection.

(2) Pay to the primary affiliated teaching hospital for the East Carolina University Brody School of Medicine, to the critical access hospitals, and to each hospital that has paid its UPL assessment for the respective quarter twenty-five percent (25%) of its UPL payment amount, as determined under subsection (c) of this section.

(3) Pay to the primary affiliated teaching hospital for the East Carolina University Brody School of Medicine, to the critical access hospitals, and to each hospital that has paid its UPL assessment for the respective quarter twenty-five percent (25%) of its UPL payment amount, as determined under subsection (c) of this section.

(c) UPL Payment Amount. - The aggregate UPL payments made to eligible hospitals that are public hospitals is the sum of the UPL gaps for all public hospitals. The aggregate UPL payments made to eligible hospitals that are not public hospitals is the sum of the UPL gaps for these hospitals. UPL payments are payable to the individual hospitals in the ratio of each hospital's Medicaid inpatient costs to the total Medicaid inpatient costs for the respective group.

(d) Refund of Assessment. - If all or any part of a payment required to be made under this section is not made to one or more hospitals when due, the Secretary must promptly refund to each such hospital the corresponding assessment proceeds collected in proportion to the amount of assessment paid by that hospital. (2011-11, s. 1; 2013-360, s. 12H.19(b).)

§ 108A-125. Deferral of assessment due date.

In the event the data necessary to calculate the assessments required under G.S. 108A-123 or the payments required under G.S. 108A-124 is not available to the Secretary in time to impose the quarterly assessments for a payment year, the Secretary may defer the due date for the assessments and payments to a subsequent quarter. (2011-11, s. 1.)

§ 108A-126. Approval of assessment program.

The Department must file a State plan amendment with the CMS that incorporates the assessment payments and distributions consistent with the provisions of this Article. Upon CMS approval, the Secretary may impose the initial assessment retroactive to the first day of the quarter in which the State Plan amended was filed, provided the Secretary remits the corresponding payments to hospitals required under G.S. 108A-124 for that quarter. If CMS approves only one component of the equity assessment, the Secretary may adjust the percentage rate on the approved component to produce the required aggregate Medicaid equity payment amounts under G.S. 108A-124. If CMS approves only one component of the UPL assessment, the Secretary may adjust the percentage rate on the approved component to produce the required aggregate UPL payment amounts under G.S. 108A-124. The Secretary may adopt rules as necessary to implement the assessment program under this Article. (2011-11, s. 1.)

§ 108A-127. Repeal.

The authority to impose an assessment under this Article is repealed in the event that CMS determines that the assessment or payment methodologies described in this Article are impermissible or CMS revokes approval of any portion of the State Plan amendment authorizing the payments required under G.S. 108A-124. (2011-11, s. 1.)

§ 108A-128. Payment for providers formerly subject to this Article.

If a hospital provider (i) is exempt from both the equity and UPL assessments under this Article, (ii) makes an intergovernmental transfer (IGT) to the Department of Health and Human Services to be used to draw down matching federal funds, and (iii) has acquired, merged, leased, or managed another provider on or after March 25, 2011, then the hospital provider shall transfer to the State an additional amount, which shall be retained by the State. The additional amount shall be twenty-five and nine-tenths percent (25.9%) of the amount of funds that (i) would be transferred to the State through such an IGT and (ii) are to be used to match additional federal funds that the hospital provider is able to receive because of the acquired, merged, leased, or managed provider. (2013-360, s. 12H.19(c).)

§ 108A-129: Reserved for future codification purposes.

§ 108A-130: Reserved for future codification purposes.

§ 108A-131: Reserved for future codification purposes.

§ 108A-132: Reserved for future codification purposes.

Vision Books Order Form

Fax Orders:	1-980-299-5965
Phone Orders:	1-704-898-0770
E-mail Orders:	www.visionbooks.org
Mail Orders:	Vision Books, LLC P.O. Box 42406 Charlotte, NC 28215

Shipp To:
Name_____
Address_____
City_____State_____Zip_____
Phone_____Fax_____
Email_____@_____

Bill To: We can bill a third party on your behalf.
Name_____
Address_____
City_____State_____Zip_____
Phone___(_____)_____Fax_____
Email_____@_____

Pamphlet Number ($15.00 Each)	Qty	Total Cost
_____	_____	_____
_____	_____	_____
_____	_____	_____
_____	_____	_____
_____	_____	_____
_____	_____	_____
_____	_____	_____
_____	_____	_____
<u>Full Volume Set 1-92</u>	<u>92 Pamphlets</u>	<u>1,380.00</u>

Free Shipping Shipping & Handling on Full Volume Orders
Add $1.00 Shipping & Handling per pamphlet $_____

Total Cost $_____

DID YOU ENJOY THIS BOOK?

Vision Books, LLC would like to hear from you! If you or someone you know has been fasely imprisoned, we would like to hear your story. If the 'North Carolina Criminal Law and Procedure' has had an effect in your life or if you have suggestions, we would like to hear from you. Send your letters to:

Vision Books, LLC
Attn: Staff Writers
P.O. Box 42406
Charlotte, NC 28215
Email: staff@visionbooks.org

Order Additional Copies:

Fax Orders: 1-980-299-5965

Phone Orders: 1-704-898-0770

E-mail Orders: www.visionbooks.org

Mail Orders: Vision Books, LLC
                       P.O. Box 42406
                       Charlotte, NC 28215

www.ingramcontent.com/pod-product-compliance
Lightning Source LLC
Chambersburg PA
CBHW051634170526
45167CB00001B/182